Miss Kobayas
Dragon m
Kanna's

story & art by
Mitsuhiro Kimura

Coolkyousinnjya

Miss Kobayashi's Dragon Maid
Kanna's Daily Life

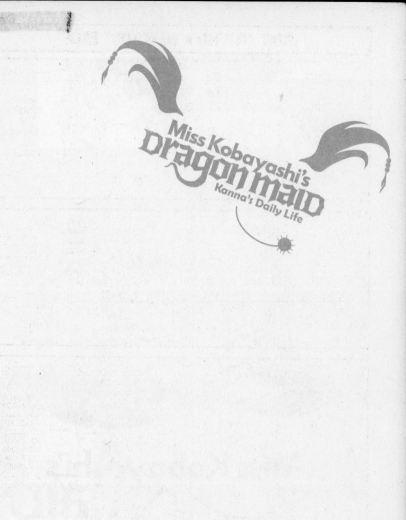

THAT "FOUND A NEW TOY" FACE

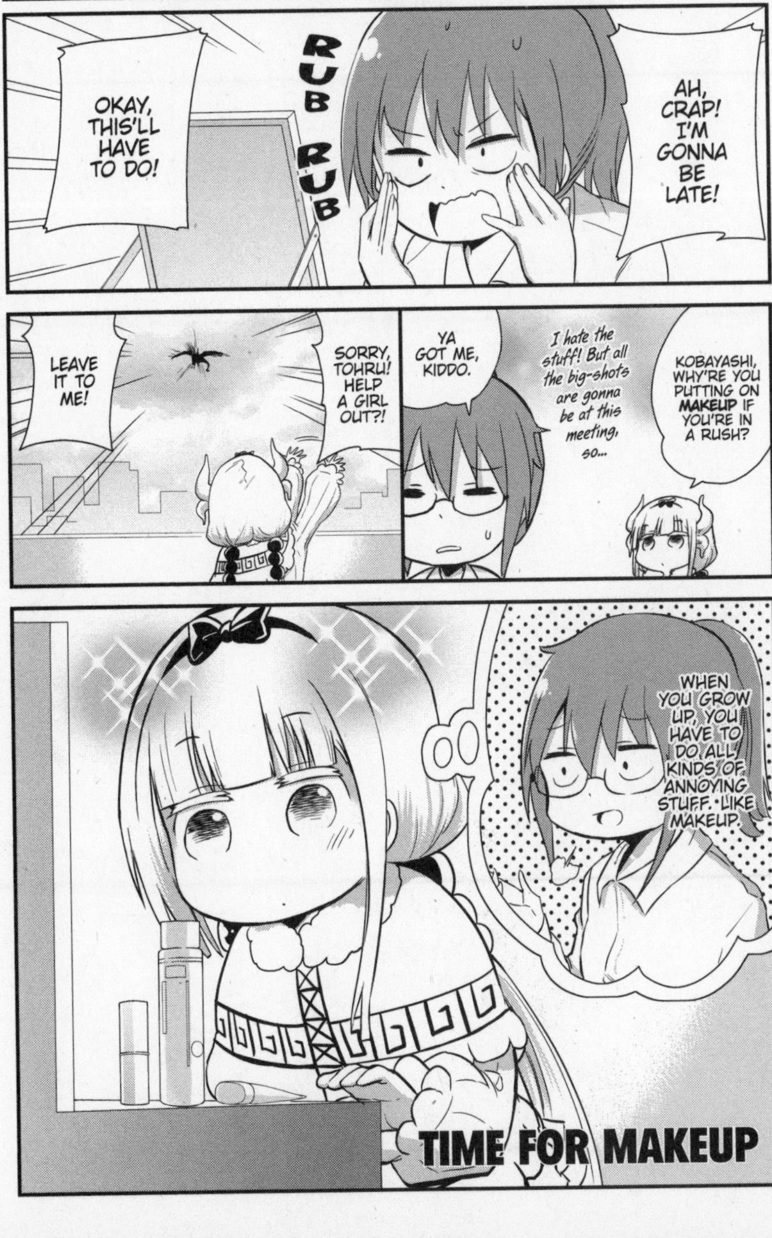
AH, CRAP! I'M GONNA BE LATE!
RUB RUB RUB
OKAY, THIS'LL HAVE TO DO!
KOBAYASHI, WHY'RE YOU PUTTING ON MAKEUP IF YOU'RE IN A RUSH?
I hate the stuff! But all the big-shots are gonna be at this meeting, so...
YA GOT ME, KIDDO.
SORRY, TOHRU! HELP A GIRL OUT?!
LEAVE IT TO ME!
WHEN YOU GROW UP, YOU HAVE TO DO ALL KINDS OF ANNOYING STUFF LIKE MAKEUP.
TIME FOR MAKEUP

CURIOSITY KILLS THE CAT

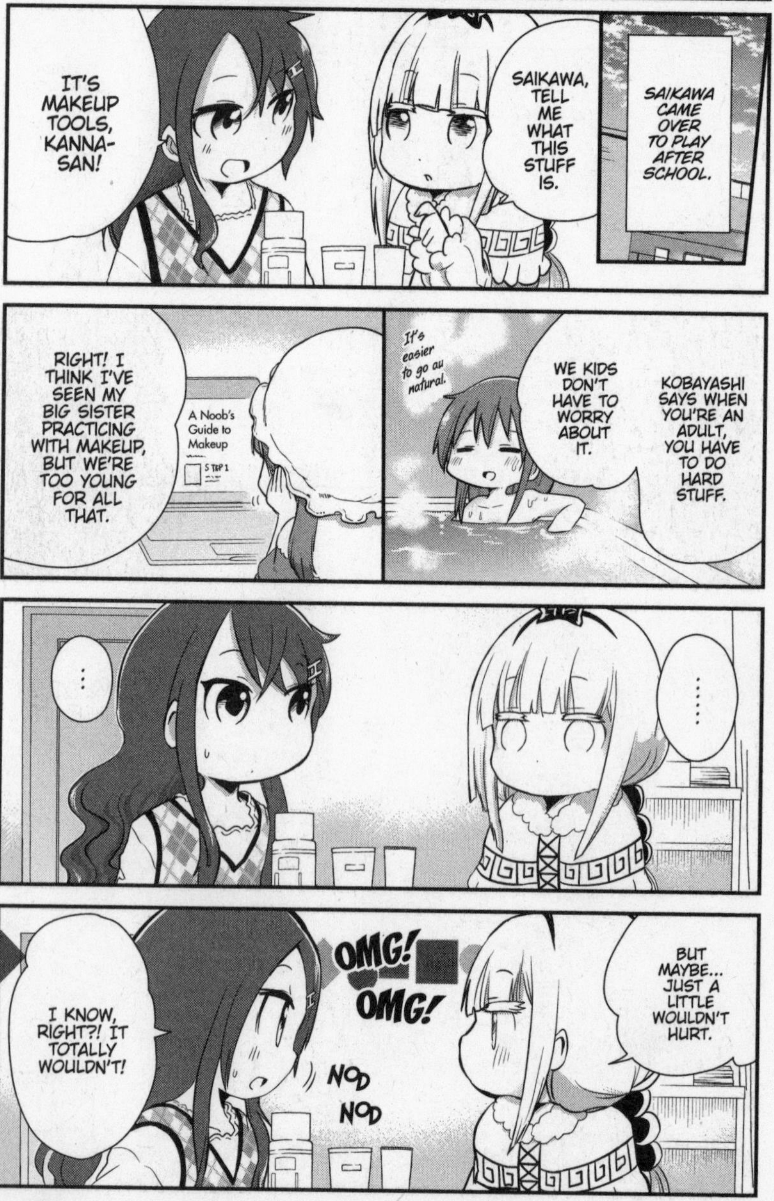
SAIKAWA CAME OVER TO PLAY AFTER SCHOOL.
SAIKAWA, TELL ME WHAT THIS STUFF IS.
IT'S MAKEUP TOOLS, KANNA-SAN!
KOBAYASHI SAYS WHEN YOU'RE AN ADULT, YOU HAVE TO DO HARD STUFF.
WE KIDS DON'T HAVE TO WORRY ABOUT IT.
It's easier to go au natural.
A Noob's Guide to Makeup
STEP 1
RIGHT! I THINK I'VE SEEN MY BIG SISTER PRACTICING WITH MAKEUP, BUT WE'RE TOO YOUNG FOR ALL THAT.
......
...
BUT MAYBE... JUST A LITTLE WOULDN'T HURT.
OMG! OMG!
NOD NOD
I KNOW, RIGHT?! IT TOTALLY WOULDN'T!

WASTE NOT, WANT NOT

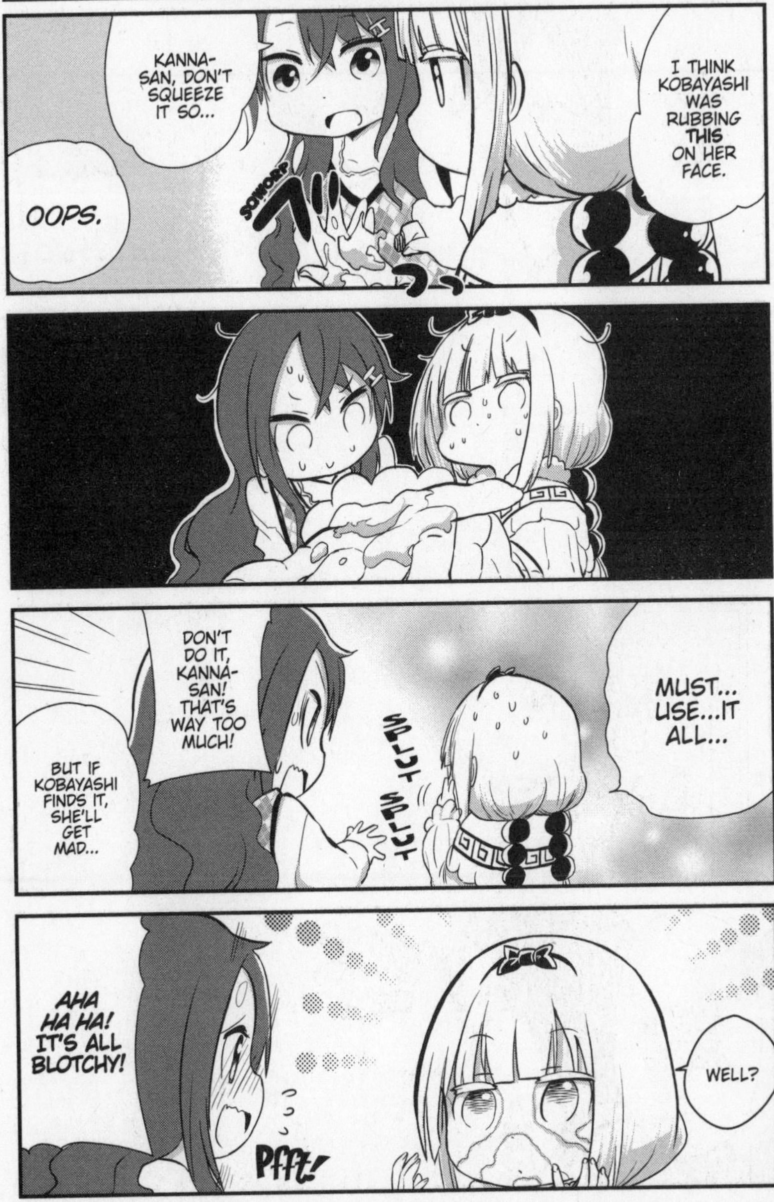

I THINK KOBAYASHI WAS RUBBING THIS ON HER FACE.
KANNA-SAN, DON'T SQUEEZE IT SO...
SQWORP
OOPS.
MUST... USE...IT ALL...
DON'T DO IT, KANNA-SAN! THAT'S WAY TOO MUCH!
SPLUT SPLUT
BUT IF KOBAYASHI FINDS IT, SHE'LL GET MAD...
WELL?
AHA HA HA! IT'S ALL BLOTCHY!
Pfft!

TARGET ACQUIRED

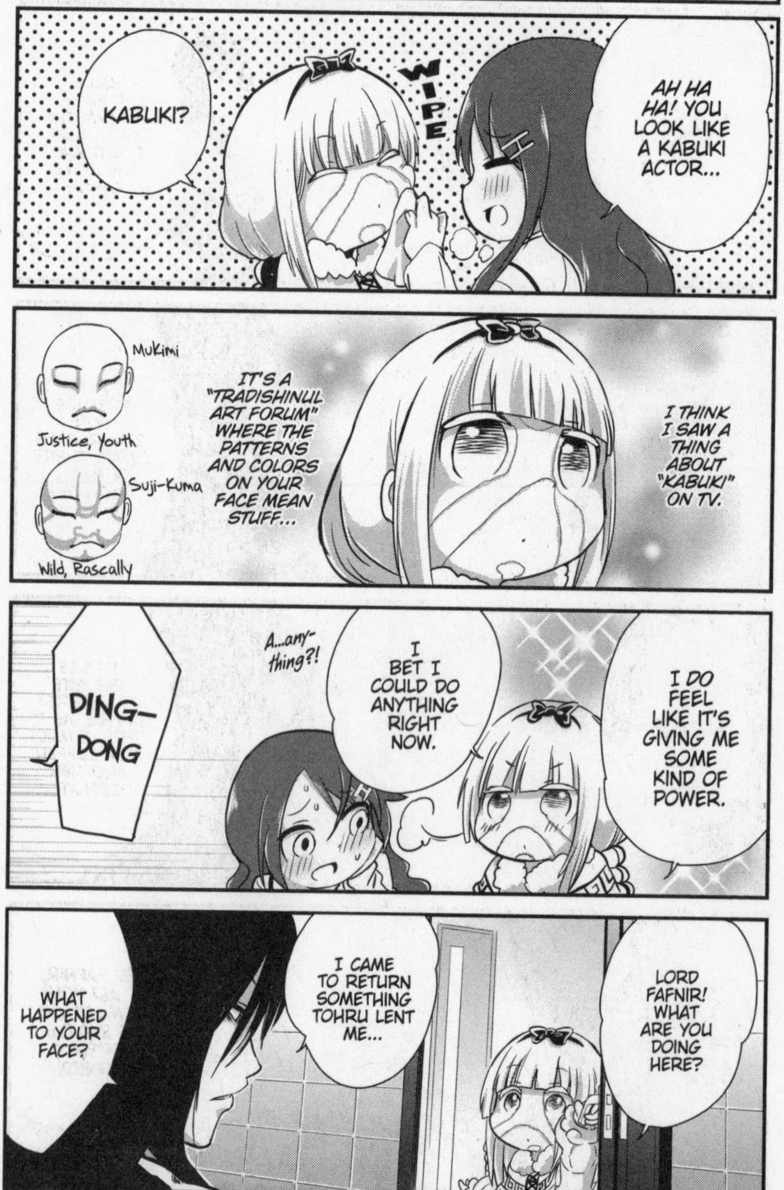
AH HA HA! YOU LOOK LIKE A KABUKI ACTOR...
WIPE
KABUKI?
I THINK I SAW A THING ABOUT "KABUKI" ON TV.
IT'S A "TRADISHINUL ART FORUM" WHERE THE PATTERNS AND COLORS ON YOUR FACE MEAN STUFF...
Mukimi
Justice, Youth
Suji-Kuma
Wild, Rascally
I DO FEEL LIKE IT'S GIVING ME SOME KIND OF POWER.
I BET I COULD DO ANYTHING RIGHT NOW.
A...anything?!
DING-DONG
LORD FAFNIR! WHAT ARE YOU DOING HERE?
I CAME TO RETURN SOMETHING TOHRU LENT ME...
WHAT HAPPENED TO YOUR FACE?

BATTLE PAINT

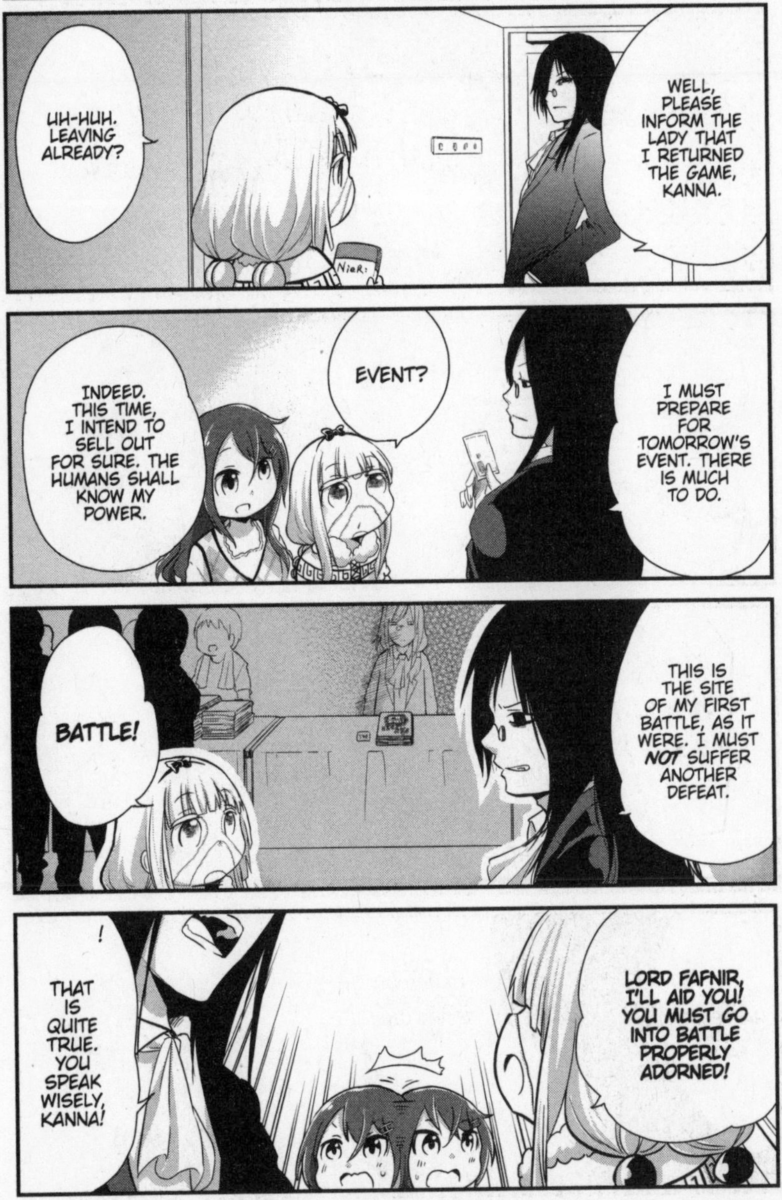
WELL, PLEASE INFORM THE LADY THAT I RETURNED THE GAME, KANNA.
UH-HUH. LEAVING ALREADY?
NieR:
I MUST PREPARE FOR TOMORROW'S EVENT. THERE IS MUCH TO DO.
EVENT?
INDEED. THIS TIME, I INTEND TO SELL OUT FOR SURE. THE HUMANS SHALL KNOW MY POWER.
THIS IS THE SITE OF MY FIRST BATTLE, AS IT WERE. I MUST NOT SUFFER ANOTHER DEFEAT.
BATTLE!
LORD FAFNIR, I'LL AID YOU! YOU MUST GO INTO BATTLE PROPERLY ADORNED!
!
THAT IS QUITE TRUE. YOU SPEAK WISELY, KANNA!

FAFNIR IS PLEASED

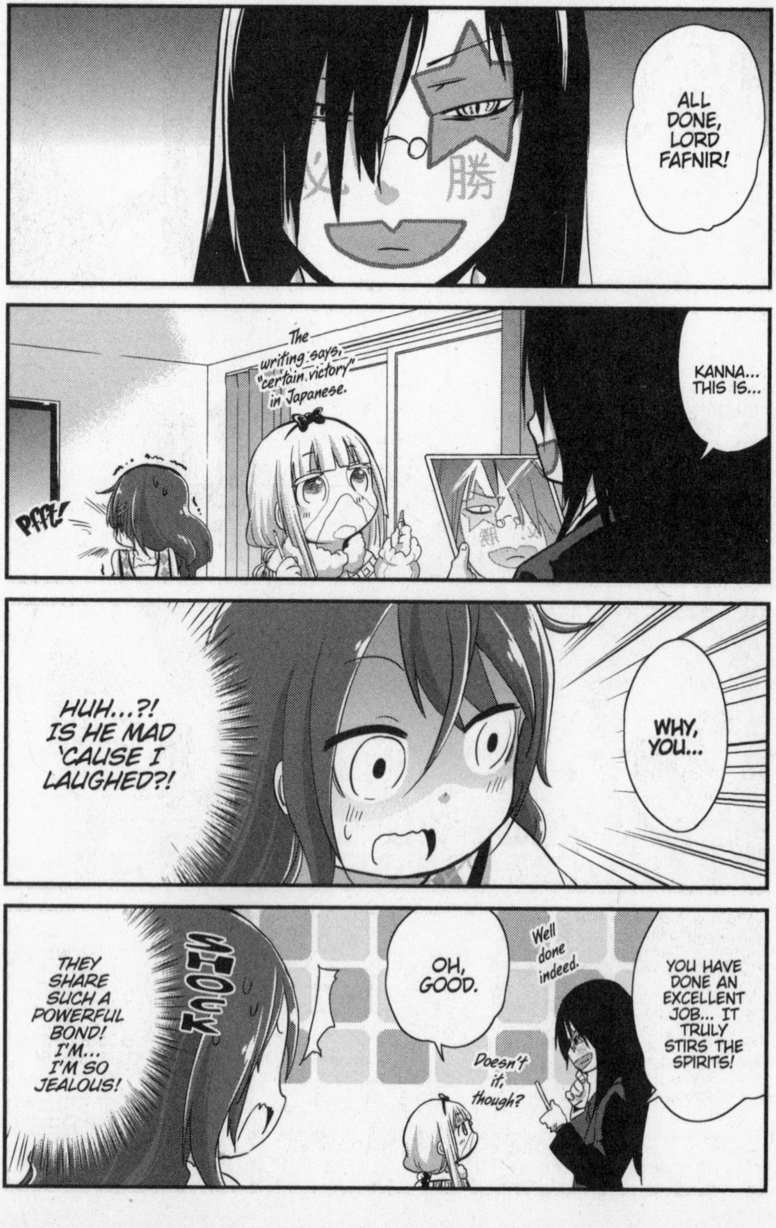
ALL DONE, LORD FAFNIR!
KANNA... THIS IS...
The writing says, "certain victory" in Japanese.
PFFT!
WHY, YOU...
HUH...?! IS HE MAD 'CAUSE I LAUGHED?!
YOU HAVE DONE AN EXCELLENT JOB... IT TRULY STIRS THE SPIRITS!
Well done indeed.
OH, GOOD.
Doesn't it, though?
SHOCK
THEY SHARE SUCH A POWERFUL BOND! I'M... I'M SO JEALOUS!

A TROUBLING DEVELOPMENT

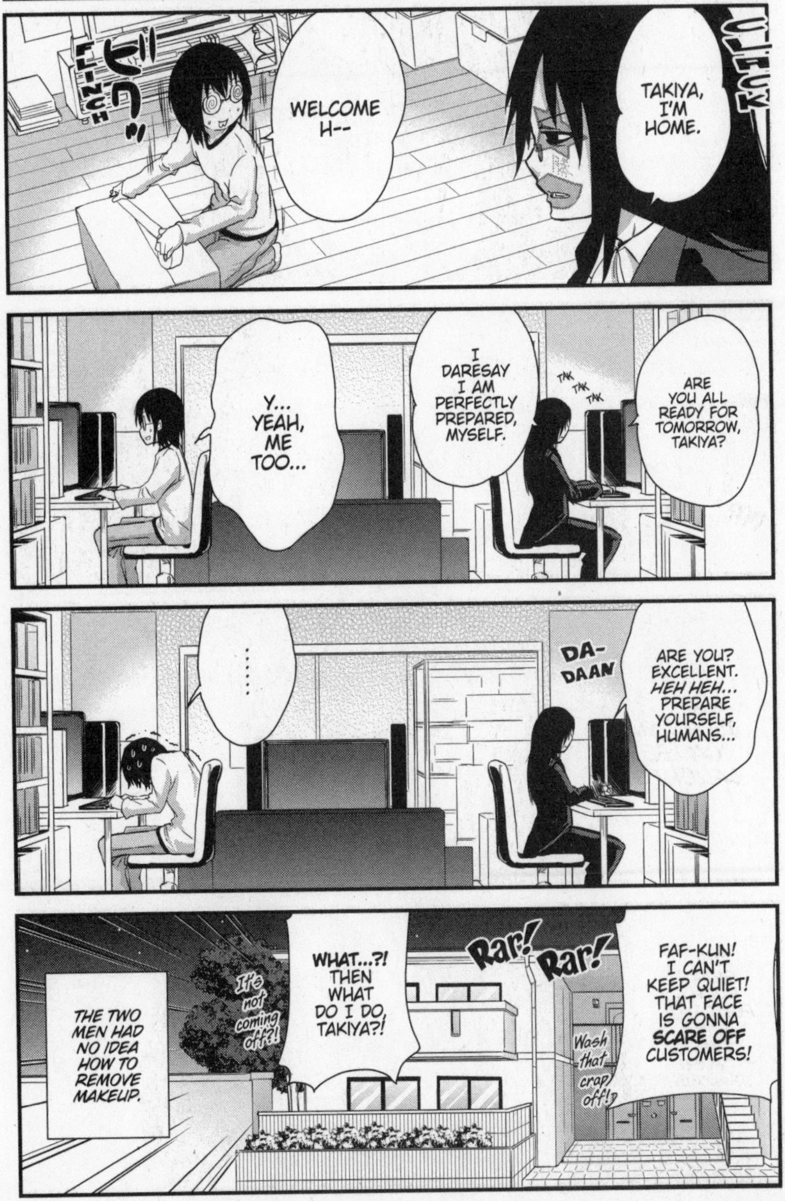
CLACK
TAKIYA, I'M HOME.
WELCOME H--
FLINCH
ARE YOU ALL READY FOR TOMORROW, TAKIYA?
TAK TAK TAK
I DARESAY I AM PERFECTLY PREPARED, MYSELF.
Y... YEAH, ME TOO...
ARE YOU? EXCELLENT. HEH HEH... PREPARE YOURSELF, HUMANS...
DA-DAAN
......
FAF-KUN! I CAN'T KEEP QUIET! THAT FACE IS GONNA SCARE OFF CUSTOMERS!
Wash that crap off!?
Rar! Rar!
WHAT...?! THEN WHAT DO I DO, TAKIYA?!
It's not coming off?!
THE TWO MEN HAD NO IDEA HOW TO REMOVE MAKEUP.

ET TU, KANNA?!

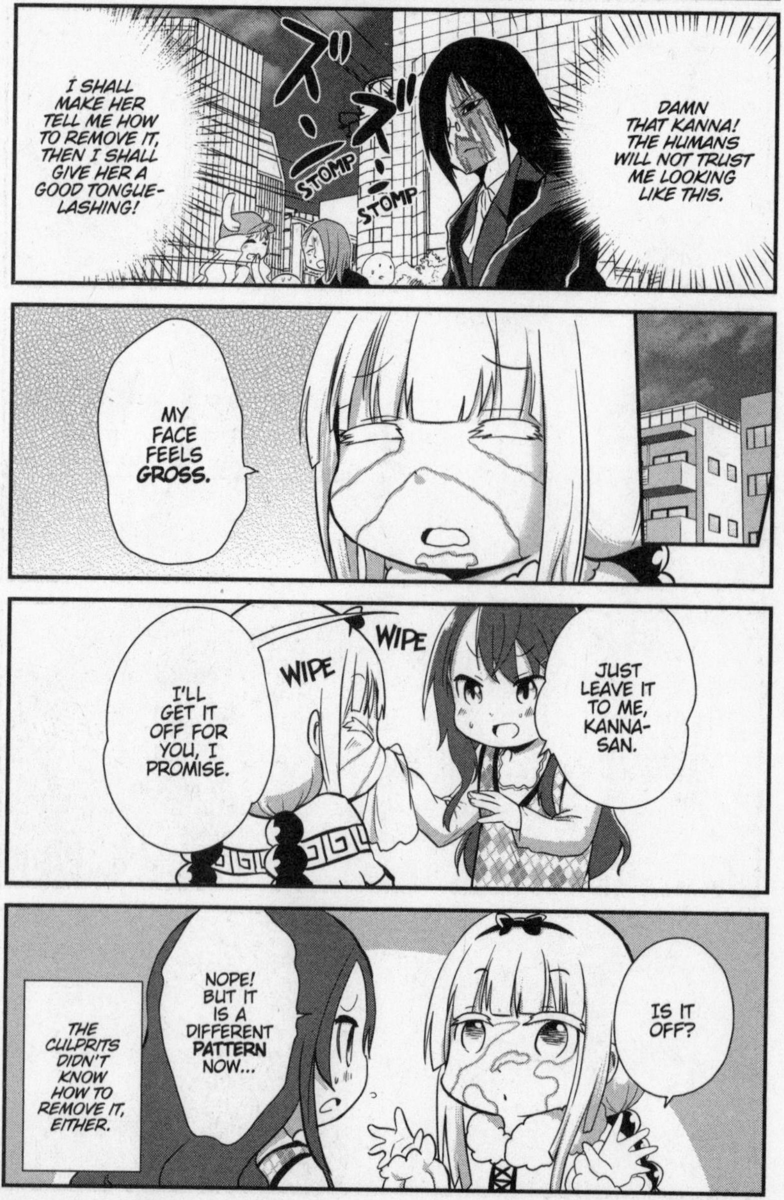
DAMN THAT KANNA! THE HUMANS WILL NOT TRUST ME LOOKING LIKE THIS.
STOMP
STOMP
I SHALL MAKE HER TELL ME HOW TO REMOVE IT, THEN I SHALL GIVE HER A GOOD TONGUE-LASHING!
MY FACE FEELS GROSS.
JUST LEAVE IT TO ME, KANNA-SAN.
WIPE
WIPE
I'LL GET IT OFF FOR YOU, I PROMISE.
IS IT OFF?
NOPE! BUT IT IS A DIFFERENT PATTERN NOW...
THE CULPRITS DIDN'T KNOW HOW TO REMOVE IT, EITHER.

PROMISES

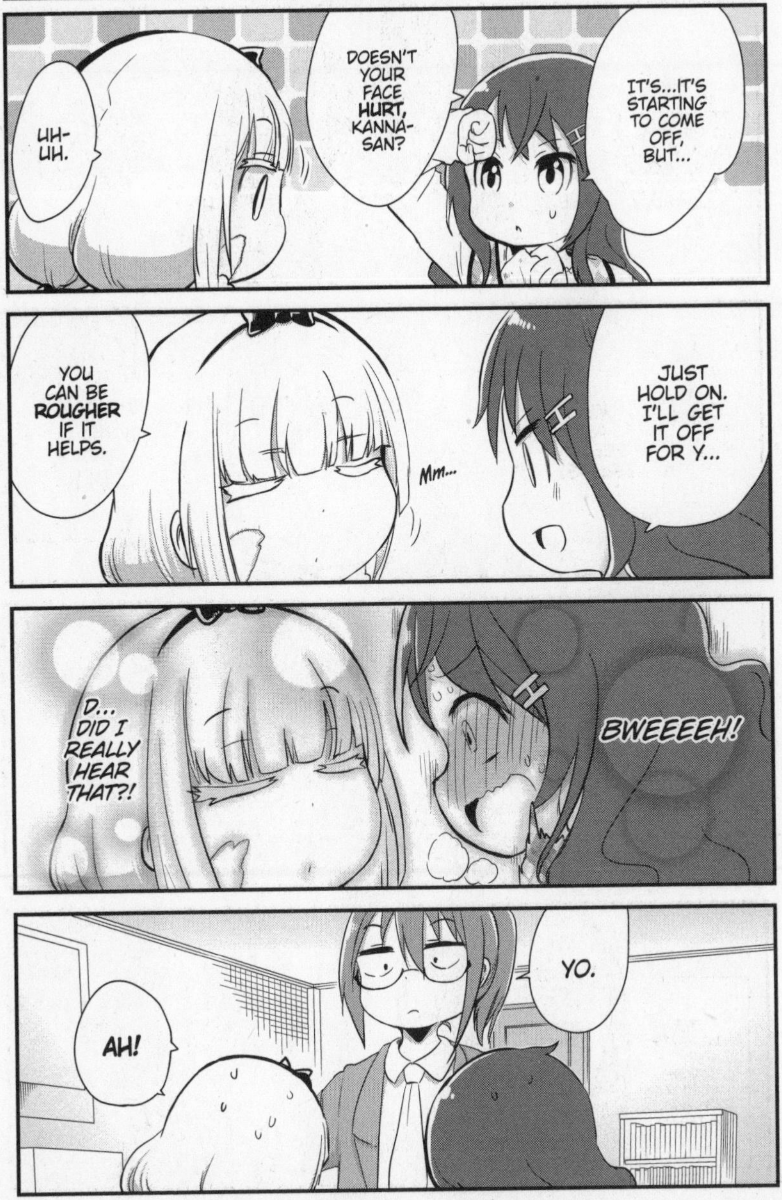
IT'S...IT'S STARTING TO COME OFF, BUT...
DOESN'T YOUR FACE HURT, KANNA-SAN?
UH-UH.
JUST HOLD ON. I'LL GET IT OFF FOR Y...
Mm...
YOU CAN BE ROUGHER IF IT HELPS.
BWEEEEH!
D... DID I REALLY HEAR THAT?!
YO.
AH!

DOING IT RIGHT

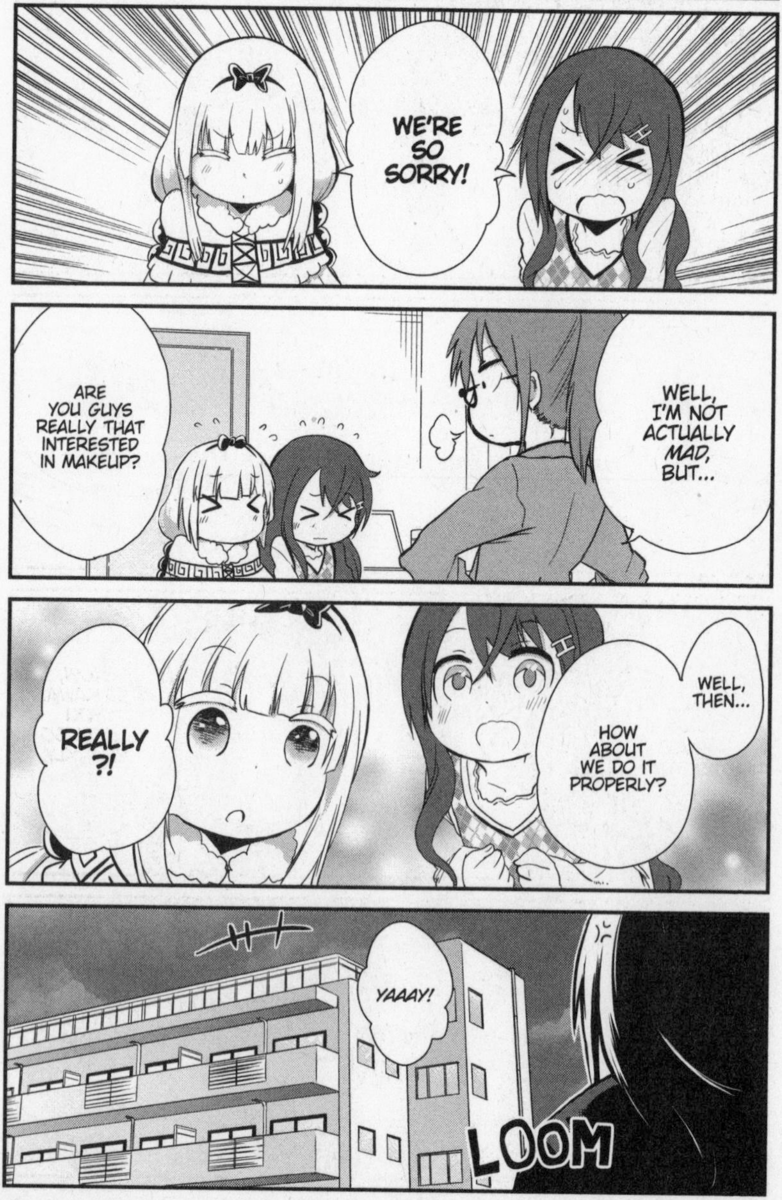
WE'RE SO SORRY!
WELL, I'M NOT ACTUALLY *MAD*, BUT...
ARE YOU GUYS REALLY THAT INTERESTED IN MAKEUP?
WELL, THEN...
HOW ABOUT WE DO IT PROPERLY?
REALLY ?!
YAAAY!
LOOM

SPARKLY MAGIC

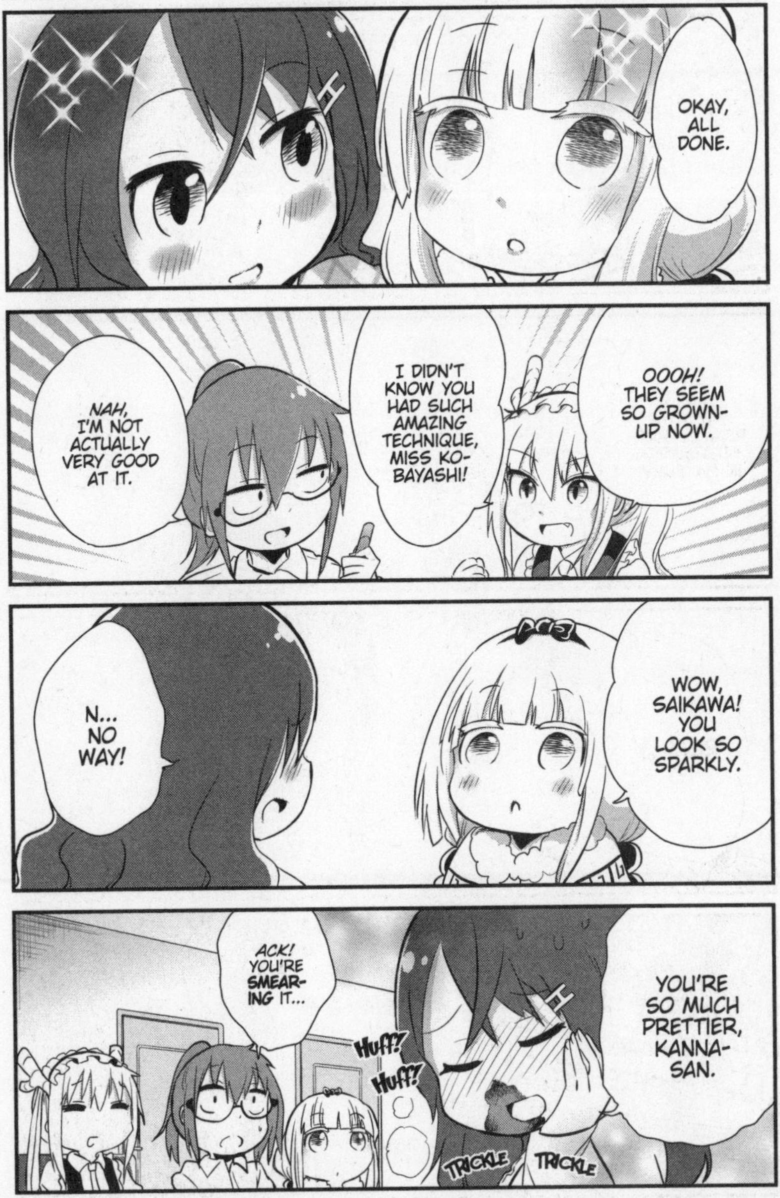
OKAY, ALL DONE.
OOOH! THEY SEEM SO GROWN-UP NOW.
I DIDN'T KNOW YOU HAD SUCH AMAZING TECHNIQUE, MISS KO-BAYASHI!
NAH, I'M NOT ACTUALLY VERY GOOD AT IT.
WOW, SAIKAWA! YOU LOOK SO SPARKLY.
N... NO WAY!
YOU'RE SO MUCH PRETTIER, KANNA-SAN.
TRICKLE
TRICKLE
HUFF!
HUFF!
ACK! YOU'RE SMEAR-ING IT...

THAT'S ALL, FOLKS

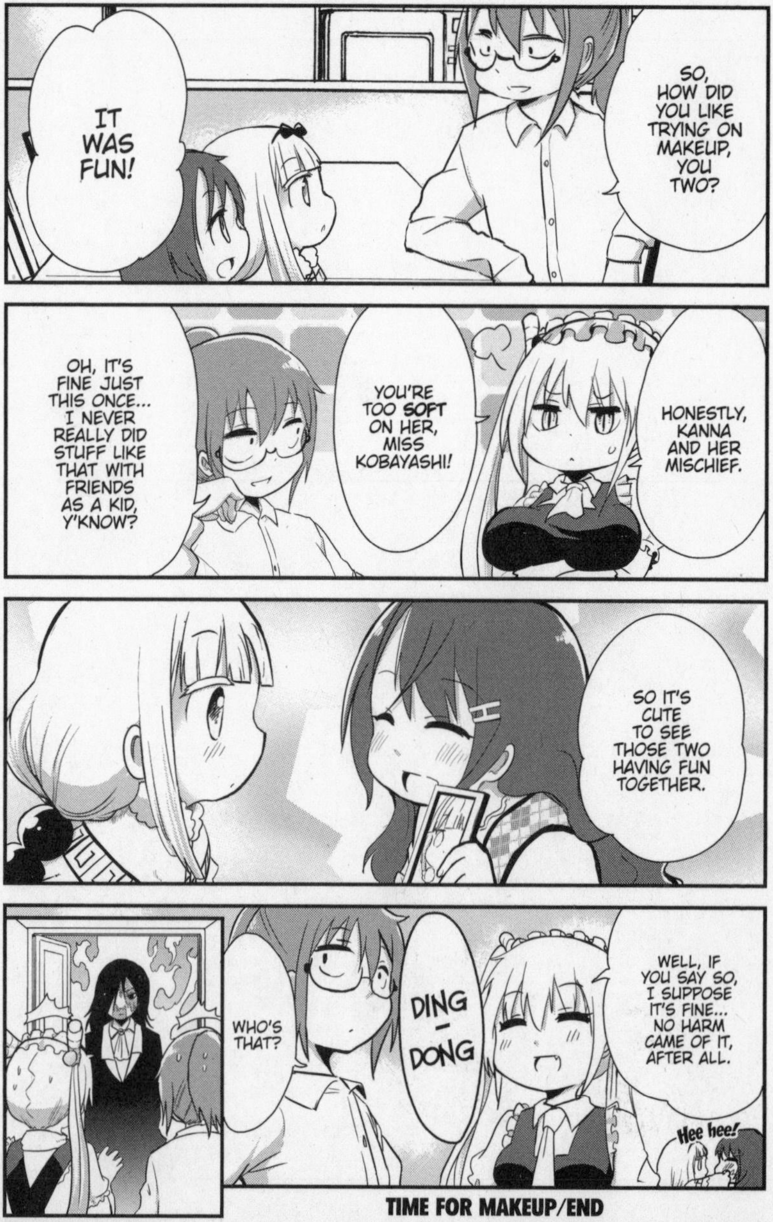
SO, HOW DID YOU LIKE TRYING ON MAKEUP, YOU TWO?
IT WAS FUN!
HONESTLY, KANNA AND HER MISCHIEF.
YOU'RE TOO SOFT ON HER, MISS KOBAYASHI!
OH, IT'S FINE JUST THIS ONCE... I NEVER REALLY DID STUFF LIKE THAT WITH FRIENDS AS A KID, Y'KNOW?
SO IT'S CUTE TO SEE THOSE TWO HAVING FUN TOGETHER.
WELL, IF YOU SAY SO, I SUPPOSE IT'S FINE... NO HARM CAME OF IT, AFTER ALL.
Hee hee!
DING-DONG
WHO'S THAT?

TIME FOR MAKEUP/END

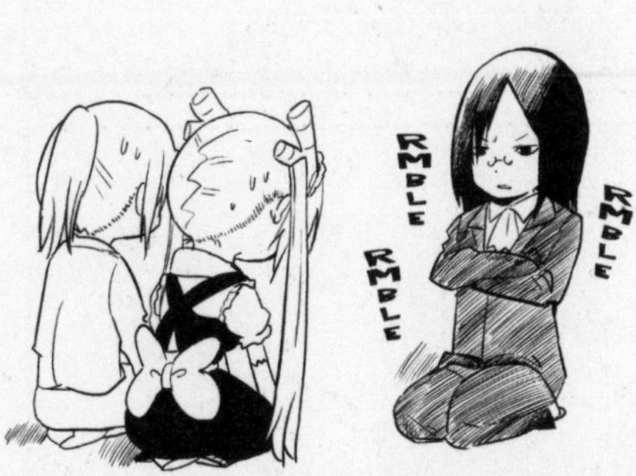
RMBLE
RMBLE
RMBLE

Miss Kobayashi's Dragon Maid

Kanna's Daily Life

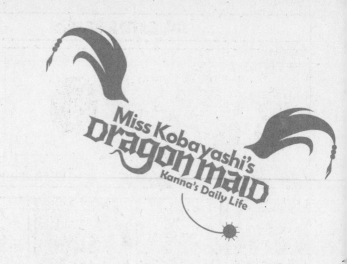

THE BATTLE BEGINS

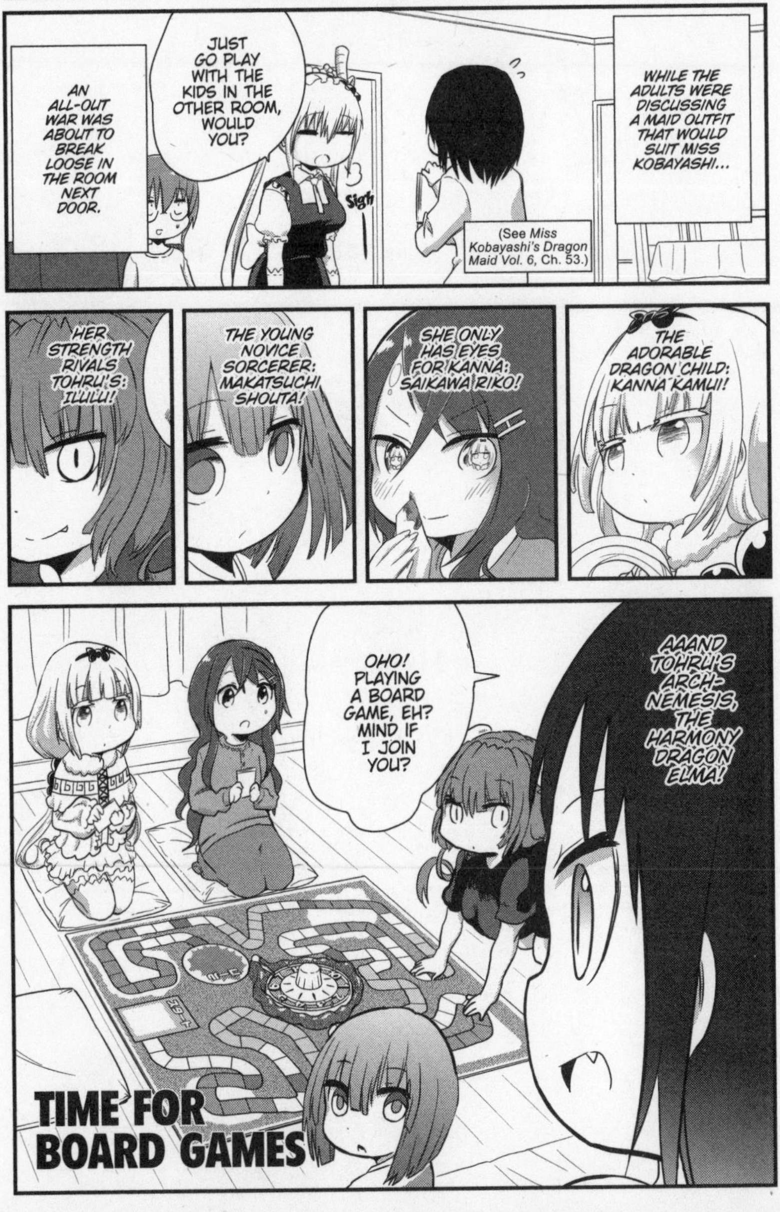
WHILE THE ADULTS WERE DISCUSSING A MAID OUTFIT THAT WOULD SUIT MISS KOBAYASHI...
(See *Miss Kobayashi's Dragon Maid* Vol. 6, Ch. 53.)
JUST GO PLAY WITH THE KIDS IN THE OTHER ROOM, WOULD YOU?
Sigh
AN ALL-OUT WAR WAS ABOUT TO BREAK LOOSE IN THE ROOM NEXT DOOR.
THE ADORABLE DRAGON CHILD: KANNA KAMUI!
SHE ONLY HAS EYES FOR KANNA: SAIKAWA RIKO!
THE YOUNG NOVICE SORCERER: MAKATSUCHI SHOUTA!
HER STRENGTH RIVALS TOHRU'S: ILULU!
AAAND TOHRU'S ARCH-NEMESIS, THE HARMONY DRAGON ELMA!
OHO! PLAYING A BOARD GAME, EH? MIND IF I JOIN YOU?
TIME FOR BOARD GAMES

SORRY, BUT THEY'RE RIGHT

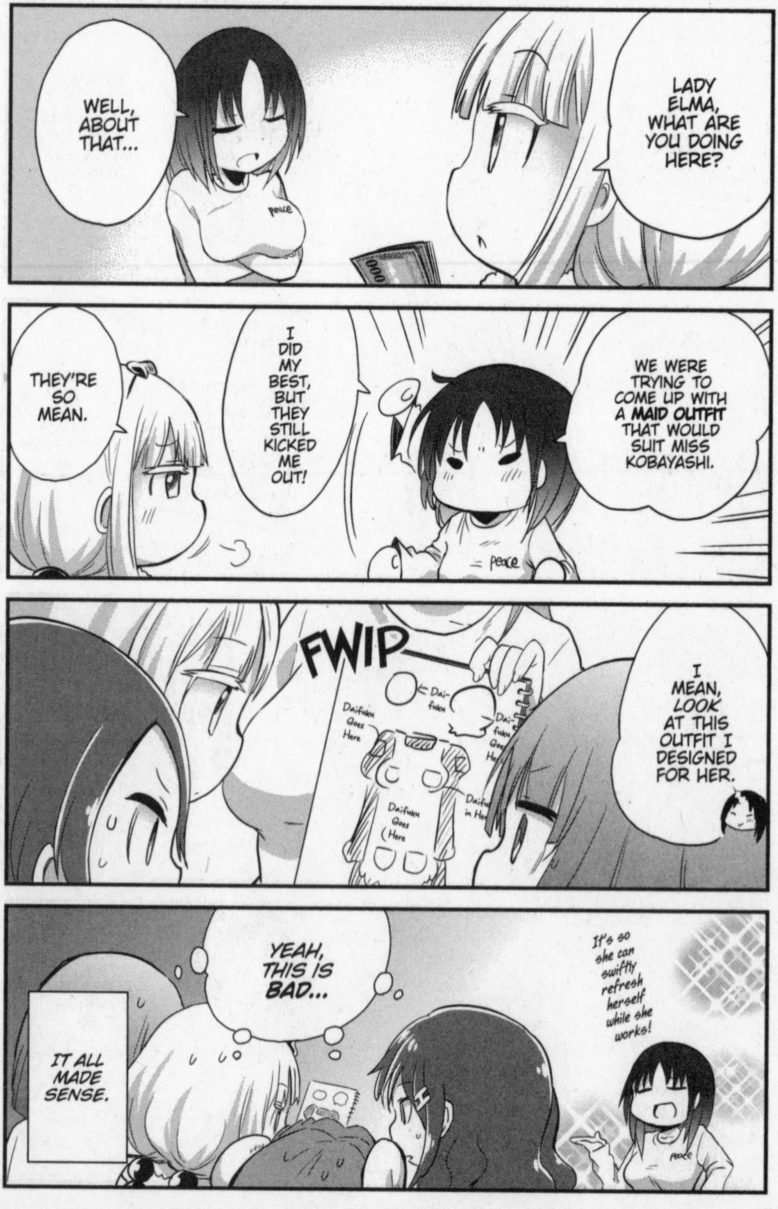
LADY ELMA, WHAT ARE YOU DOING HERE?
WELL, ABOUT THAT...
WE WERE TRYING TO COME UP WITH A **MAID OUTFIT** THAT WOULD SUIT MISS KOBAYASHI.
I DID MY BEST, BUT THEY STILL KICKED ME OUT!
THEY'RE SO MEAN.
I MEAN, *LOOK* AT THIS OUTFIT I DESIGNED FOR HER.
FWIP
Dai-fuku
Daifuku Goes Here
Daifuku Goes Here
It's so she can swiftly refresh herself while she works!
YEAH, THIS IS BAD...
IT ALL MADE SENSE.

OFF TO A GOOD START

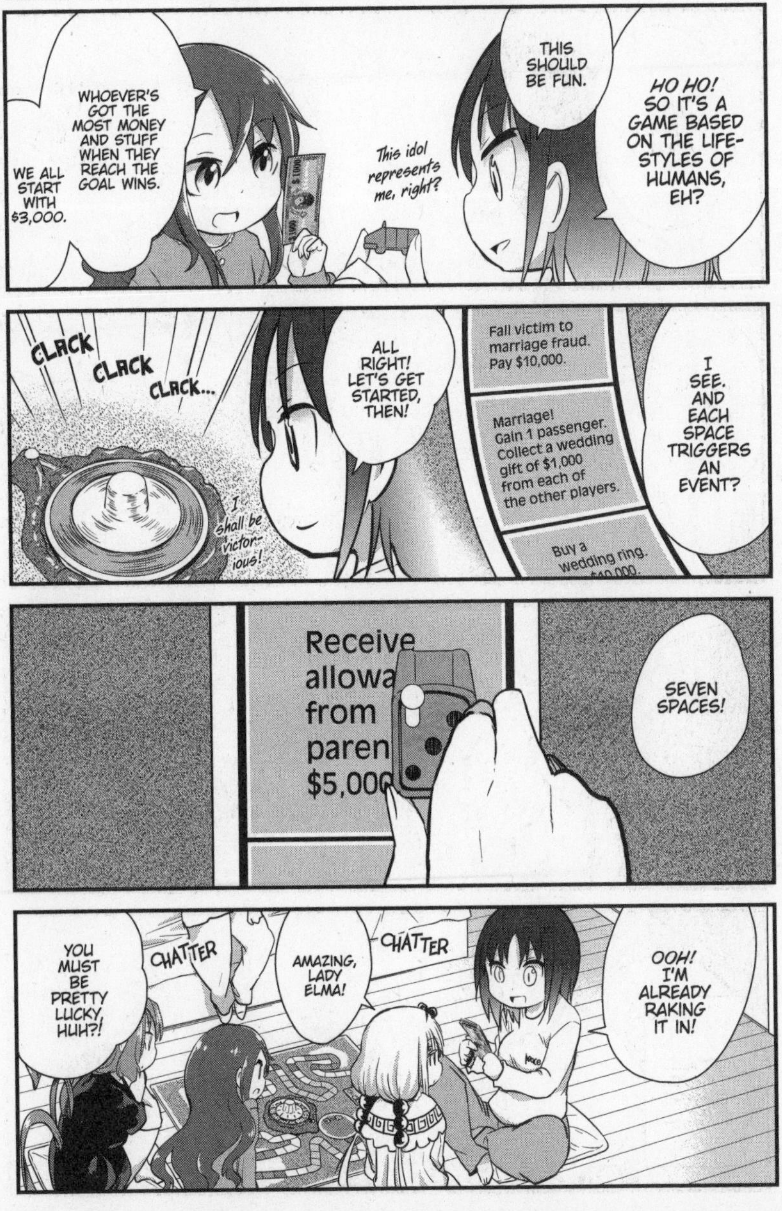
HO HO! SO IT'S A GAME BASED ON THE LIFE-STYLES OF HUMANS, EH?
THIS SHOULD BE FUN.
This idol represents me, right?
WHOEVER'S GOT THE MOST MONEY AND STUFF WHEN THEY REACH THE GOAL WINS.
WE ALL START WITH $3,000.
I SEE. AND EACH SPACE TRIGGERS AN EVENT?
Fall victim to marriage fraud. Pay $10,000.
Marriage! Gain 1 passenger. Collect a wedding gift of $1,000 from each of the other players.
Buy a wedding ring.
ALL RIGHT! LET'S GET STARTED, THEN!
I shall be victorious!
CLACK
CLACK
CLACK...
SEVEN SPACES!
Receive allowa from paren $5,000
OOH! I'M ALREADY RAKING IT IN!
CHATTER
AMAZING, LADY ELMA!
CHATTER
YOU MUST BE PRETTY LUCKY, HUH?!

KANNA'S HOT STREAK

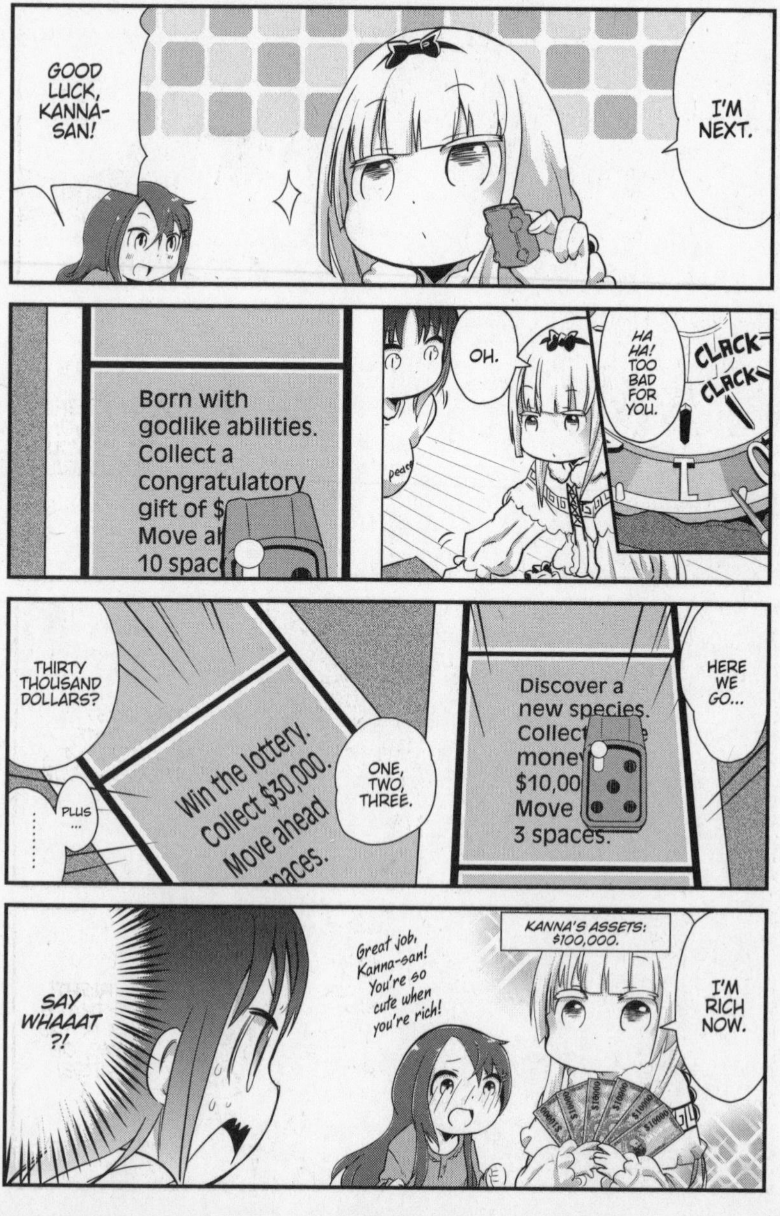

I'M NEXT.
GOOD LUCK, KANNA-SAN!
CLACK
CLACK
HA HA! TOO BAD FOR YOU.
OH.
Born with godlike abilities. Collect a congratulatory gift of $
Move a
10 spac
HERE WE GO...
Discover a new species. Collect
mone
$10,00
Move
3 spaces.
ONE, TWO, THREE.
Win the lottery. Collect $30,000. Move ahead
spaces.
THIRTY THOUSAND DOLLARS?
PLUS...
......
KANNA'S ASSETS: $100,000.
I'M RICH NOW.
Great job, Kanna-san! You're so cute when you're rich!
SAY WHAAAT?!

SHOUTA-KUN IS POPULAR

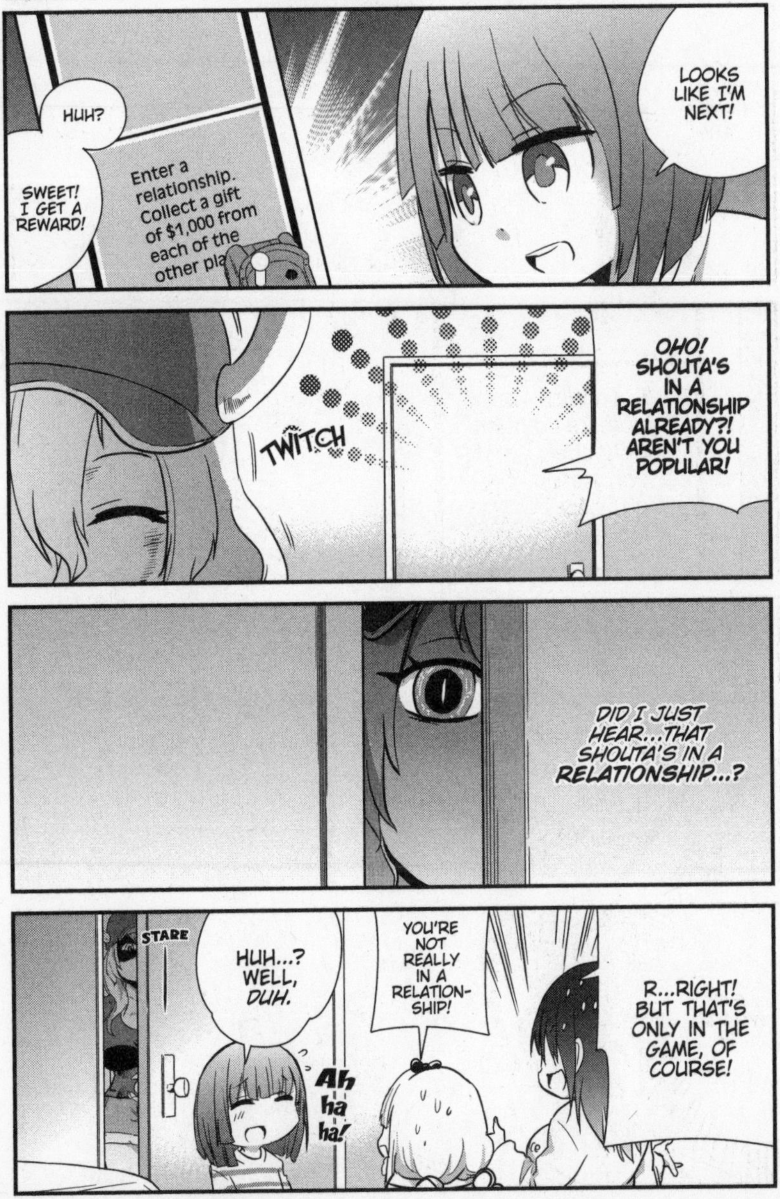
LOOKS LIKE I'M NEXT!
HUH?
Enter a relationship. Collect a gift of $1,000 from each of the other pla
SWEET! I GET A REWARD!
OHO! SHOUTA'S IN A RELATIONSHIP ALREADY?! AREN'T YOU POPULAR!
TWITCH
DID I JUST HEAR...THAT SHOUTA'S IN A RELATIONSHIP...?
R...RIGHT! BUT THAT'S ONLY IN THE GAME, OF COURSE!
YOU'RE NOT REALLY IN A RELATION-SHIP!
Ah ha ha!
HUH...? WELL, DUH.
STARE

TOO MUCH INFORMATION

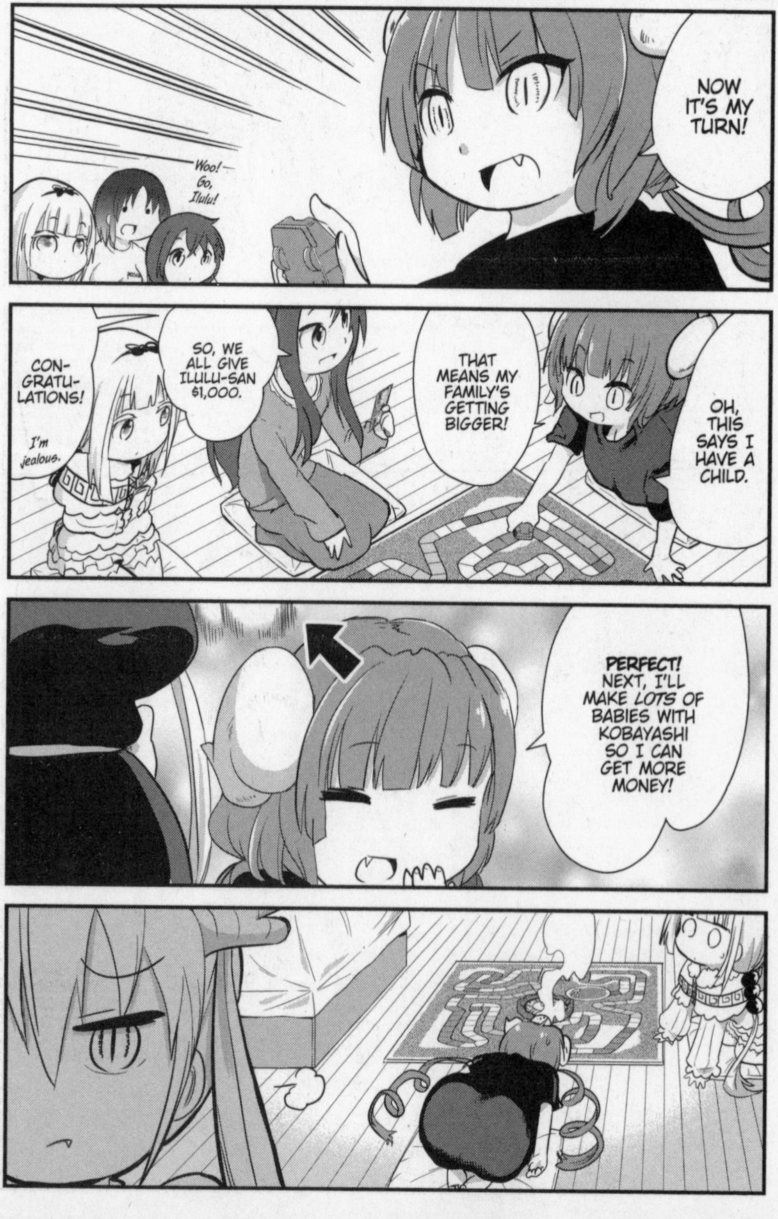
NOW IT'S MY TURN!
Woo! Go, Ilulu!
OH, THIS SAYS I HAVE A CHILD.
THAT MEANS MY FAMILY'S GETTING BIGGER!
SO, WE ALL GIVE ILULU-SAN $1,000.
CONGRATULATIONS!
I'm jealous.
PERFECT! NEXT, I'LL MAKE LOTS OF BABIES WITH KOBAYASHI SO I CAN GET MORE MONEY!

SAIKAWA-SAN'S REAL GOAL

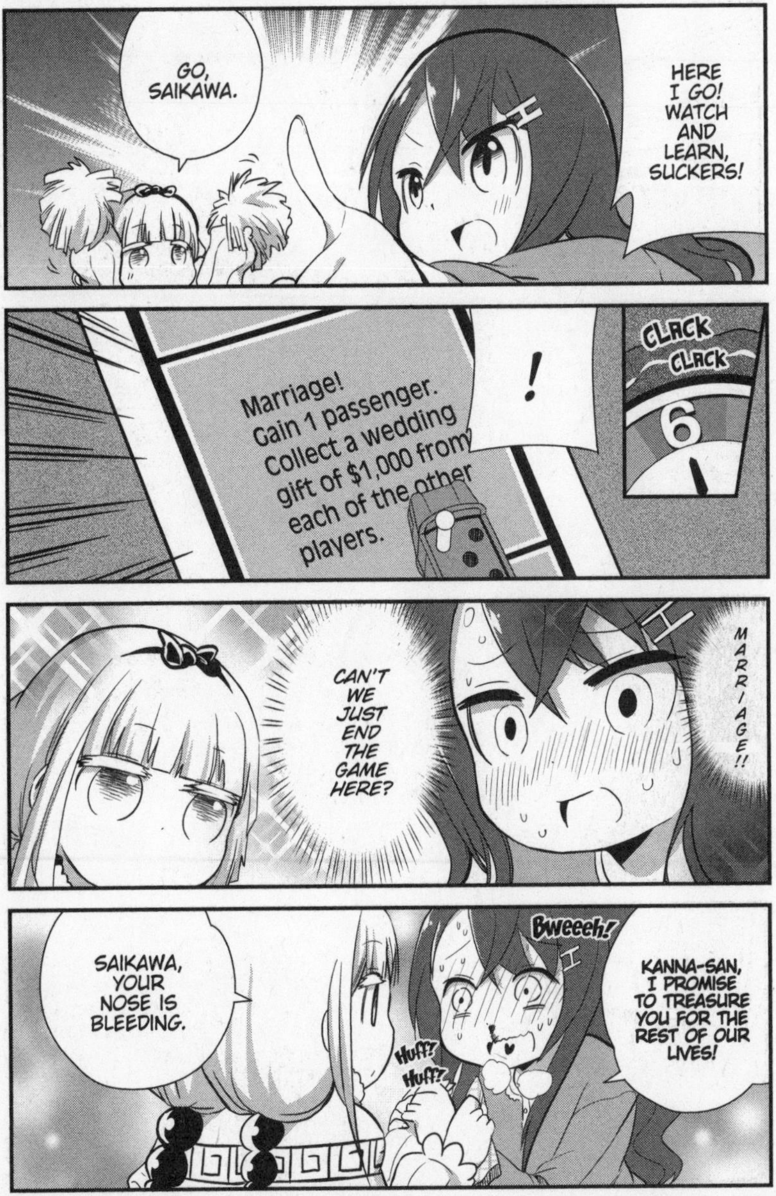
HERE I GO! WATCH AND LEARN, SUCKERS!
GO, SAIKAWA.
CLACK
CLACK
6
!
Marriage! Gain 1 passenger. Collect a wedding gift of $1,000 from each of the other players.
MARRIAGE!!
CAN'T WE JUST END THE GAME HERE?
Bweeeh!
KANNA-SAN, I PROMISE TO TREASURE YOU FOR THE REST OF OUR LIVES!
Huff! Huff!
SAIKAWA, YOUR NOSE IS BLEEDING.

PRIORITIES

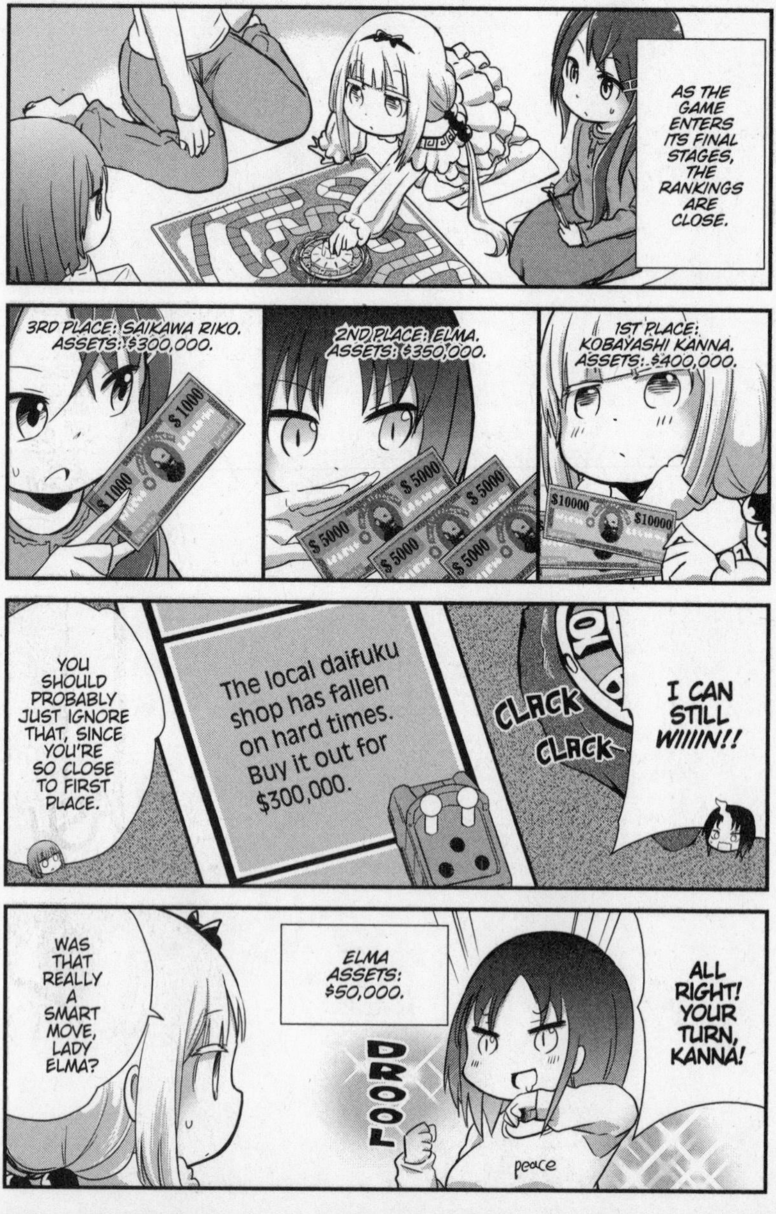
AS THE GAME ENTERS ITS FINAL STAGES, THE RANKINGS ARE CLOSE.
1ST PLACE: KOBAYASHI KANNA. ASSETS: $400,000.
$10000
$10000
2ND PLACE: ELMA. ASSETS: $350,000.
$ 5000
$ 5000
$ 5000
$ 5000
$ 5000
3RD PLACE: SAIKAWA RIKO. ASSETS: $300,000.
$ 1000
$ 1000
I CAN STILL WIIIIN!!
CLACK
CLACK
The local daifuku shop has fallen on hard times. Buy it out for $300,000.
YOU SHOULD PROBABLY JUST IGNORE THAT, SINCE YOU'RE SO CLOSE TO FIRST PLACE.
ALL RIGHT! YOUR TURN, KANNA!
ELMA ASSETS: $50,000.
DROOL
peace
WAS THAT REALLY A SMART MOVE, LADY ELMA?

GLUTTONY PAYS?

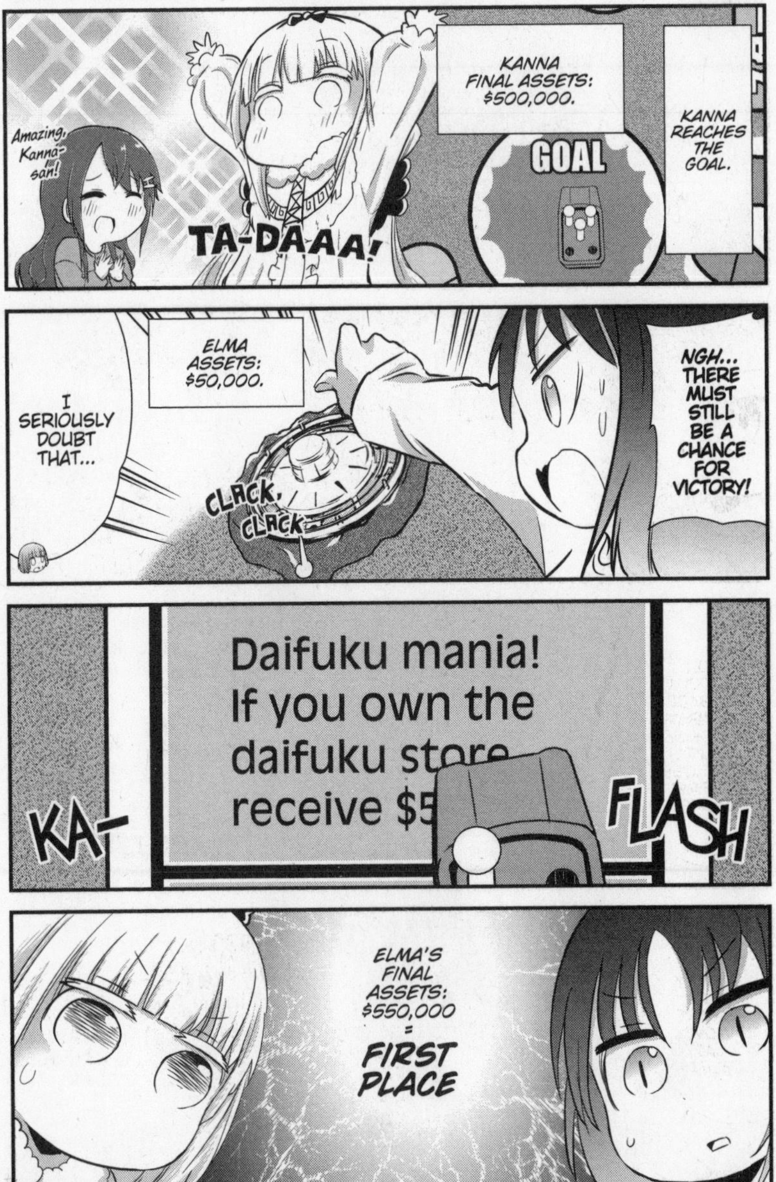
KANNA REACHES THE GOAL.
KANNA FINAL ASSETS: $500,000.
GOAL
Amazing, Kanna-san!
TA-DAAA!
NGH... THERE MUST STILL BE A CHANCE FOR VICTORY!
ELMA ASSETS: $50,000.
I SERIOUSLY DOUBT THAT...
CLACK, CLACK
FLASH
Daifuku mania! If you own the daifuku store receive $5
KA-
ELMA'S FINAL ASSETS: $550,000 = FIRST PLACE

KANNA VS. ELMA

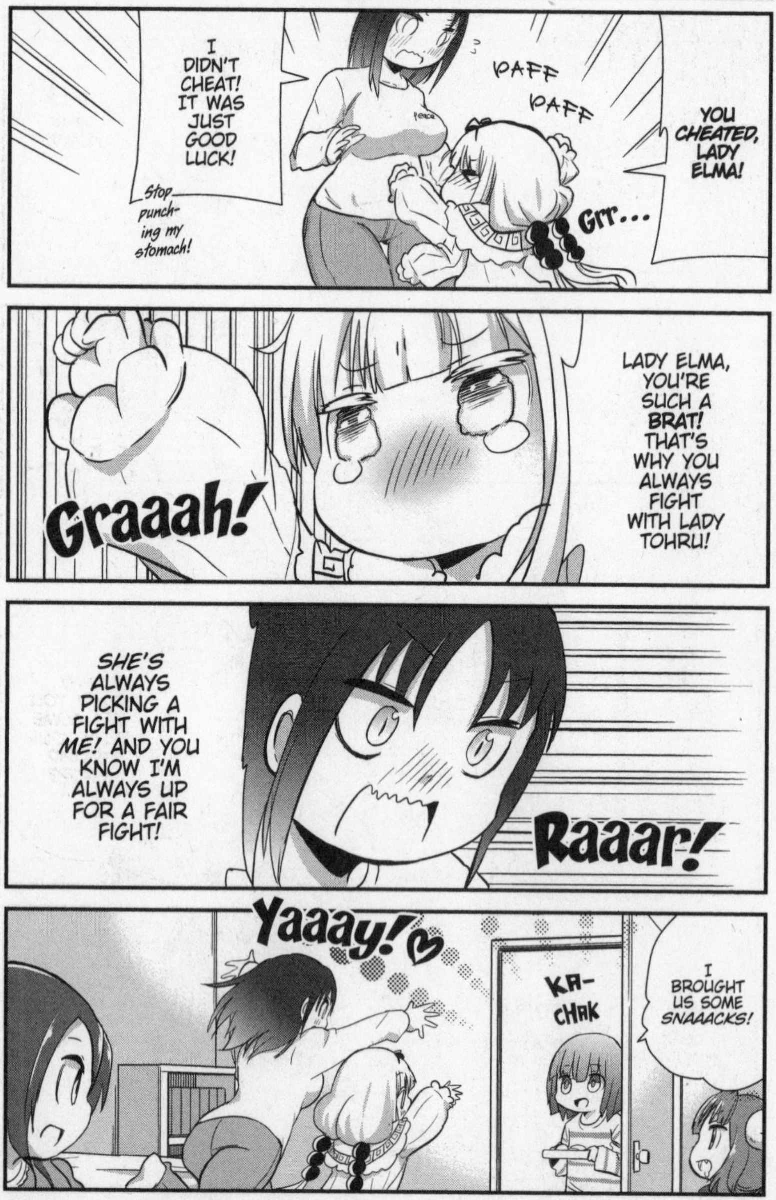
YOU CHEATED, LADY ELMA!
Grr...
PAFF
PAFF
I DIDN'T CHEAT! IT WAS JUST GOOD LUCK!
Stop punching my stomach!
LADY ELMA, YOU'RE SUCH A BRAT! THAT'S WHY YOU ALWAYS FIGHT WITH LADY TOHRU!
Graaah!
Raaar!
SHE'S ALWAYS PICKING A FIGHT WITH *ME!* AND YOU KNOW I'M ALWAYS UP FOR A FAIR FIGHT!
I BROUGHT US SOME *SNAAACKS!*
KA-CHAK
Yaaay!♡

DAIFUKU TRIUMPHANT

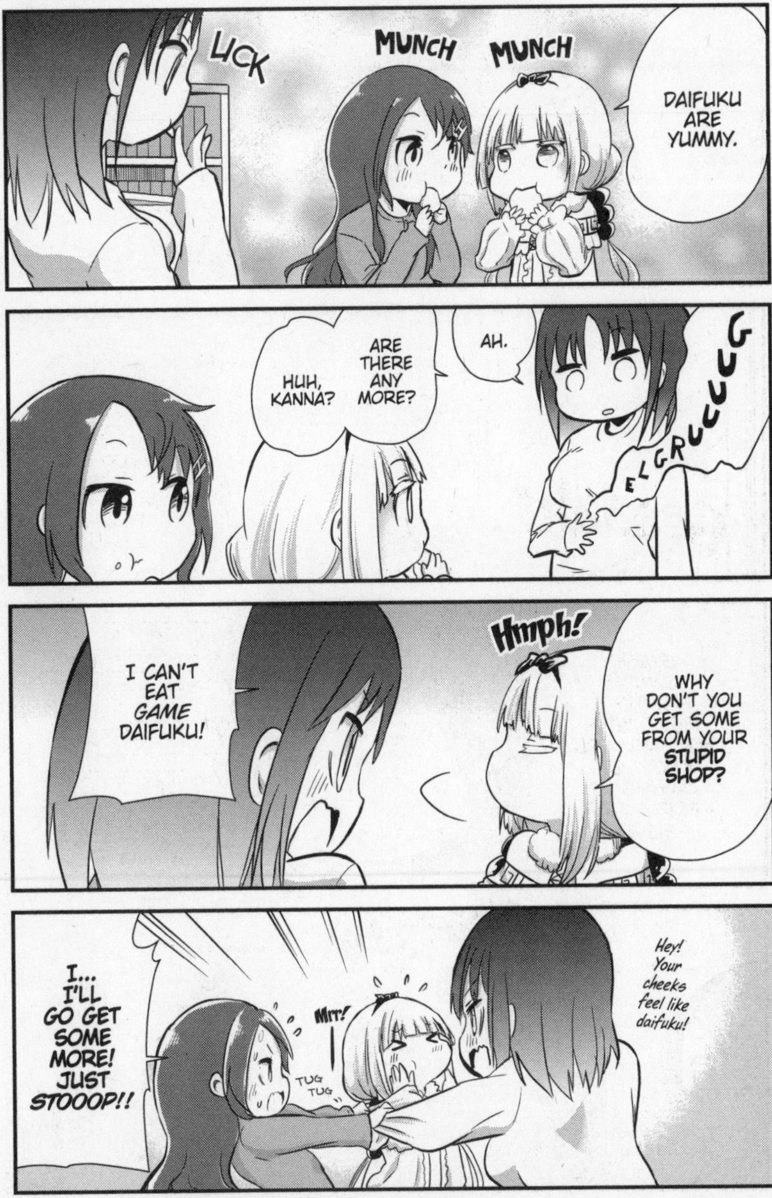
DAIFUKU ARE YUMMY.
MUNCH
MUNCH
LICK
ELGRUUUUG
AH.
HUH, KANNA? ARE THERE ANY MORE?
Hmph!
WHY DON'T YOU GET SOME FROM YOUR STUPID SHOP?
I CAN'T EAT GAME DAIFUKU!
Hey! Your cheeks feel like daifuku!
Mrr!
TUG TUG
I... I'LL GO GET SOME MORE! JUST STOOOP!!

ELMA DOESN'T FOOL AROUND

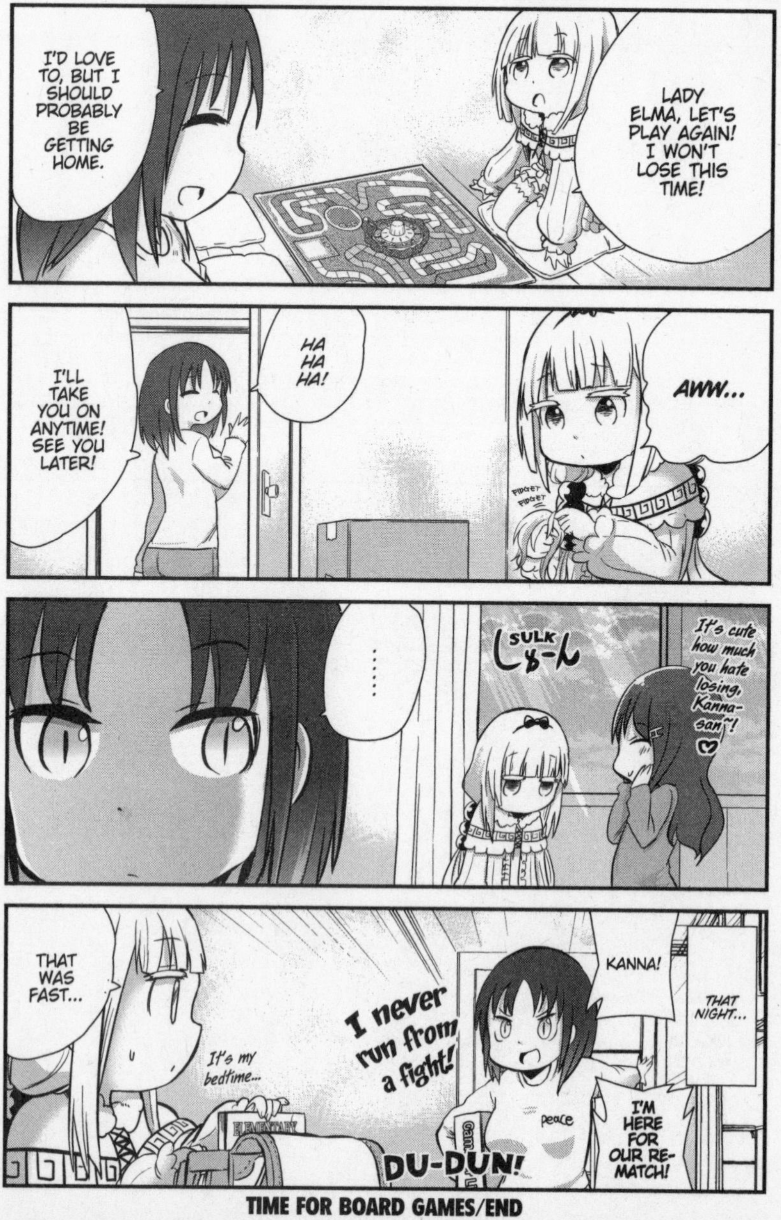
LADY ELMA, LET'S PLAY AGAIN! I WON'T LOSE THIS TIME!
I'D LOVE TO, BUT I SHOULD PROBABLY BE GETTING HOME.
AWW...
FIDGET FIDGET
HA HA HA!
I'LL TAKE YOU ON ANYTIME! SEE YOU LATER!
It's cute how much you hate losing, Kanna-san~!
SULK
......
THAT NIGHT...
KANNA!
I'M HERE FOR OUR RE-MATCH!
DU-DUN!
I never run from a fight!
peace
ELEMENTARY
It's my bedtime...
THAT WAS FAST...

TIME FOR BOARD GAMES/END

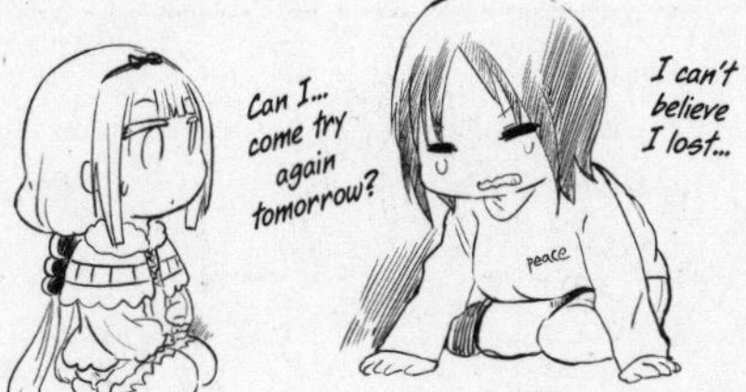
I can't believe I lost...
peace
Can I... come try again tomorrow?

Miss Kobayashi's Dragon Maid
Kanna's Daily Life

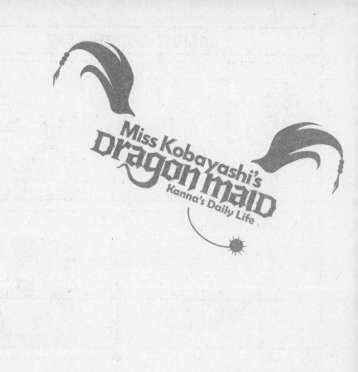

ALMOST MOTHER'S DAY

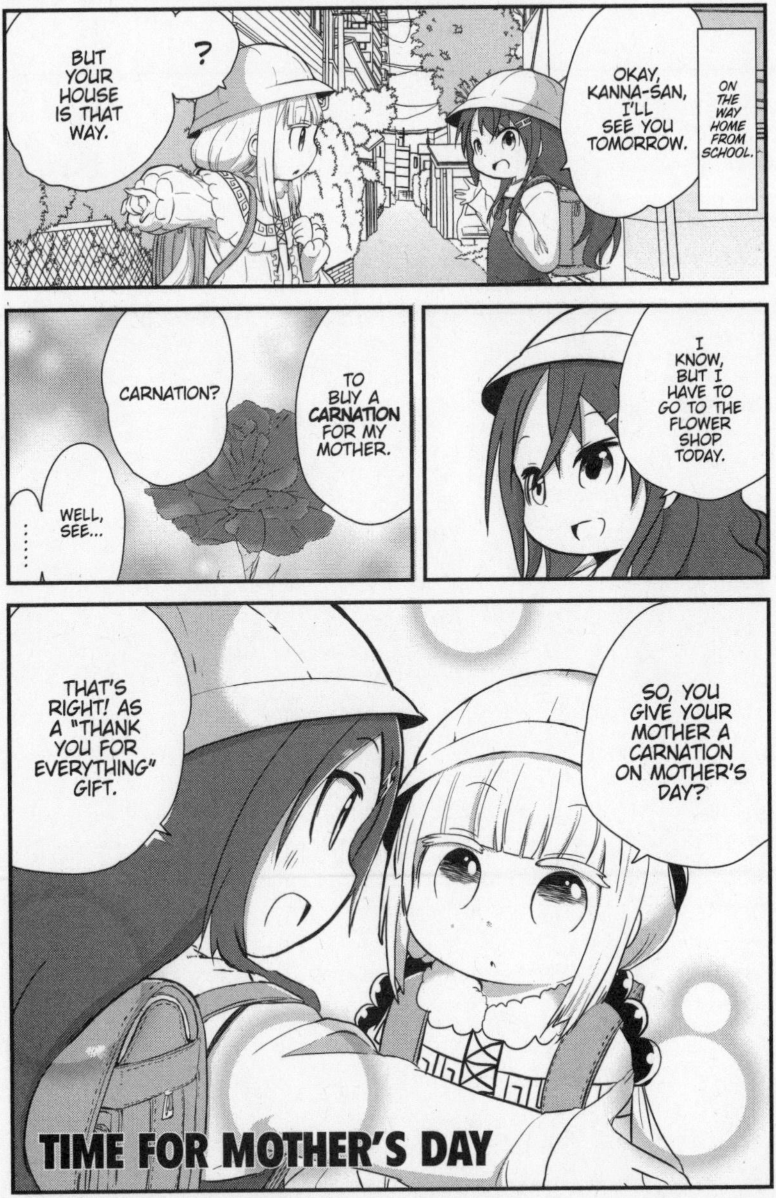
ON THE WAY HOME FROM SCHOOL.
OKAY, KANNA-SAN, I'LL SEE YOU TOMORROW.
?
BUT YOUR HOUSE IS THAT WAY.
I KNOW, BUT I HAVE TO GO TO THE FLOWER SHOP TODAY.
TO BUY A CARNATION FOR MY MOTHER.
CARNATION?
WELL, SEE...
......
SO, YOU GIVE YOUR MOTHER A CARNATION ON MOTHER'S DAY?
THAT'S RIGHT! AS A "THANK YOU FOR EVERYTHING" GIFT.
TIME FOR MOTHER'S DAY

CAN'T GO THERE

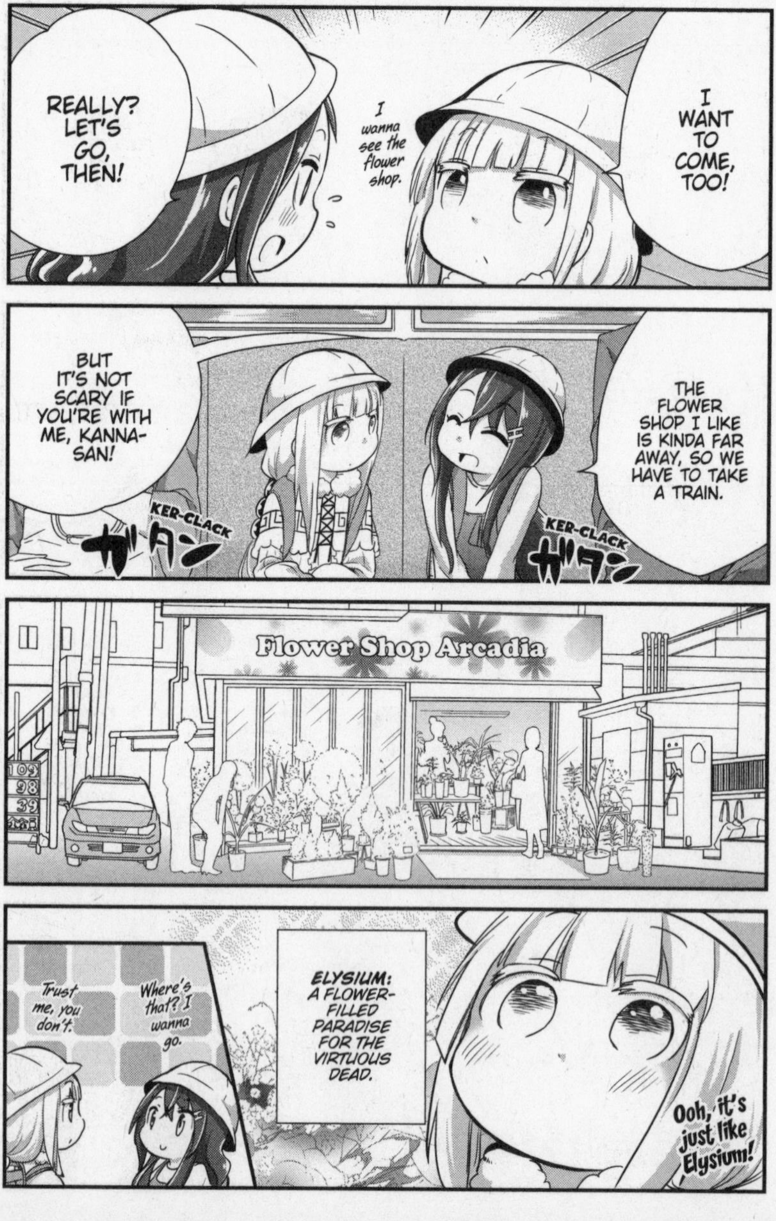
I WANT TO COME, TOO!
I wanna see the flower shop.
REALLY? LET'S GO, THEN!
THE FLOWER SHOP I LIKE IS KINDA FAR AWAY, SO WE HAVE TO TAKE A TRAIN.
KER-CLACK
BUT IT'S NOT SCARY IF YOU'RE WITH ME, KANNA-SAN!
KER-CLACK
Flower Shop Arcadia
Ooh, it's just like Elysium!
ELYSIUM: A FLOWER-FILLED PARADISE FOR THE VIRTUOUS DEAD.
Where's that? I wanna go.
Trust me, you don't.

WAS JUST TAGGING ALONG, BUT...

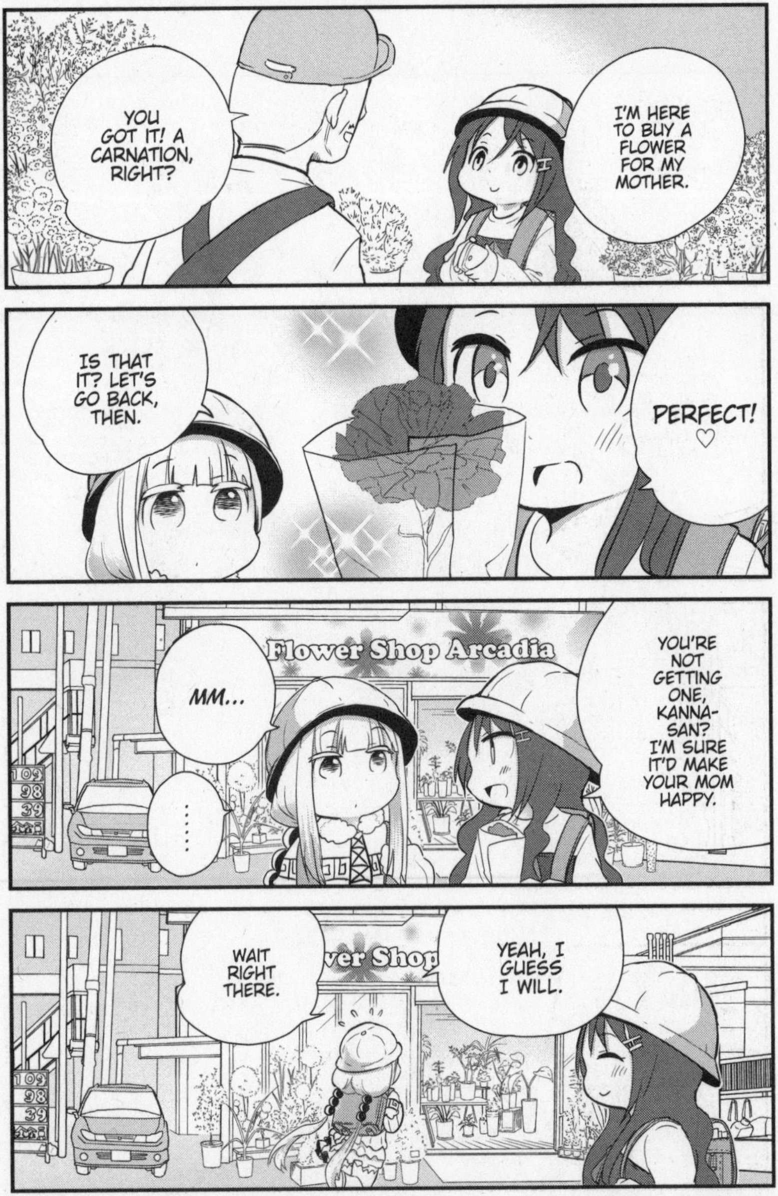
I'M HERE TO BUY A FLOWER FOR MY MOTHER.
YOU GOT IT! A CARNATION, RIGHT?
PERFECT! ♡
IS THAT IT? LET'S GO BACK, THEN.
YOU'RE NOT GETTING ONE, KANNA-SAN? I'M SURE IT'D MAKE YOUR MOM HAPPY.
Flower Shop Arcadia
MM...
......
109
98
39
YEAH, I GUESS I WILL.
ver Shop
WAIT RIGHT THERE.

TROUBLE IN PARADISE

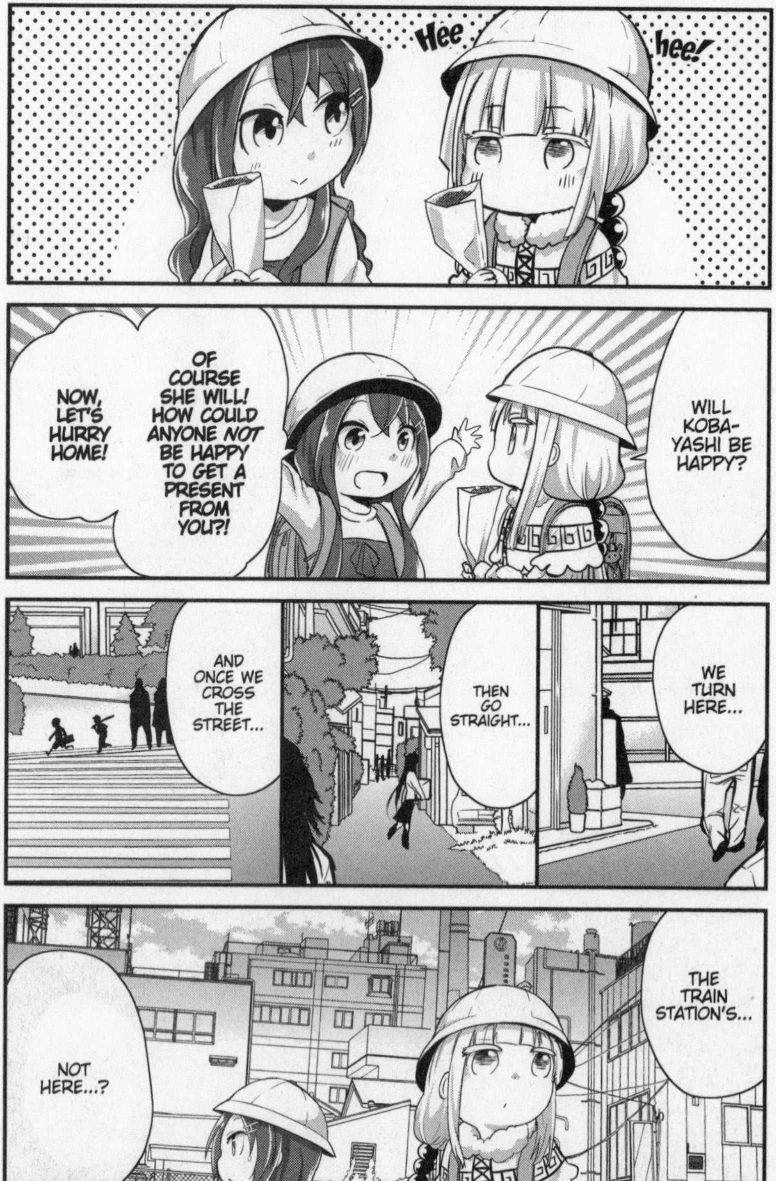
Hee hee!
WILL KOBAYASHI BE HAPPY?
OF COURSE SHE WILL! HOW COULD ANYONE *NOT* BE HAPPY TO GET A PRESENT FROM YOU?!
NOW, LET'S HURRY HOME!
WE TURN HERE...
THEN GO STRAIGHT...
AND ONCE WE CROSS THE STREET...
THE TRAIN STATION'S...
NOT HERE...?

DEEPER AND DEEPER

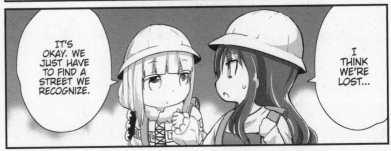

I THINK WE'RE LOST...
IT'S OKAY. WE JUST HAVE TO FIND A STREET WE RECOGNIZE.
Y... YOU'RE RIGHT! STANDING AROUND PANICKING WON'T GET US HOME.
LET'S SING AS WE WALK. WE'LL BE BACK ON TRACK BEFORE WE KNOW IT.
WHERE... ARE WE?

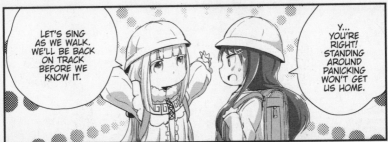

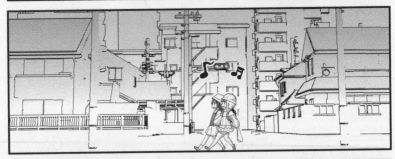

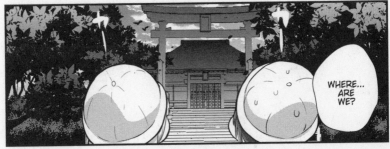

ALL ALONE

My feet hurt.

I WONDER IF MY MOM'LL BE WORRIED...

DON'T WORRY.

OR MAYBE SHE'LL BE ANGRY...

IT'S OKAY. I'M GLAD I'M WITH YOU.

SORRY I GOT US BOTH LOST, KANNA-SAN.

Kanna-san, you're so brave~!

WHAT SHOULD I DO?

SINCE I'M WITH SAIKAWA, I CAN'T USE MY DRAGON FORM TO FLY AND LOOK FOR THE STATION...

TOUCHED A NERVE

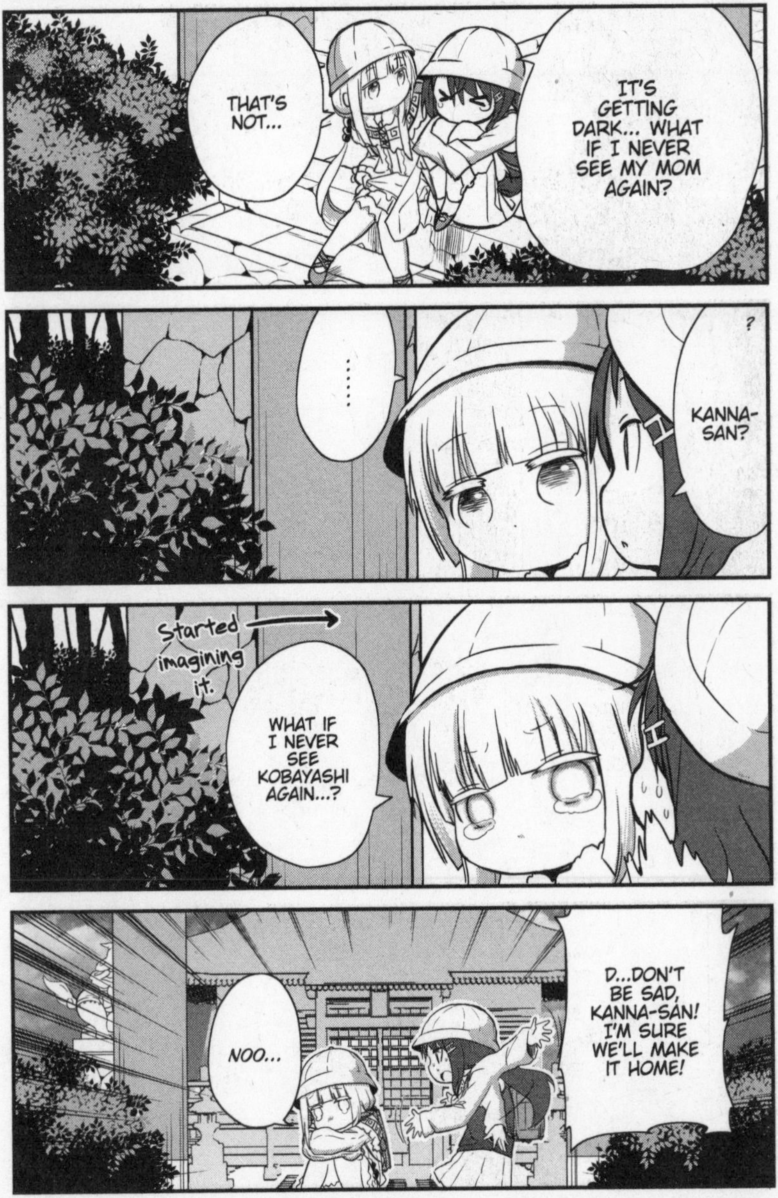
IT'S GETTING DARK... WHAT IF I NEVER SEE MY MOM AGAIN?
THAT'S NOT...
?
KANNA-SAN?
......
WHAT IF I NEVER SEE KOBAYASHI AGAIN...?
Started imagining it.
D...DON'T BE SAD, KANNA-SAN! I'M SURE WE'LL MAKE IT HOME!
NOO...

SMELLS LIKE KOBAYASHI SPIRIT

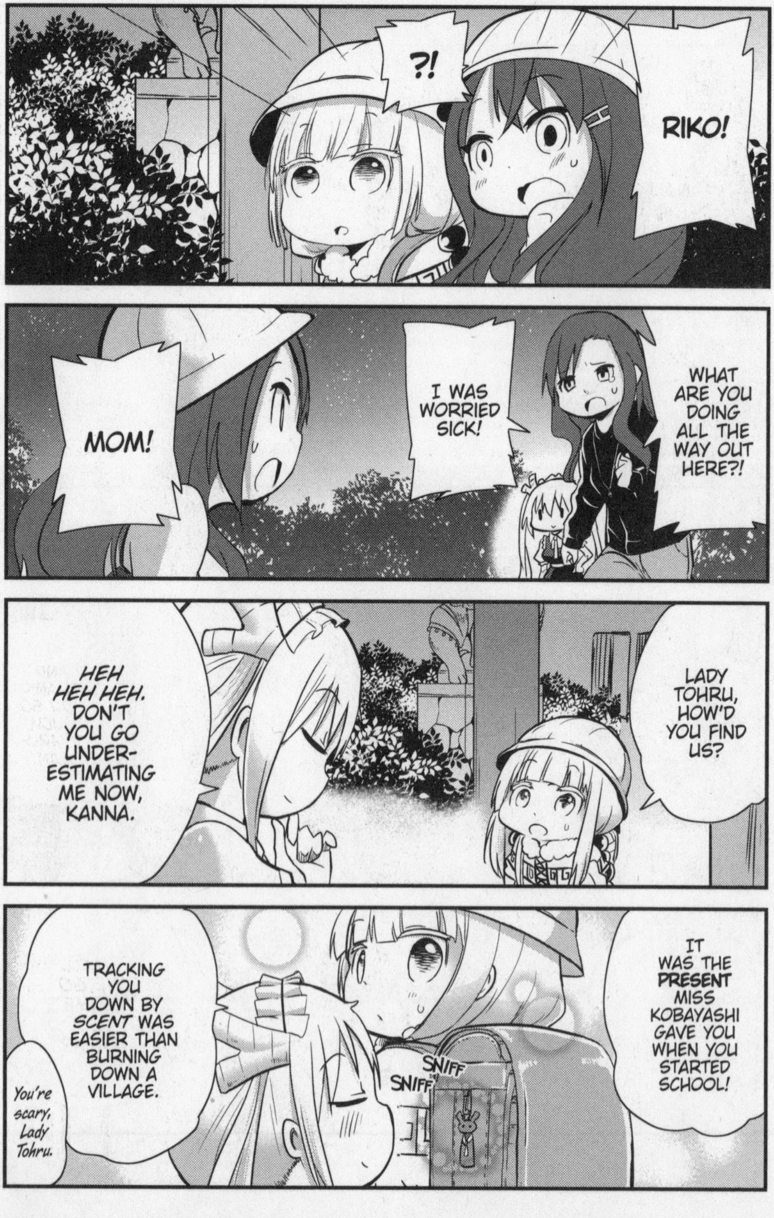
RIKO!
?!
WHAT ARE YOU DOING ALL THE WAY OUT HERE?!
I WAS WORRIED SICK!
MOM!
LADY TOHRU, HOW'D YOU FIND US?
HEH HEH HEH. DON'T YOU GO UNDER-ESTIMATING ME NOW, KANNA.
IT WAS THE PRESENT MISS KOBAYASHI GAVE YOU WHEN YOU STARTED SCHOOL!
SNIFF SNIFF
TRACKING YOU DOWN BY SCENT WAS EASIER THAN BURNING DOWN A VILLAGE.
You're scary, Lady Tohru.

FORGIVEN

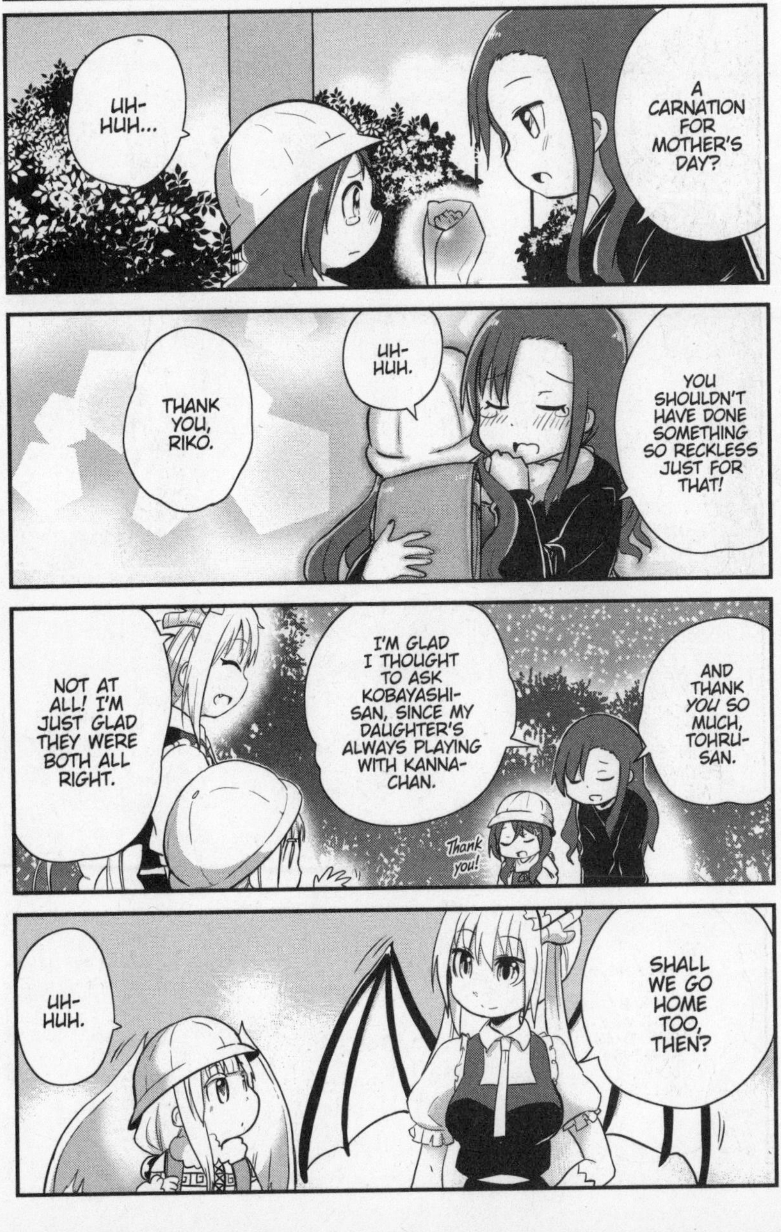
A CARNATION FOR MOTHER'S DAY?
UH-HUH...
YOU SHOULDN'T HAVE DONE SOMETHING SO RECKLESS JUST FOR THAT!
UH-HUH.
THANK YOU, RIKO.
AND THANK *YOU* SO MUCH, TOHRU-SAN.
I'M GLAD I THOUGHT TO ASK KOBAYASHI-SAN, SINCE MY DAUGHTER'S ALWAYS PLAYING WITH KANNA-CHAN.
Thank you!
NOT AT ALL! I'M JUST GLAD THEY WERE BOTH ALL RIGHT.
SHALL WE GO HOME TOO, THEN?
UH-HUH.

KANNA-CHAN'S CONFLICT

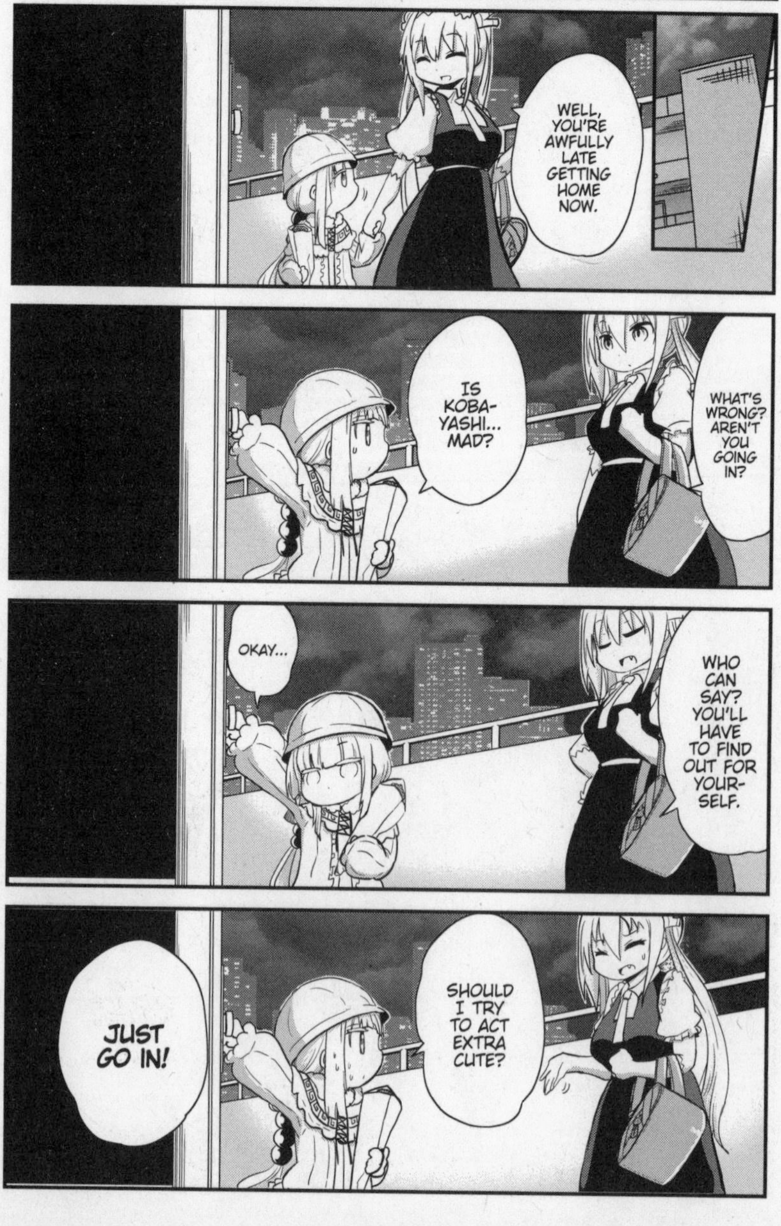
WELL, YOU'RE AWFULLY LATE GETTING HOME NOW.
WHAT'S WRONG? AREN'T YOU GOING IN?
IS KOBA-YASHI... MAD?
WHO CAN SAY? YOU'LL HAVE TO FIND OUT FOR YOUR-SELF.
OKAY...
SHOULD I TRY TO ACT EXTRA CUTE?
JUST GO IN!

Fresno Tarzana Branch
10/19/2019   1:24:14 PM

PATRON RECEIPT
CHARGES

1   Item Number: 37344226764968
Title: Kinko mosaic   2?
Due Date: 11/9/2019

2   Item Number: 37344236649001
Title: Miss Kobayashi's dragon maid   2. Kanr
Due Date: 11/9/2019

To Renew: www.lapl.org or 888-577-5275

Free online tutoring with your library card for
K-12 and adult learners.
lapl.org/online/tutor

--Please retain this slip as your receipt--

THE PROPER ORDER OF THINGS

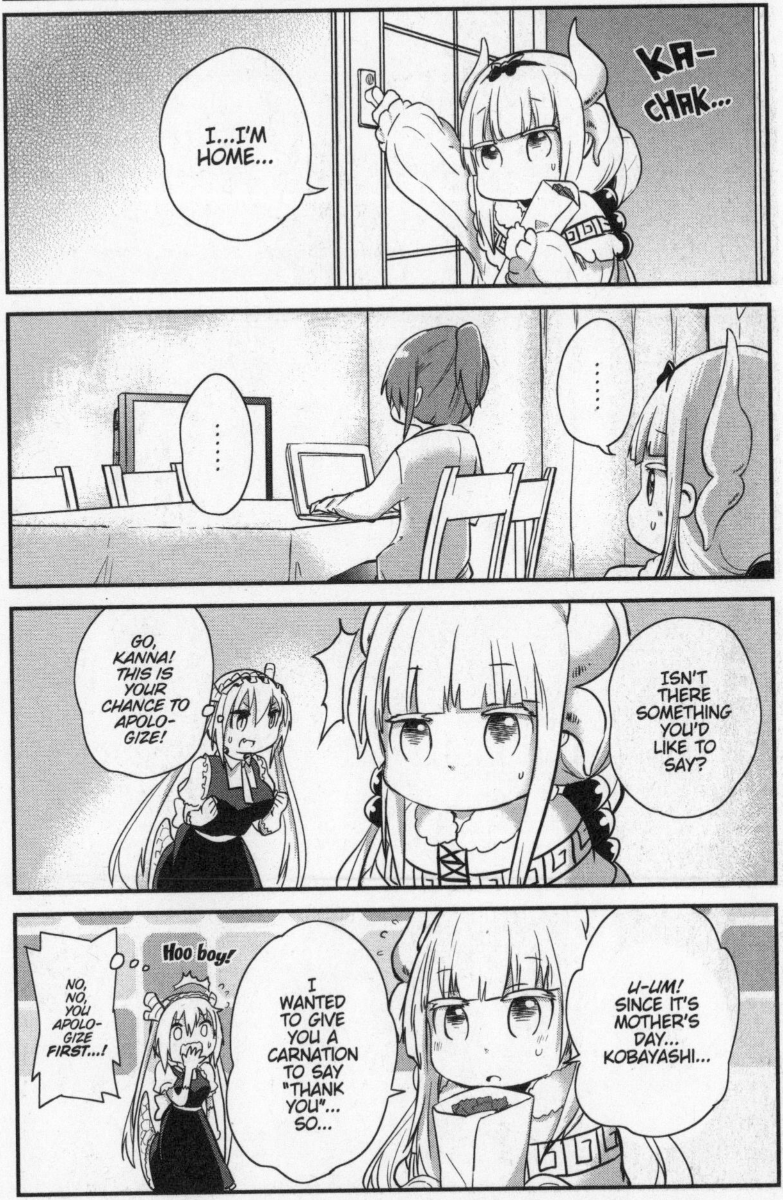
KA-CHAK...
I...I'M HOME...
......
......
ISN'T THERE SOMETHING YOU'D LIKE TO SAY?
GO, KANNA! THIS IS YOUR CHANCE TO APOLOGIZE!
U-UM! SINCE IT'S MOTHER'S DAY... KOBAYASHI...
I WANTED TO GIVE YOU A CARNATION TO SAY "THANK YOU"... SO...
Hoo boy!
NO, NO, YOU APOLOGIZE FIRST...!

THE PERFECT GIFT

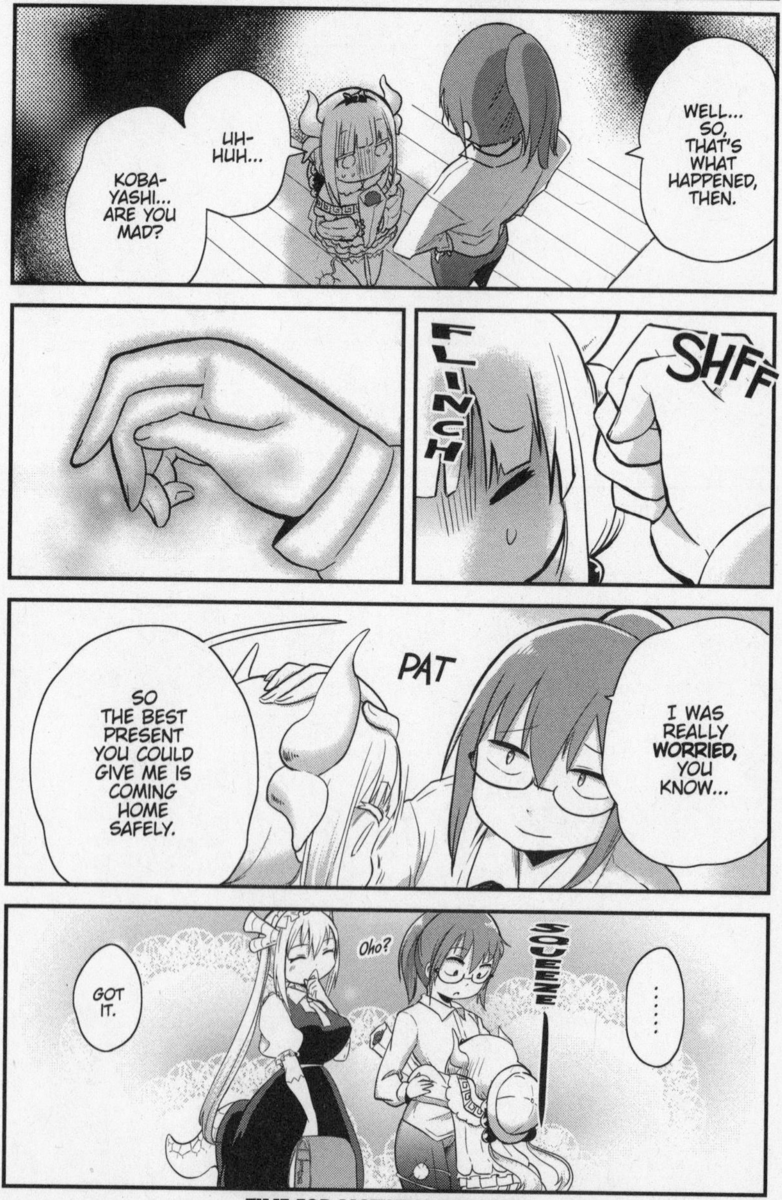
WELL... SO, THAT'S WHAT HAPPENED, THEN.
UH-HUH...
KOBA-YASHI... ARE YOU MAD?
SHFF
FLINCH
I WAS REALLY WORRIED, YOU KNOW...
PAT
SO THE BEST PRESENT YOU COULD GIVE ME IS COMING HOME SAFELY.
......
SQUEEZE
Oho?
GOT IT.

TIME FOR MOTHER'S DAY/END

Miss Kobayashi's Dragon Maid
Kanna's Daily Life

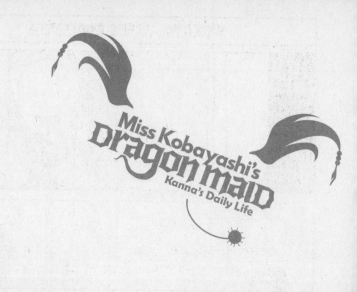

SAIKAWA-SAN'S CHALLENGE

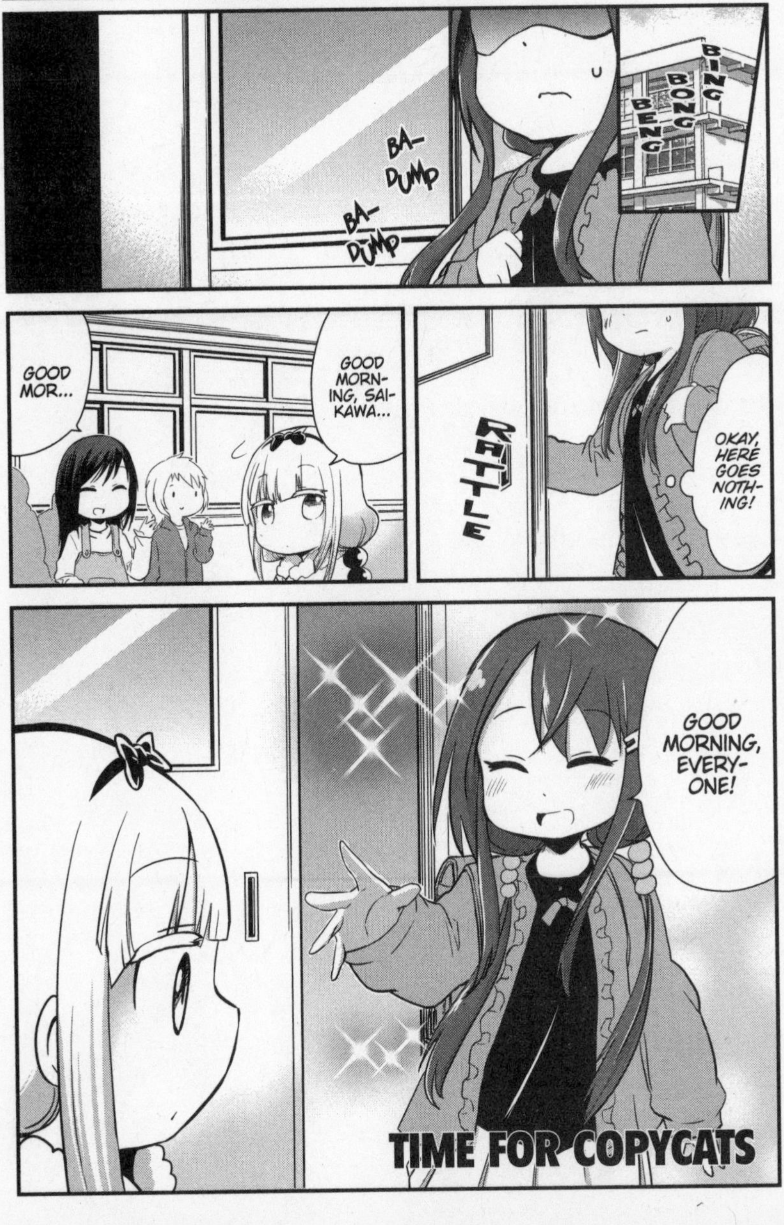
BING
BONG
BENG
BA-DUMP
BA-DUMP
RATTLE
OKAY, HERE GOES NOTHING!
GOOD MORNING, SAIKAWA...
GOOD MOR...
GOOD MORNING, EVERYONE!
TIME FOR COPYCATS

LOOKING GOOD, SAIKAWA-SAN!

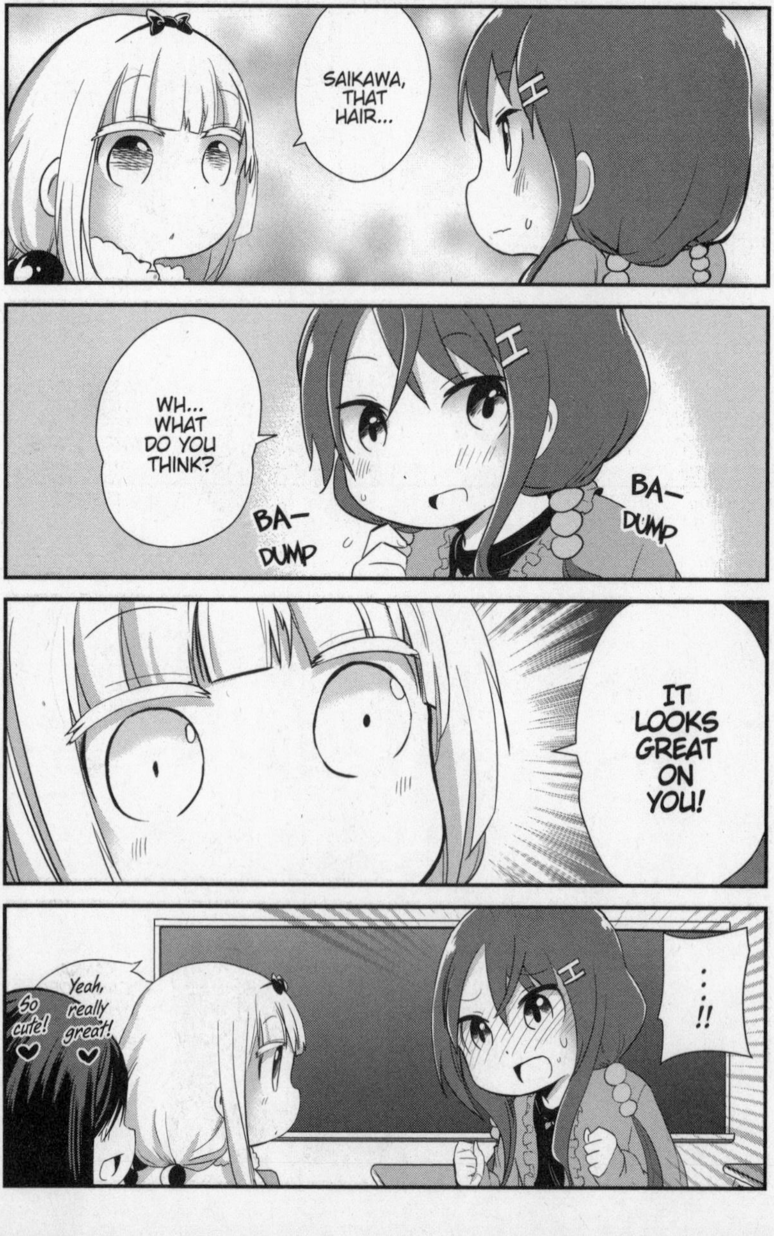

SAIKAWA, THAT HAIR...
WH... WHAT DO YOU THINK?
BA-DUMP
BA-DUMP
IT LOOKS GREAT ON YOU!
...!!
Yeah, really great! ❤
So cute! ❤

OVERTHINKING IT

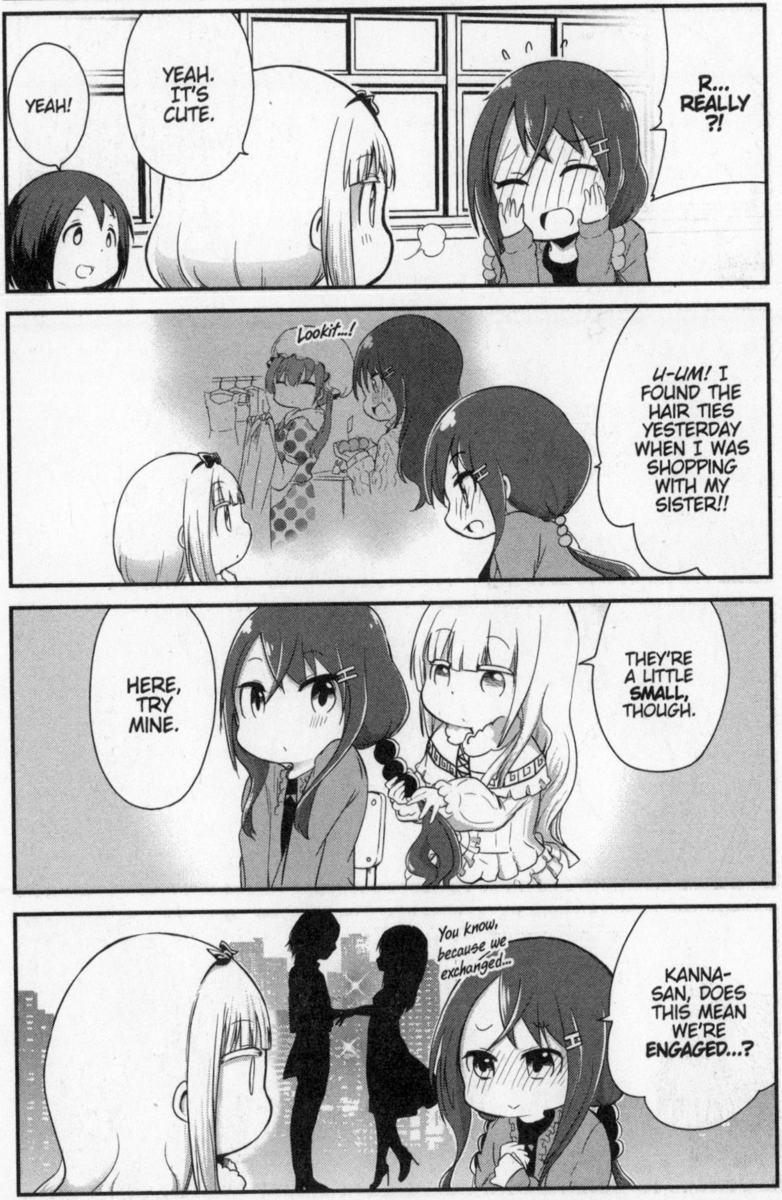
R... REALLY ?!
YEAH. IT'S CUTE.
YEAH!
U-UM! I FOUND THE HAIR TIES YESTERDAY WHEN I WAS SHOPPING WITH MY SISTER!!
Lookit...!
THEY'RE A LITTLE SMALL, THOUGH.
HERE, TRY MINE.
KANNA-SAN, DOES THIS MEAN WE'RE ENGAGED...?
You know, because we exchanged...

A LIFE WELL LIVED!

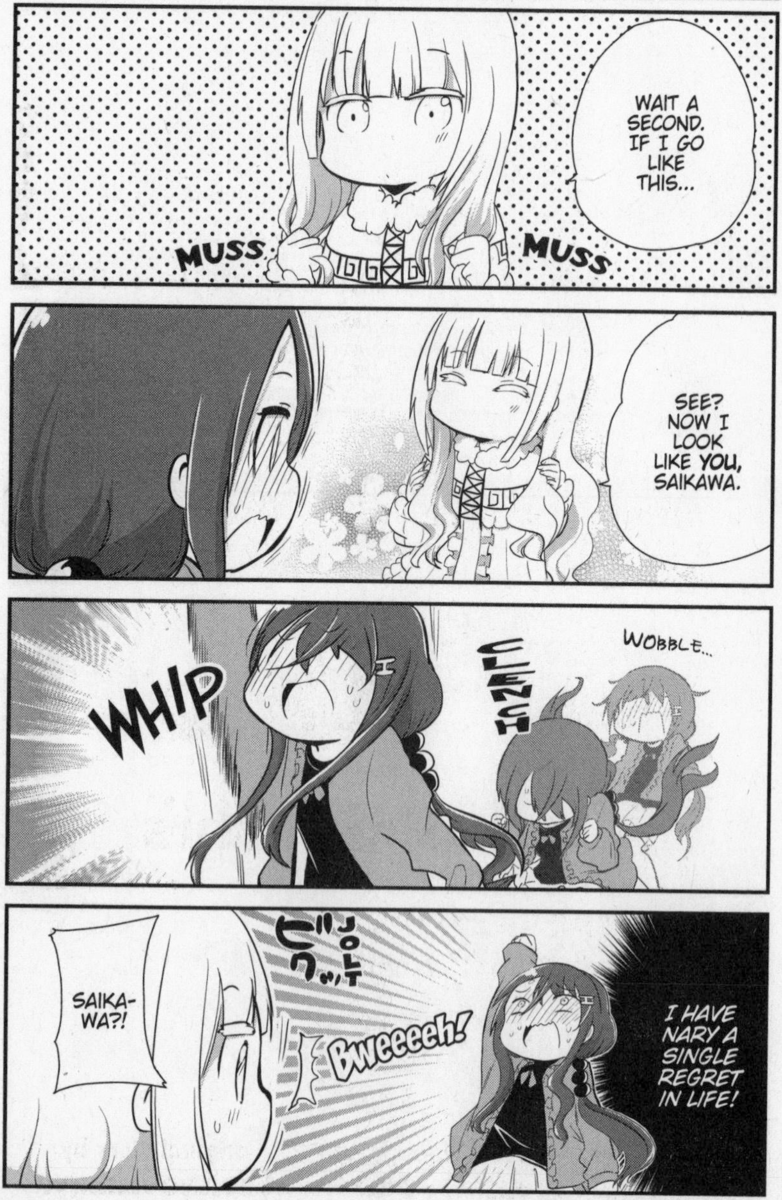

WAIT A SECOND. IF I GO LIKE THIS...
MUSS
MUSS
SEE? NOW I LOOK LIKE YOU, SAIKAWA.
WOBBLE...
CLENCH
WHIP
I HAVE NARY A SINGLE REGRET IN LIFE!
ビクッ
JOLT
Bweeeeh!
SAIKA-WA?!

CHILD PRODIGY

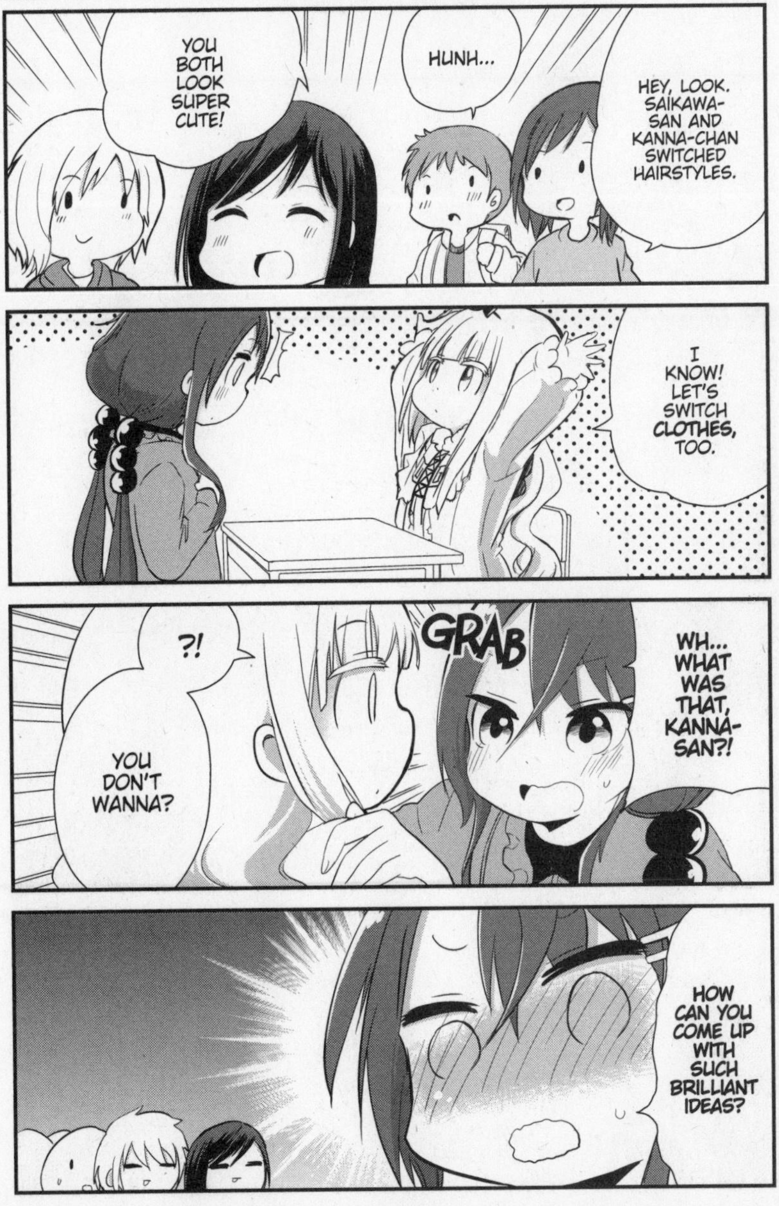
HEY, LOOK. SAIKAWA-SAN AND KANNA-CHAN SWITCHED HAIRSTYLES.
HUNH...
YOU BOTH LOOK SUPER CUTE!
I KNOW! LET'S SWITCH CLOTHES, TOO.
WH... WHAT WAS THAT, KANNA-SAN?!
GRAB
?!
YOU DON'T WANNA?
HOW CAN YOU COME UP WITH SUCH BRILLIANT IDEAS?

YEAH, THIS IS A LITTLE EMBARRASSING

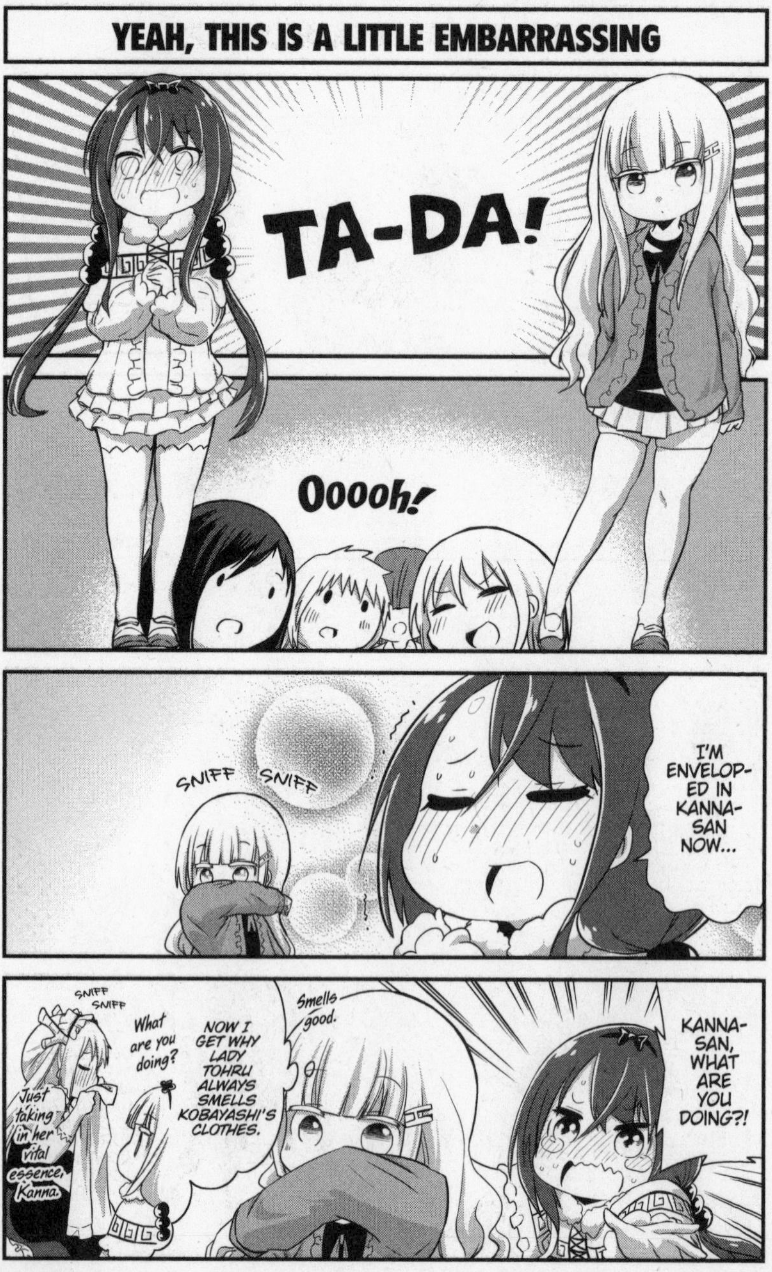

TA-DA!
Ooooh!
I'M ENVELOPED IN KANNA-SAN NOW...
SNIFF SNIFF
KANNA-SAN, WHAT ARE YOU DOING?!
Smells good.
NOW I GET WHY LADY TOHRU ALWAYS SMELLS KOBAYASHI'S CLOTHES.
What are you doing?
SNIFF SNIFF
Just taking in her vital essence, Kanna.

SAIKAWA-SAN'S FASHION TIPS

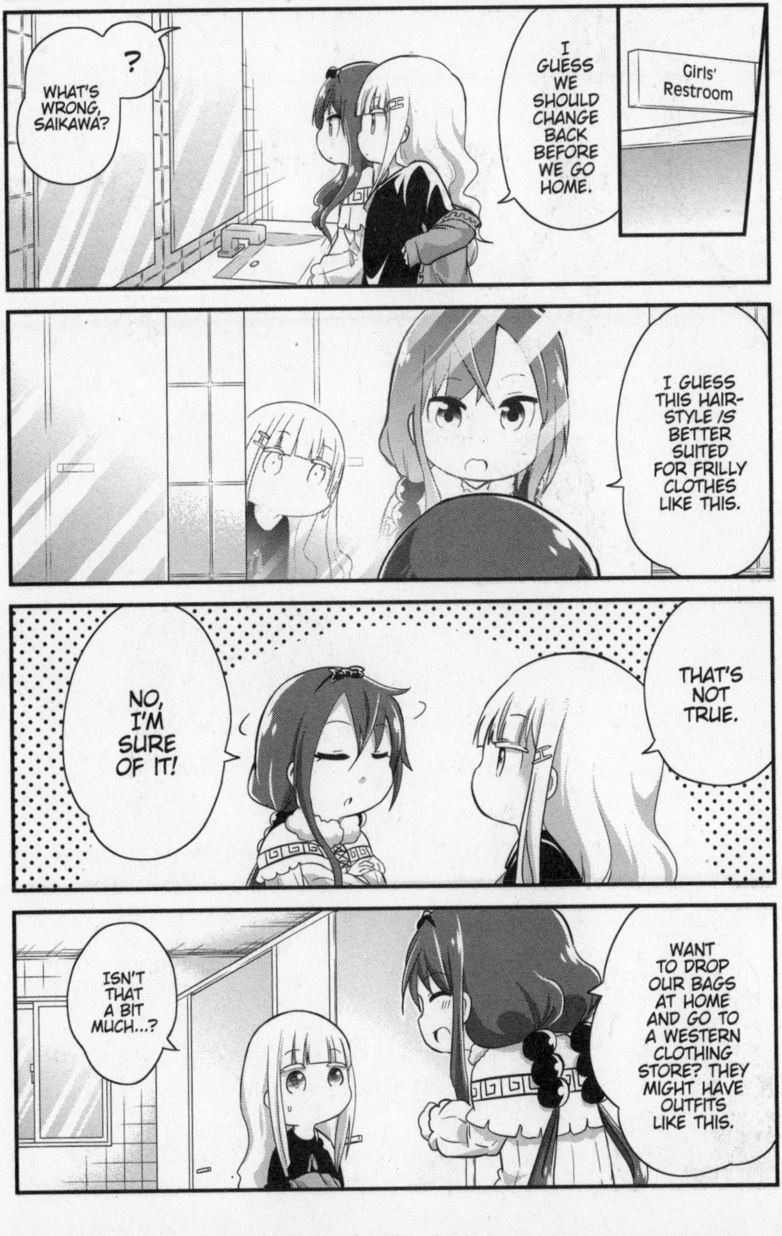
Girls' Restroom
I GUESS WE SHOULD CHANGE BACK BEFORE WE GO HOME.
?
WHAT'S WRONG, SAIKAWA?
I GUESS THIS HAIR-STYLE IS BETTER SUITED FOR FRILLY CLOTHES LIKE THIS.
THAT'S NOT TRUE.
NO, I'M SURE OF IT!
WANT TO DROP OUR BAGS AT HOME AND GO TO A WESTERN CLOTHING STORE? THEY MIGHT HAVE OUTFITS LIKE THIS.
ISN'T THAT A BIT MUCH...?

THE PERFECT MATCH

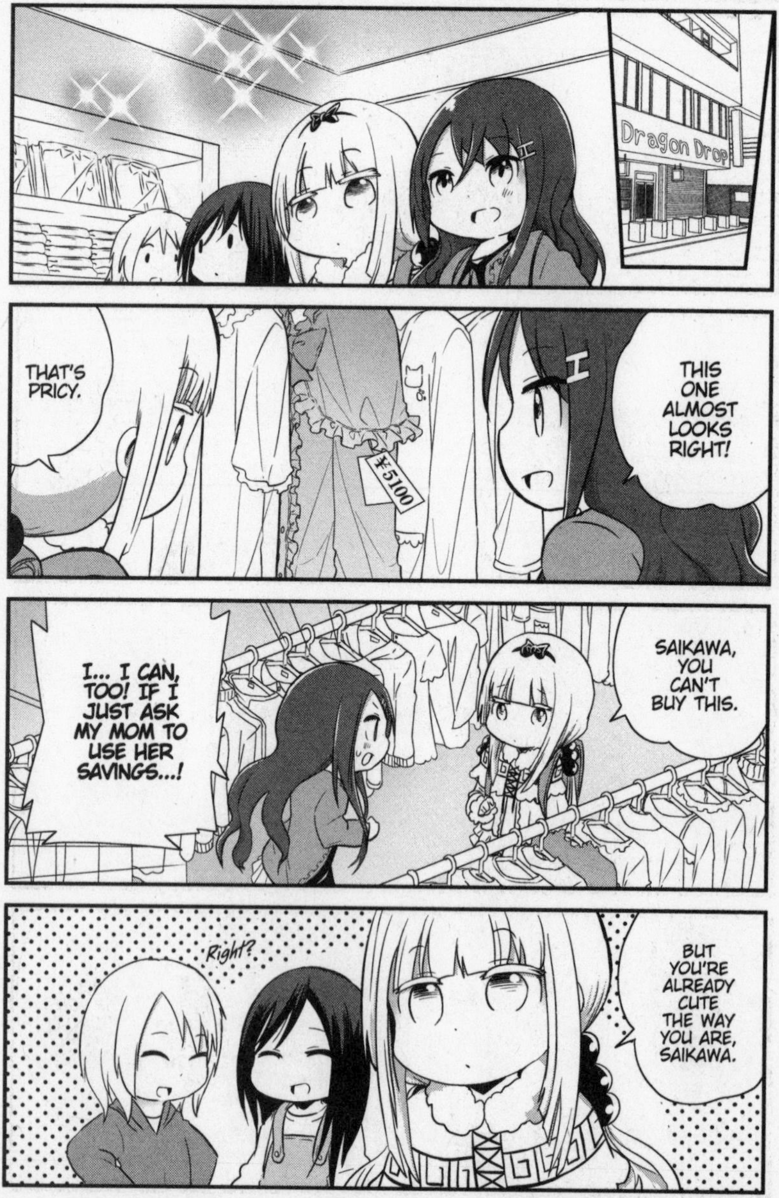

Dragon Drop
THIS ONE ALMOST LOOKS RIGHT!
¥5100
THAT'S PRICY.
SAIKAWA, YOU CAN'T BUY THIS.
I... I CAN, TOO! IF I JUST ASK MY MOM TO USE HER SAVINGS...!
BUT YOU'RE ALREADY CUTE THE WAY YOU ARE, SAIKAWA.
Right?

FRILLS ARE FOR LITTLE GIRLS

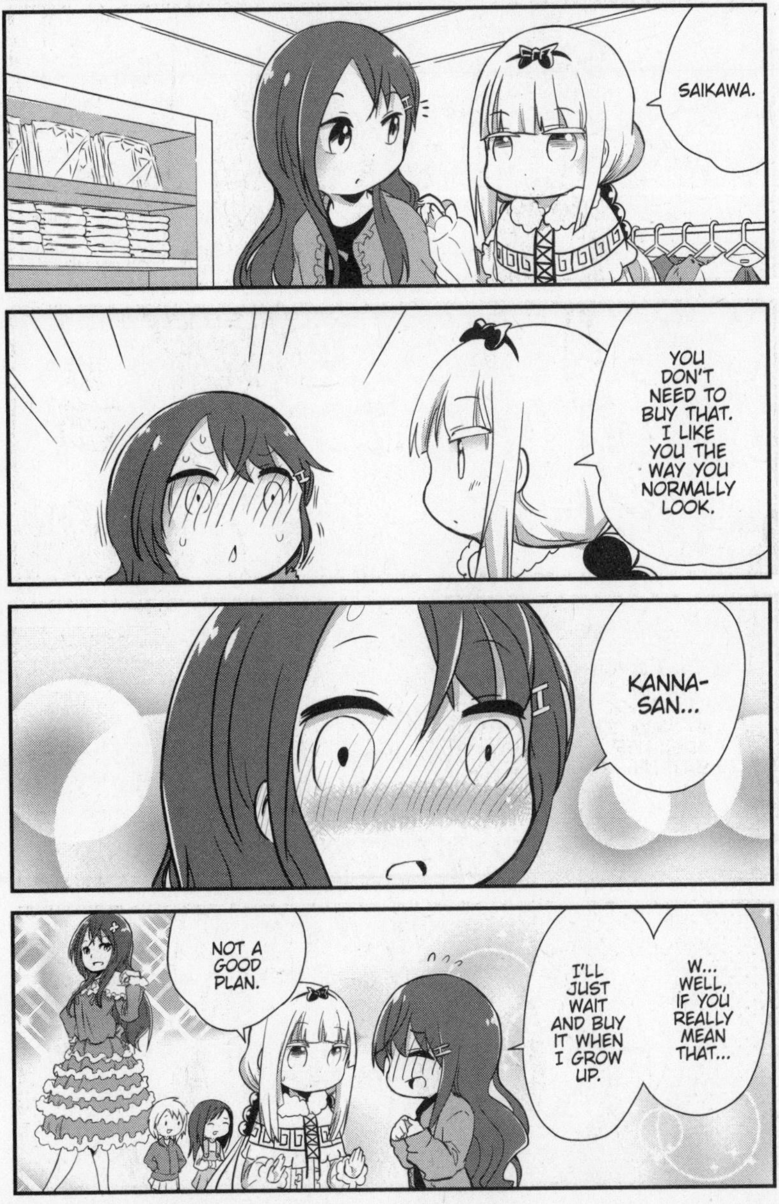
SAIKAWA.
YOU DON'T NEED TO BUY THAT. I LIKE YOU THE WAY YOU NORMALLY LOOK.
KANNA-SAN...
W... WELL, IF YOU REALLY MEAN THAT...
I'LL JUST WAIT AND BUY IT WHEN I GROW UP.
NOT A GOOD PLAN.

WITH OUR ALLOWANCES COMBINED

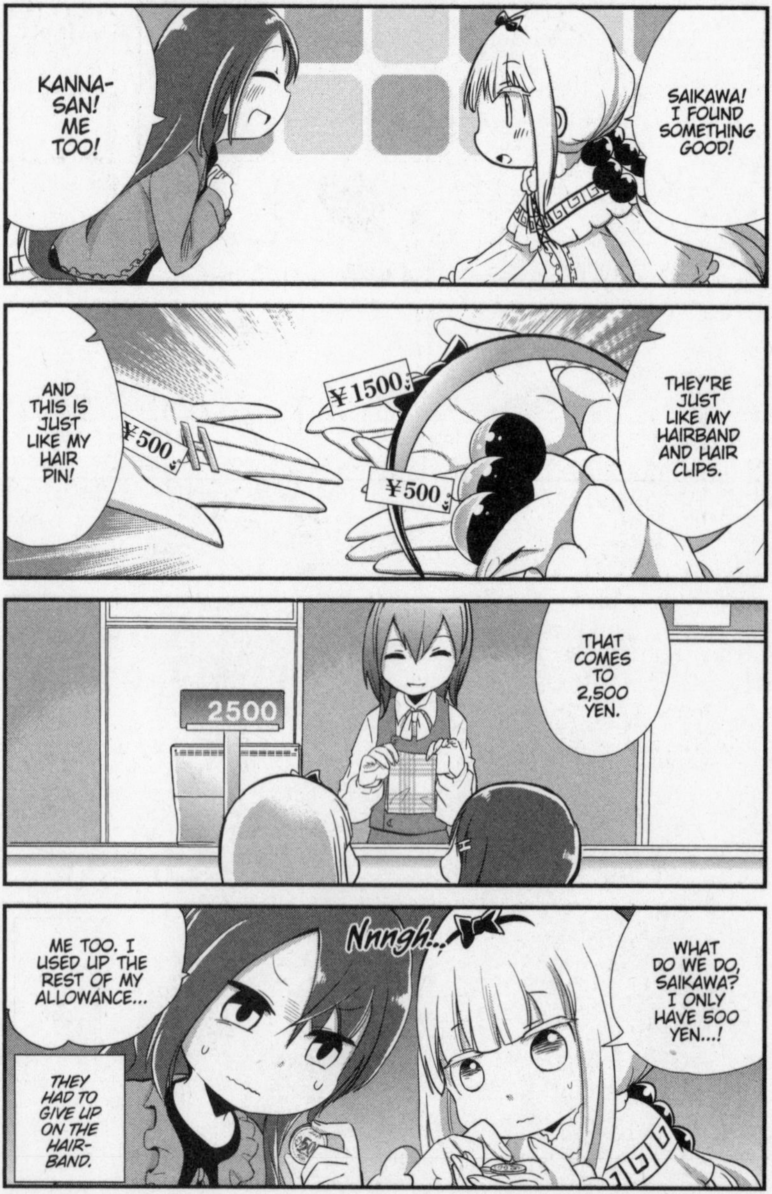
SAIKAWA! I FOUND SOMETHING GOOD!
KANNA-SAN! ME TOO!
THEY'RE JUST LIKE MY HAIRBAND AND HAIR CLIPS.
¥1500
¥500
¥500
AND THIS IS JUST LIKE MY HAIR PIN!
THAT COMES TO 2,500 YEN.
2500
WHAT DO WE DO, SAIKAWA? I ONLY HAVE 500 YEN...!
Nnngh...
ME TOO. I USED UP THE REST OF MY ALLOWANCE...
THEY HAD TO GIVE UP ON THE HAIR-BAND.

PRESENTS TO EACH OTHER

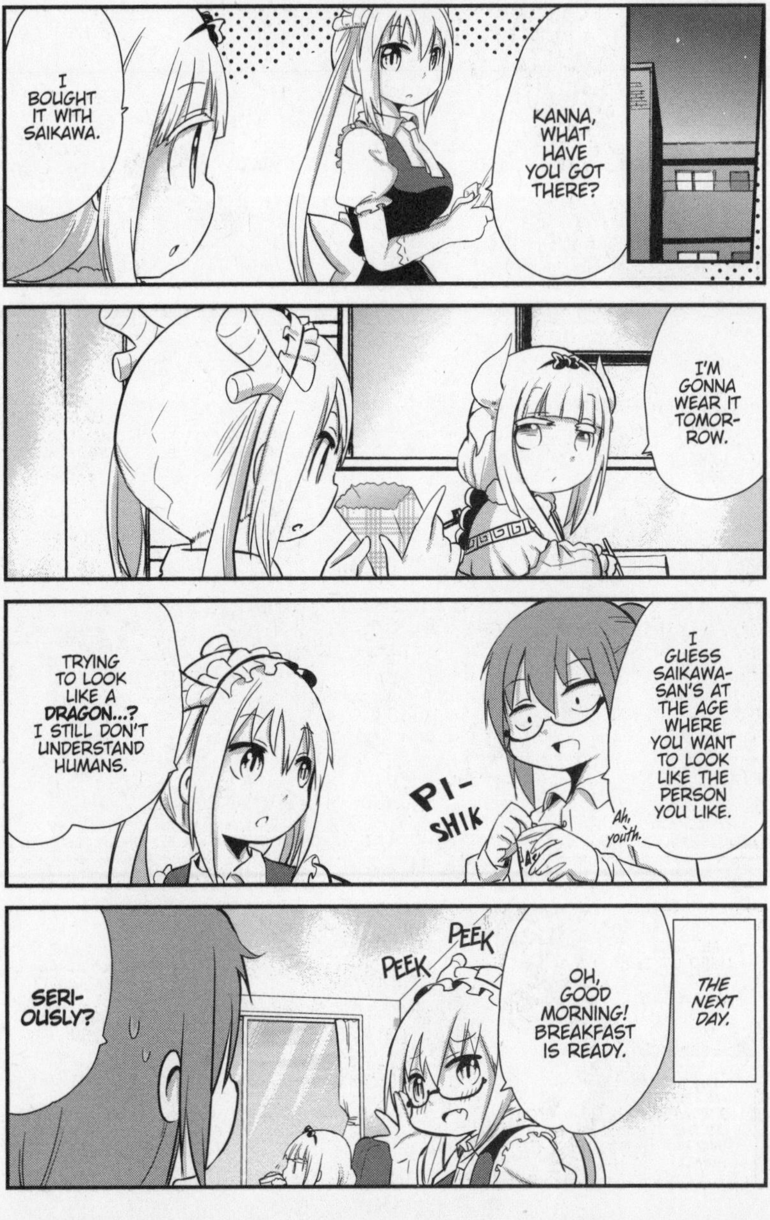
KANNA, WHAT HAVE YOU GOT THERE?
I BOUGHT IT WITH SAIKAWA.
I'M GONNA WEAR IT TOMORROW.
I GUESS SAIKAWA-SAN'S AT THE AGE WHERE YOU WANT TO LOOK LIKE THE PERSON YOU LIKE.
Ah, youth.
PI-SHIK
TRYING TO LOOK LIKE A DRAGON...? I STILL DON'T UNDERSTAND HUMANS.
THE NEXT DAY.
OH, GOOD MORNING! BREAKFAST IS READY.
PEEK
PEEK
SERI-OUSLY?

OUR LITTLE SECRET

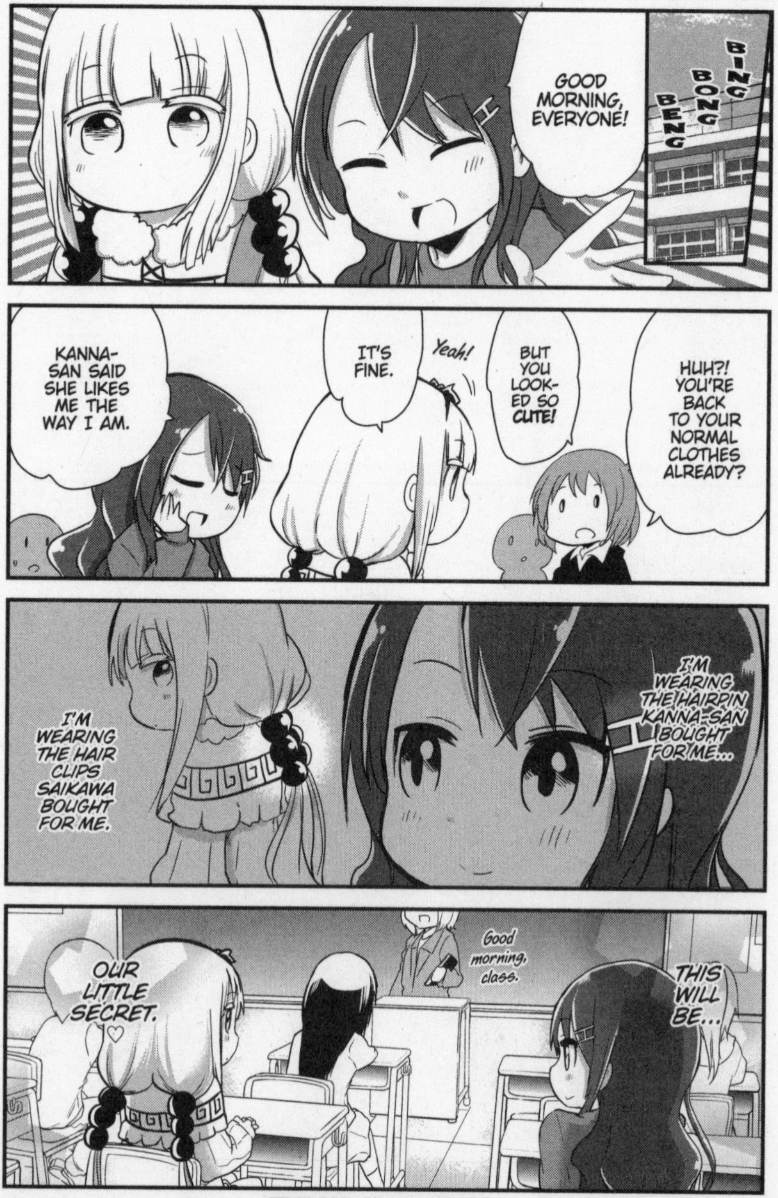
BING
BONG
BENG
GOOD MORNING, EVERYONE!
HUH?! YOU'RE BACK TO YOUR NORMAL CLOTHES ALREADY?
BUT YOU LOOKED SO CUTE!
Yeah!
IT'S FINE.
KANNA-SAN SAID SHE LIKES ME THE WAY I AM.
I'M WEARING THE HAIRPIN KANNA-SAN BOUGHT FOR ME...
I'M WEARING THE HAIR CLIPS SAIKAWA BOUGHT FOR ME.
THIS WILL BE...
Good morning, class.
OUR LITTLE SECRET. ♡

TIME FOR COPYCATS/END

Miss Kobayashi's Dragon Maid
Kanna's Daily Life

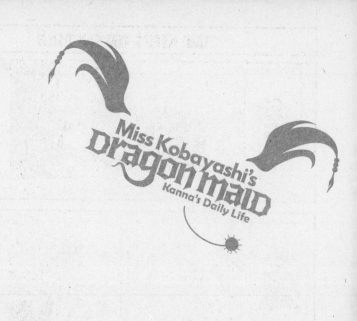

TIME KEEPS ON SLIPPING

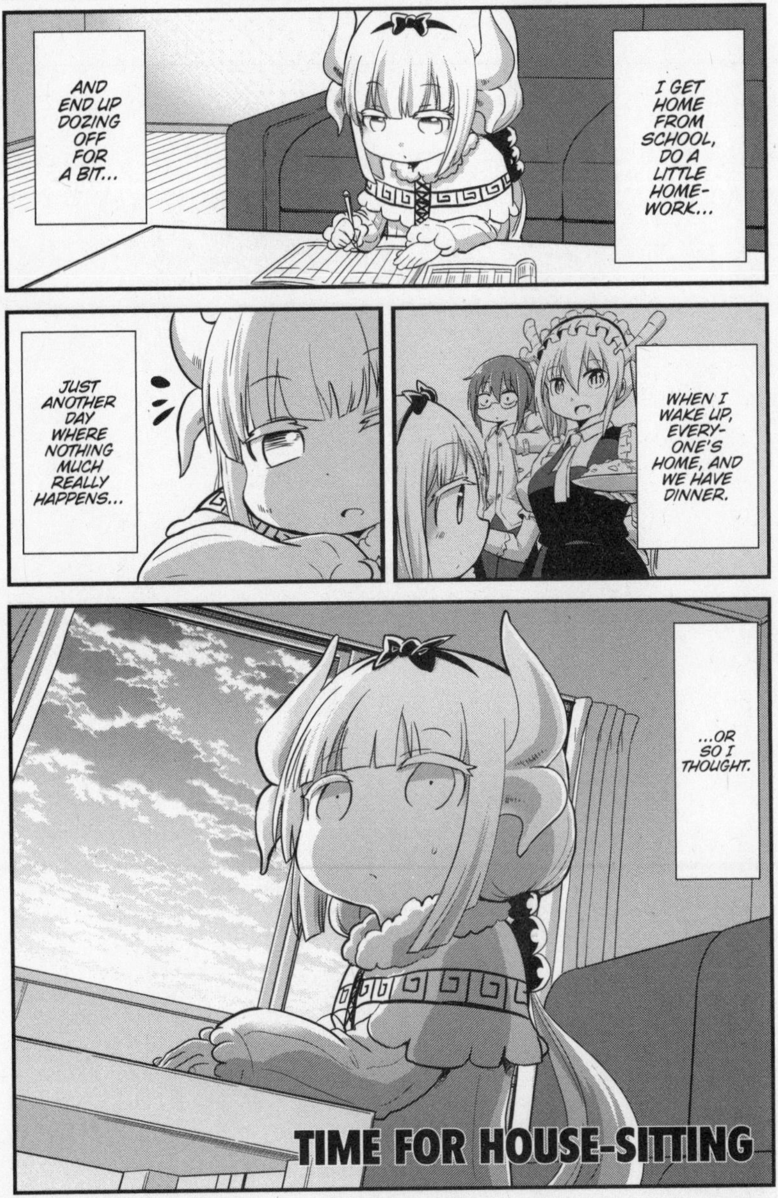
I GET HOME FROM SCHOOL, DO A LITTLE HOME-WORK...
AND END UP DOZING OFF FOR A BIT...
WHEN I WAKE UP, EVERY-ONE'S HOME, AND WE HAVE DINNER.
JUST ANOTHER DAY WHERE NOTHING MUCH REALLY HAPPENS...
...OR SO I THOUGHT.
TIME FOR HOUSE-SITTING

HIGH ANXIETY

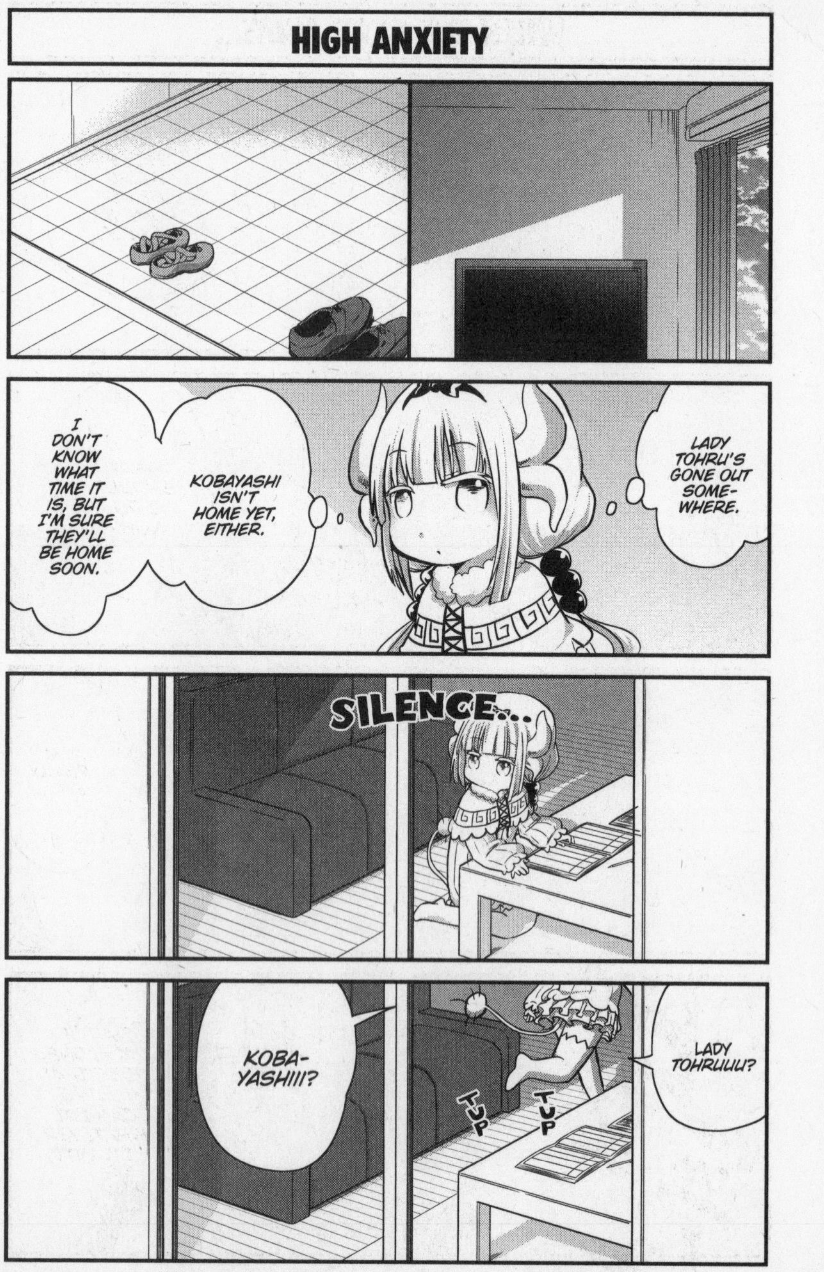
LADY TOHRU'S GONE OUT SOME-WHERE.
KOBAYASHI ISN'T HOME YET, EITHER.
I DON'T KNOW WHAT TIME IT IS, BUT I'M SURE THEY'LL BE HOME SOON.
SILENCE...
LADY TOHRUUU?
TUP
TUP
KOBA-YASHIII?

WHEN THE CAT'S AWAY...

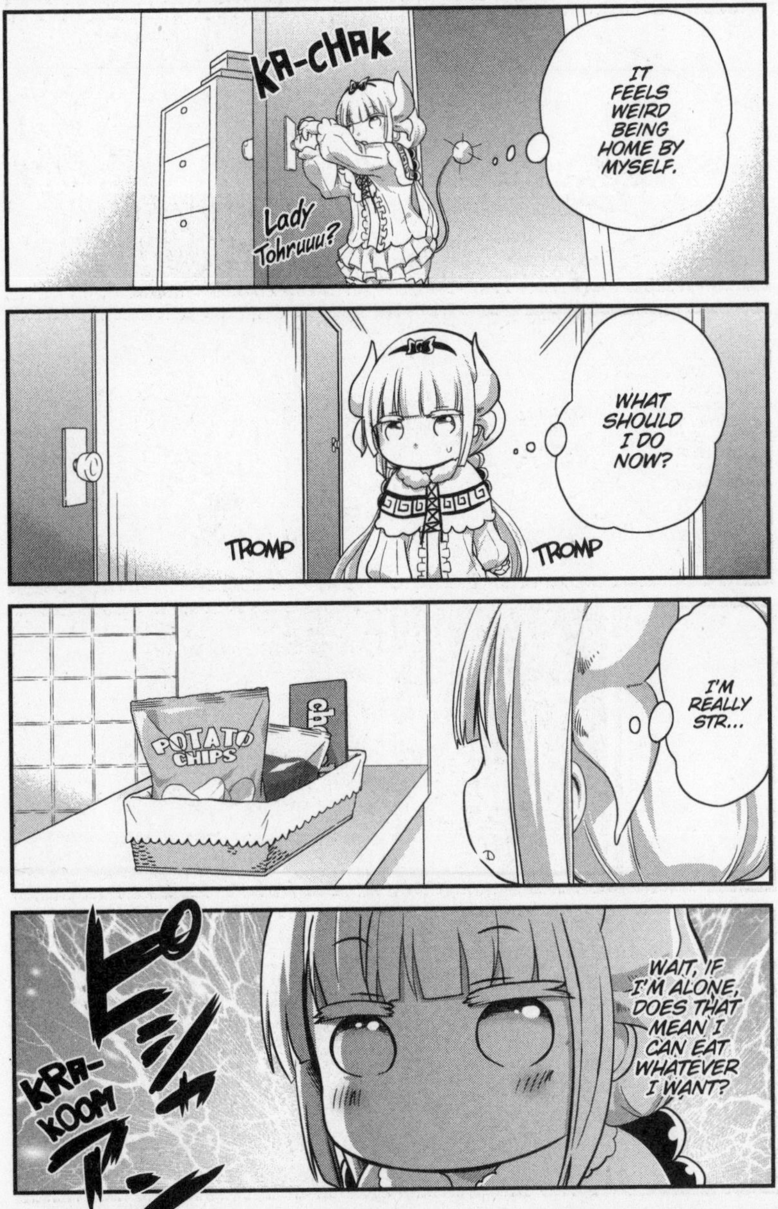
IT FEELS WEIRD BEING HOME BY MYSELF.
KA-CHAK
Lady Tohruuu?
WHAT SHOULD I DO NOW?
TROMP
TROMP
I'M REALLY STR…
POTATO CHIPS
WAIT, IF I'M ALONE, DOES THAT MEAN I CAN EAT WHATEVER I WANT?
ピシャアーン
KRA-KOOM

CAN'T SHAKE THE FEELING

NOM
NOM
NOM

YAY! ♡

Whew!

LADY TOHRU ALWAYS TELLS ME NOT TO EAT TOO MANY SNACKS, BUT TODAY I GOT TO EAT A WHOLE BUNCH.

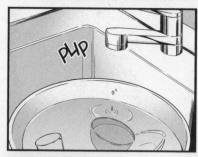

PLIP

Whaaat?!

That's as far as you go!

WHAT AM I GONNA DO IF THEY NEVER COME HOME?

SHI

VER

OF ALL TIMES...

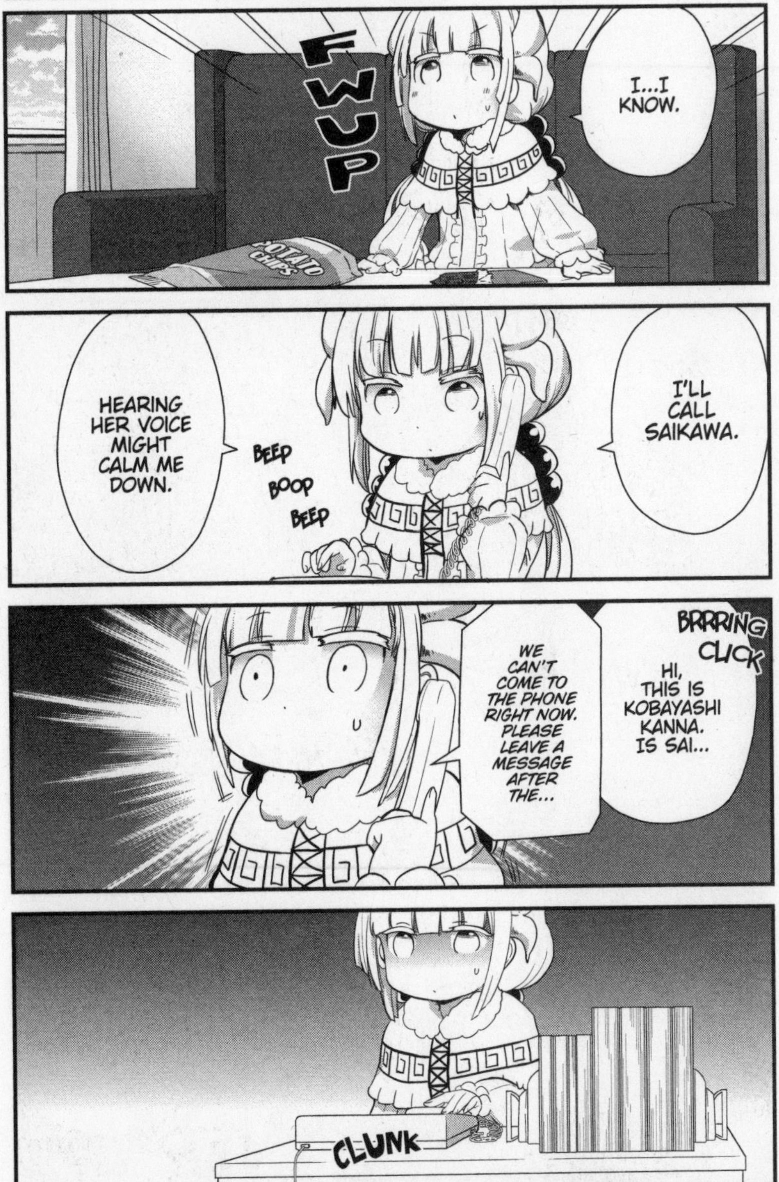
I...I KNOW.
FWUP
POTATO CHIPS
I'LL CALL SAIKAWA.
BEEP BOOP BEEP
HEARING HER VOICE MIGHT CALM ME DOWN.
BRRRING CLICK
HI, THIS IS KOBAYASHI KANNA. IS SAI...
WE CAN'T COME TO THE PHONE RIGHT NOW. PLEASE LEAVE A MESSAGE AFTER THE...
CLUNK

FLY, KANNA!

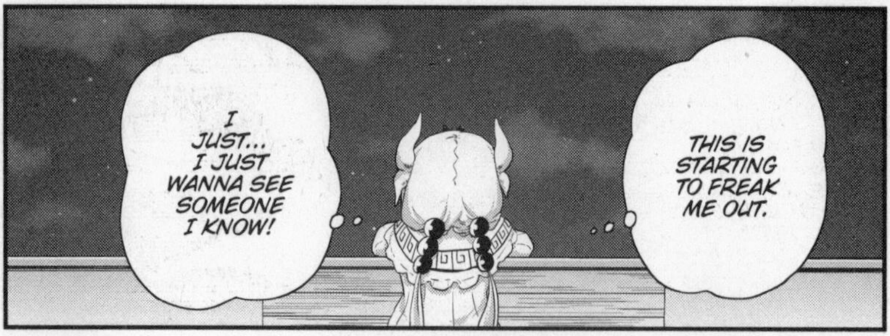
THIS IS STARTING TO FREAK ME OUT.
I JUST... I JUST WANNA SEE SOMEONE I KNOW!

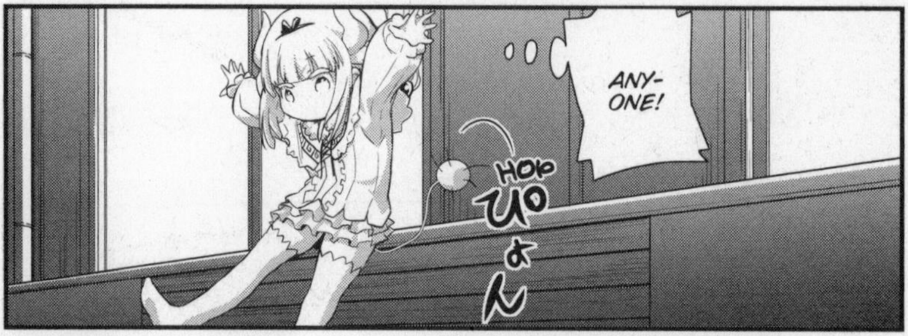
ANY-ONE!
HOP
ぴょん

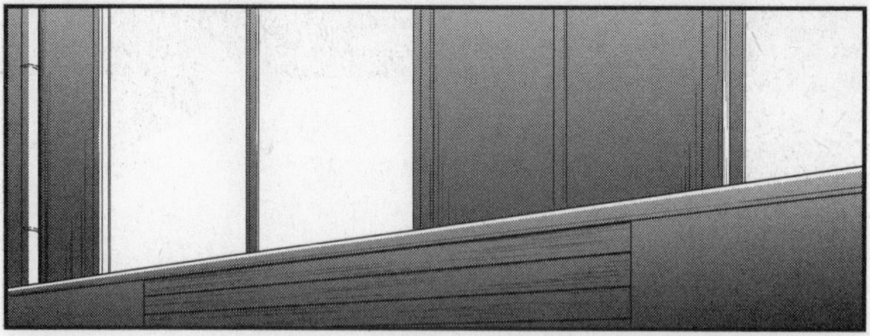

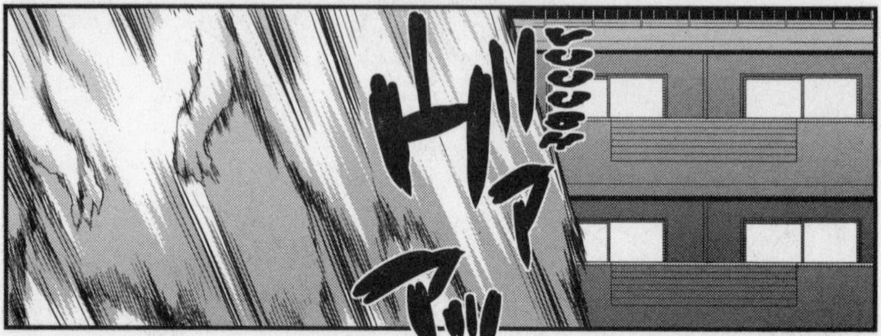

DESPERATION MOVE!

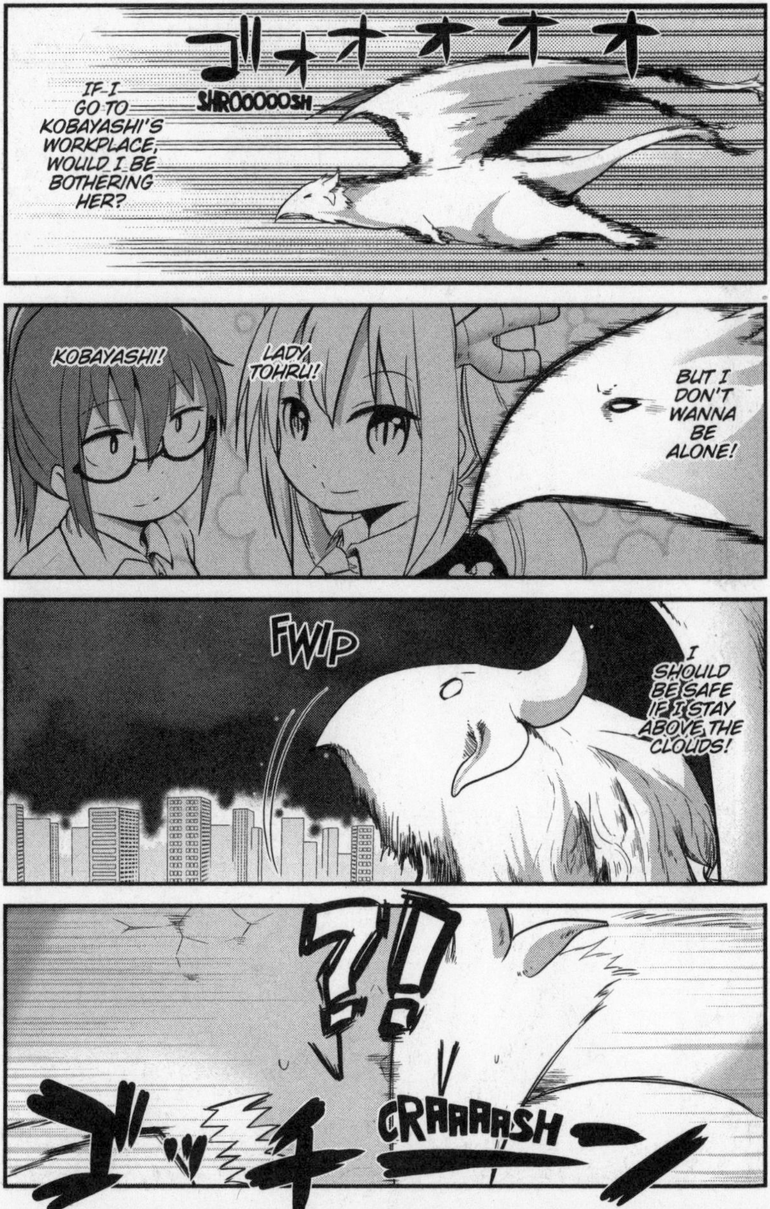
ゴォオオオオ
SHROOOOOSH
IF I GO TO KOBAYASHI'S WORKPLACE, WOULD I BE BOTHERING HER?
BUT I DON'T WANNA BE ALONE!
LADY TOHRU!
KOBAYASHI!
I SHOULD BE SAFE IF I STAY ABOVE THE CLOUDS!
FWIP
?!
ゴッチ
CRAAAASH

REMEMBER YOUR PASSENGER!

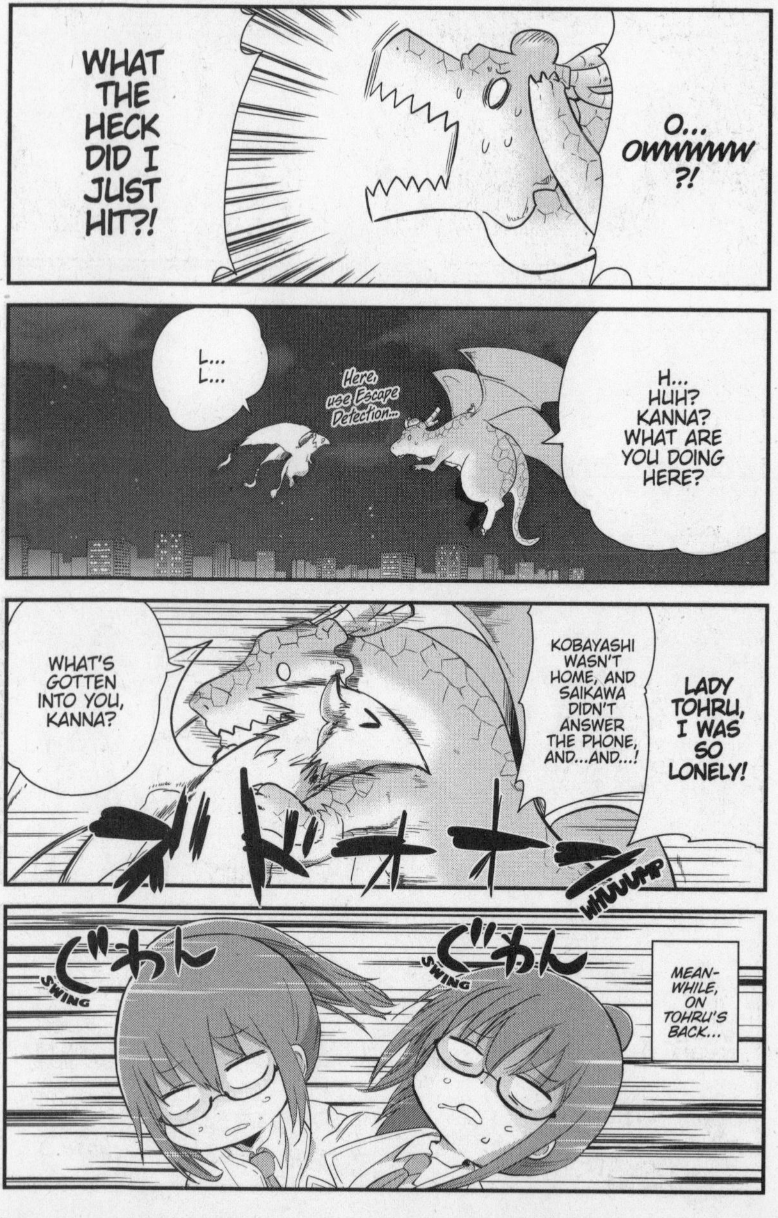
O... OWWWWW?!
WHAT THE HECK DID I JUST HIT?!
H... HUH? KANNA? WHAT ARE YOU DOING HERE?
Here, use Escape Detection...
L... L...
LADY TOHRU, I WAS SO LONELY!
KOBAYASHI WASN'T HOME, AND SAIKAWA DIDN'T ANSWER THE PHONE, AND...AND...!
WHAT'S GOTTEN INTO YOU, KANNA?
WHUUUMP
MEAN-WHILE, ON TOHRU'S BACK...
ぐわん
SWING
ぐわん
SWING

CHILDHOOD FEARS

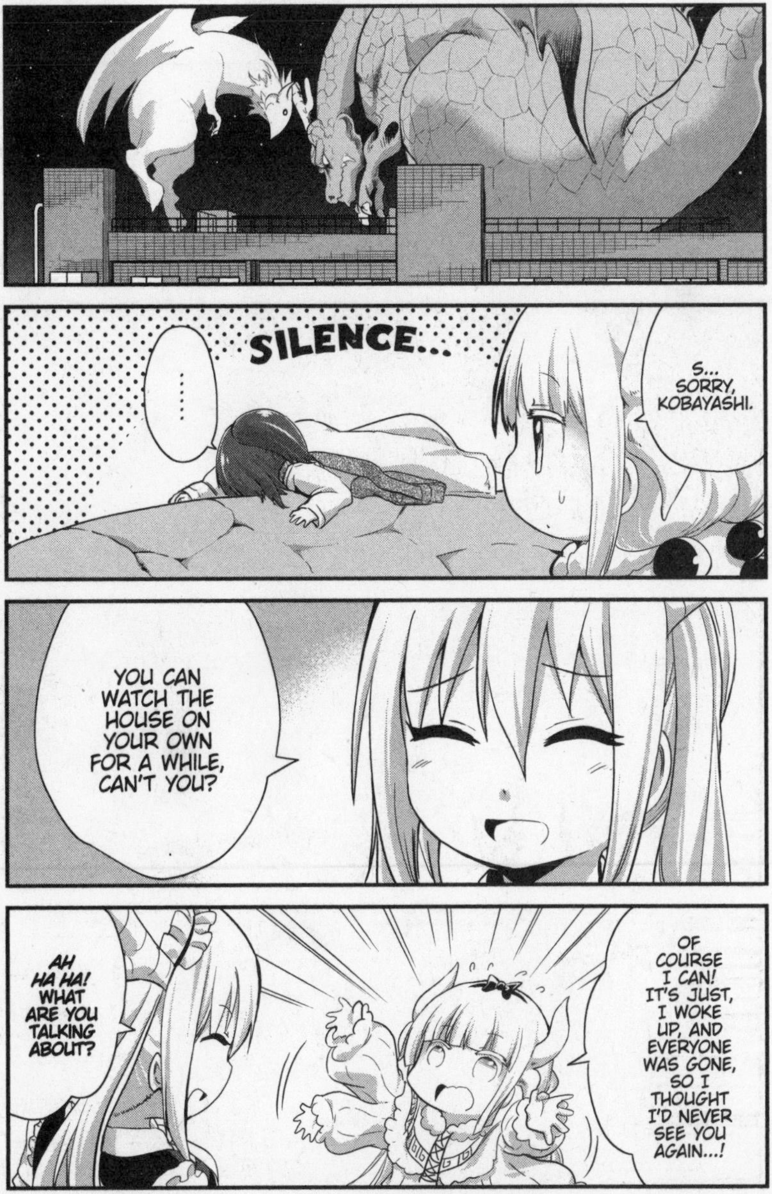
S... SORRY, KOBAYASHI.
SILENCE...
......
YOU CAN WATCH THE HOUSE ON YOUR OWN FOR A WHILE, CAN'T YOU?
OF COURSE I CAN! IT'S JUST, I WOKE UP, AND EVERYONE WAS GONE, SO I THOUGHT I'D NEVER SEE YOU AGAIN...!
AH HA HA! WHAT ARE YOU TALKING ABOUT?

BUSTED

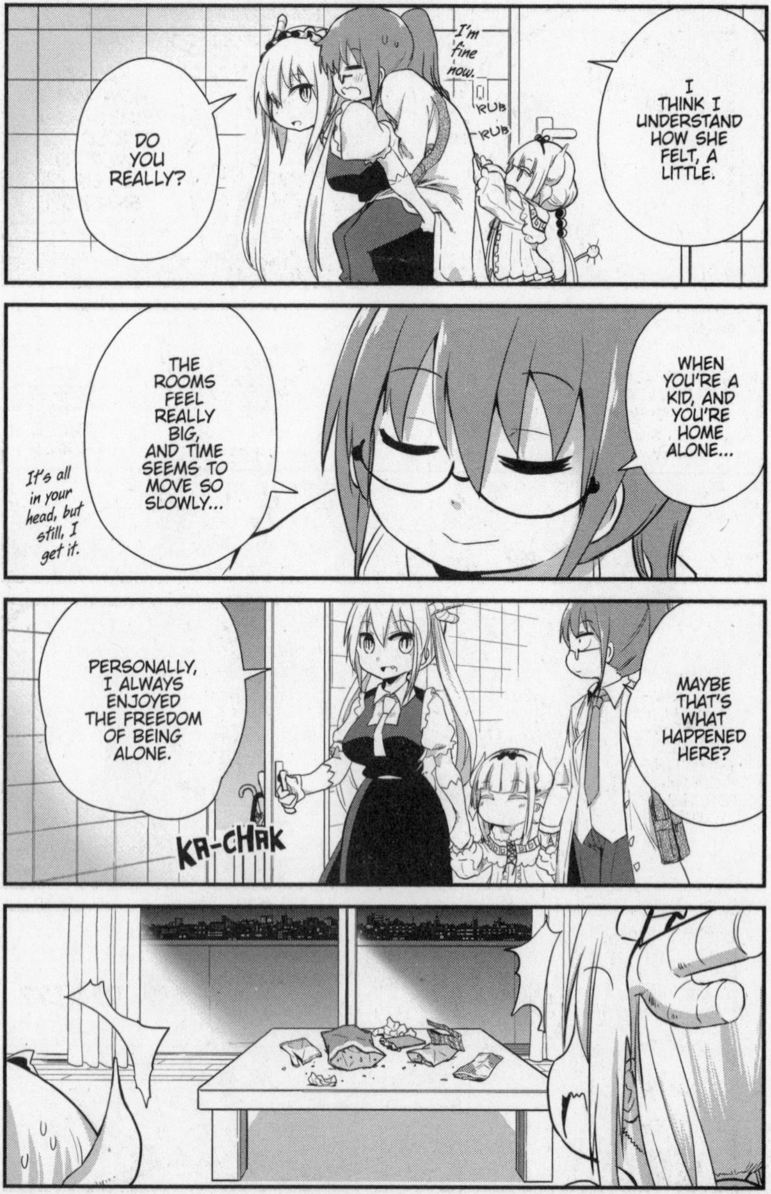
I THINK I UNDERSTAND HOW SHE FELT, A LITTLE.
I'm fine now.
RUB
RUB
DO YOU REALLY?
WHEN YOU'RE A KID, AND YOU'RE HOME ALONE...
THE ROOMS FEEL REALLY BIG, AND TIME SEEMS TO MOVE SO SLOWLY...
It's all in your head, but still, I get it.
MAYBE THAT'S WHAT HAPPENED HERE?
PERSONALLY, I ALWAYS ENJOYED THE FREEDOM OF BEING ALONE.
KA-CHAK

CHILDREN RECOVER VERY QUICKLY

I'm sorry!!

FLINCH

KANNA! HOW MANY TIMES HAVE I TOLD YOU *NOT* TO FILL UP ON SNACKS?!

REALLY! YOU'RE TOO **SOFT**, MISS KOBAYASHI.

SHE MIGHT BE A DRAGON, BUT SHE'S STILL JUST A KID.

TOHRU, I THINK THAT'S ENOUGH.

CHEER UP, KANNA-CHAN. WHY DON'T WE GO GET SOMETHING SPECIAL FOR DINNER TONIGHT?

SULK

This kid...

PERK

REALLY?

EPILOGUE: SAIKAWA-SAN'S DISTRESS

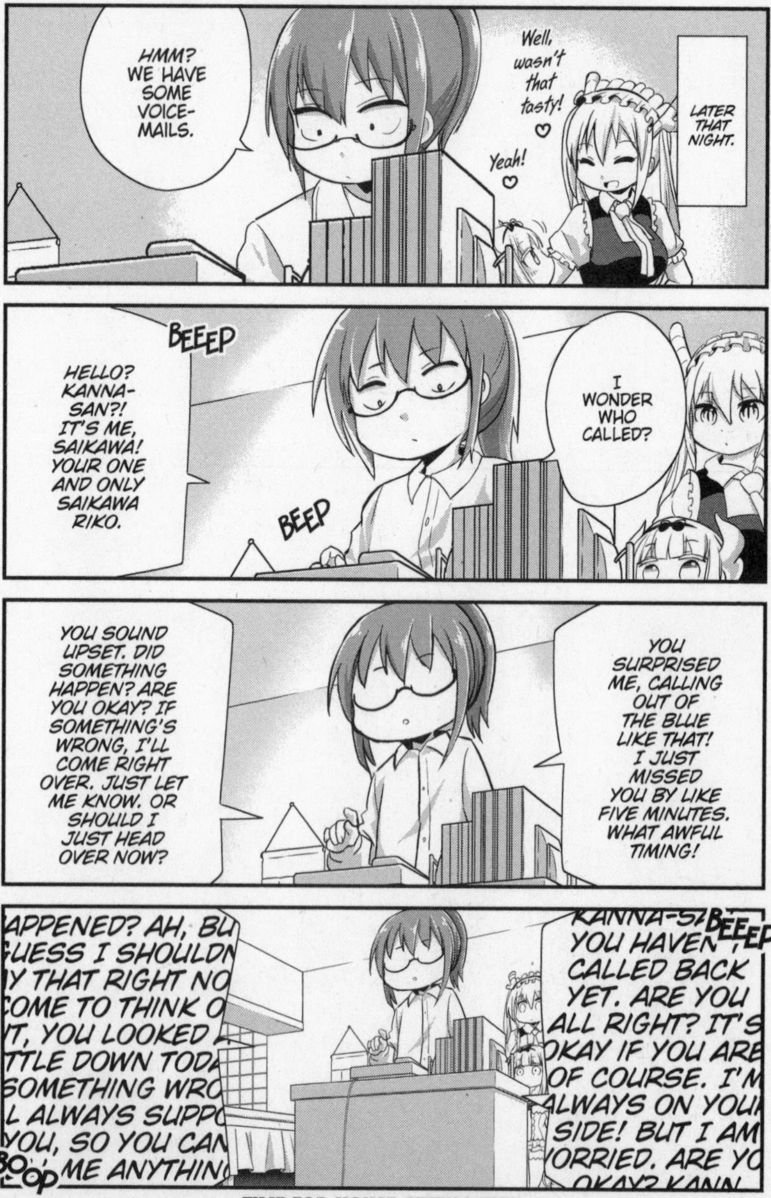

LATER THAT NIGHT.
Well, wasn't that tasty! ♡
Yeah! ♡
HMM? WE HAVE SOME VOICE-MAILS.
I WONDER WHO CALLED?
BEEP
BEEEP
HELLO? KANNA-SAN?! IT'S ME, SAIKAWA! YOUR ONE AND ONLY SAIKAWA RIKO.
YOU SURPRISED ME, CALLING OUT OF THE BLUE LIKE THAT! I JUST MISSED YOU BY LIKE FIVE MINUTES. WHAT AWFUL TIMING!
YOU SOUND UPSET. DID SOMETHING HAPPEN? ARE YOU OKAY? IF SOMETHING'S WRONG, I'LL COME RIGHT OVER. JUST LET ME KNOW. OR SHOULD I JUST HEAD OVER NOW?
BEEEP
KANNA-SA YOU HAVEN CALLED BACK YET. ARE YOU ALL RIGHT? IT'S OKAY IF YOU ARE OF COURSE. I'M ALWAYS ON YOU SIDE! BUT I AM WORRIED. ARE YO OKAY? KANN
APPENED? AH, BU UESS I SHOULDN Y THAT RIGHT NO OME TO THINK O T, YOU LOOKED TTLE DOWN TODA OMETHING WRO L ALWAYS SUPP YOU, SO YOU CAN ME ANYTHIN
BOOP

TIME FOR HOUSE-SITTING/END

Kanna-san?! Talk to me!!

Miss Kobayashi's Dragon Maid

Kanna's Daily Life

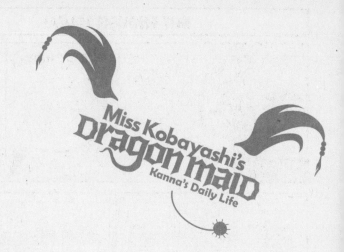

NOT ENOUGH MANA!

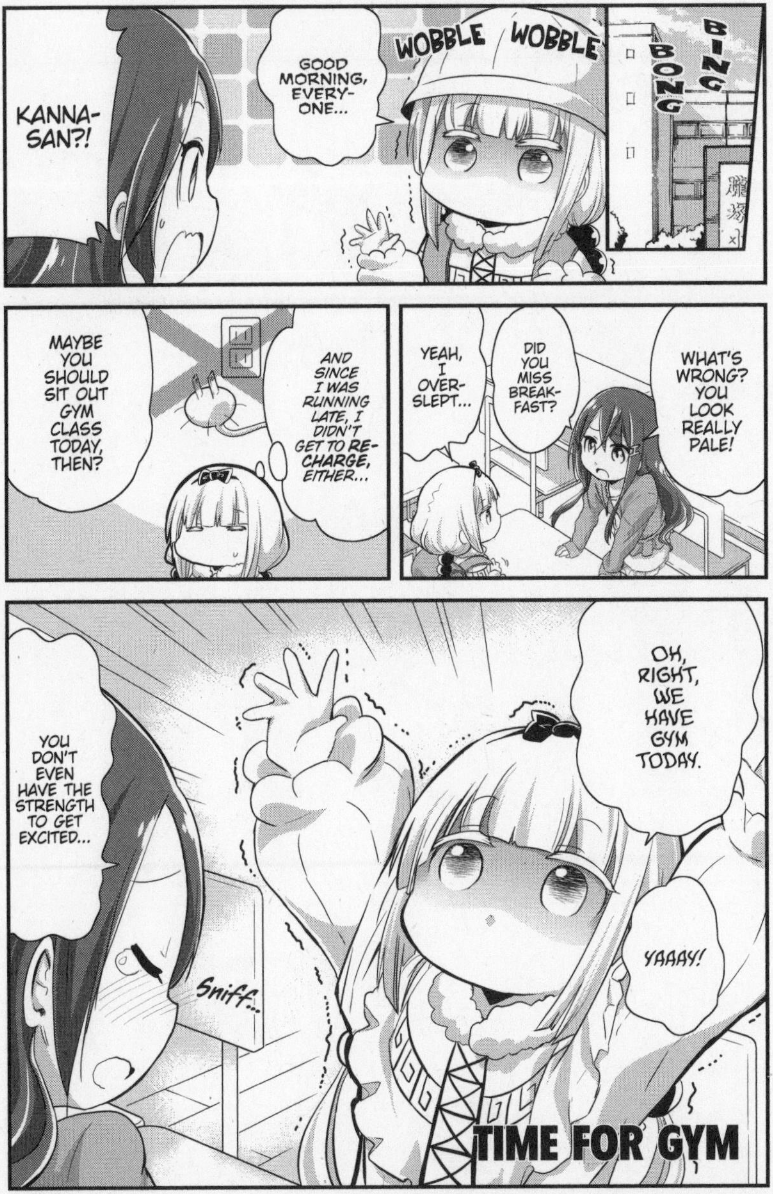
BING BONG
WOBBLE WOBBLE
GOOD MORNING, EVERY-ONE...
KANNA-SAN?!
WHAT'S WRONG? YOU LOOK REALLY PALE!
DID YOU MISS BREAK-FAST?
YEAH, I OVER-SLEPT...
AND SINCE I WAS RUNNING LATE, I DIDN'T GET TO RE-CHARGE, EITHER...
MAYBE YOU SHOULD SIT OUT GYM CLASS TODAY, THEN?
OH, RIGHT, WE HAVE GYM TODAY.
YAAAY!
YOU DON'T EVEN HAVE THE STRENGTH TO GET EXCITED...
Sniff...
TIME FOR GYM

CHALLENGE ACCEPTED

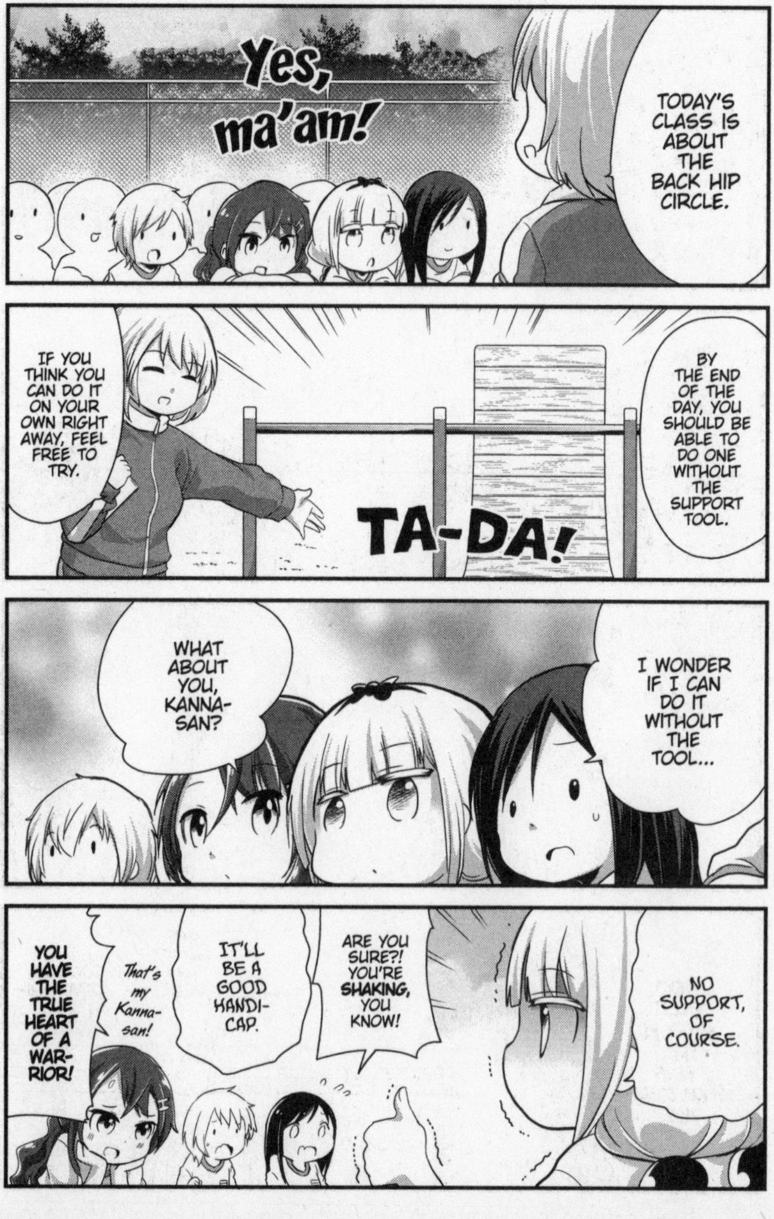
TODAY'S CLASS IS ABOUT THE BACK HIP CIRCLE.
Yes, ma'am!
BY THE END OF THE DAY, YOU SHOULD BE ABLE TO DO ONE WITHOUT THE SUPPORT TOOL.
TA-DA!
IF YOU THINK YOU CAN DO IT ON YOUR OWN RIGHT AWAY, FEEL FREE TO TRY.
I WONDER IF I CAN DO IT WITHOUT THE TOOL...
WHAT ABOUT YOU, KANNA-SAN?
NO SUPPORT, OF COURSE.
ARE YOU SURE?! YOU'RE SHAKING, YOU KNOW!
IT'LL BE A GOOD HANDI-CAP.
That's my Kanna-san!
YOU HAVE THE TRUE HEART OF A WAR-RIOR!

BACK HIP FLOP

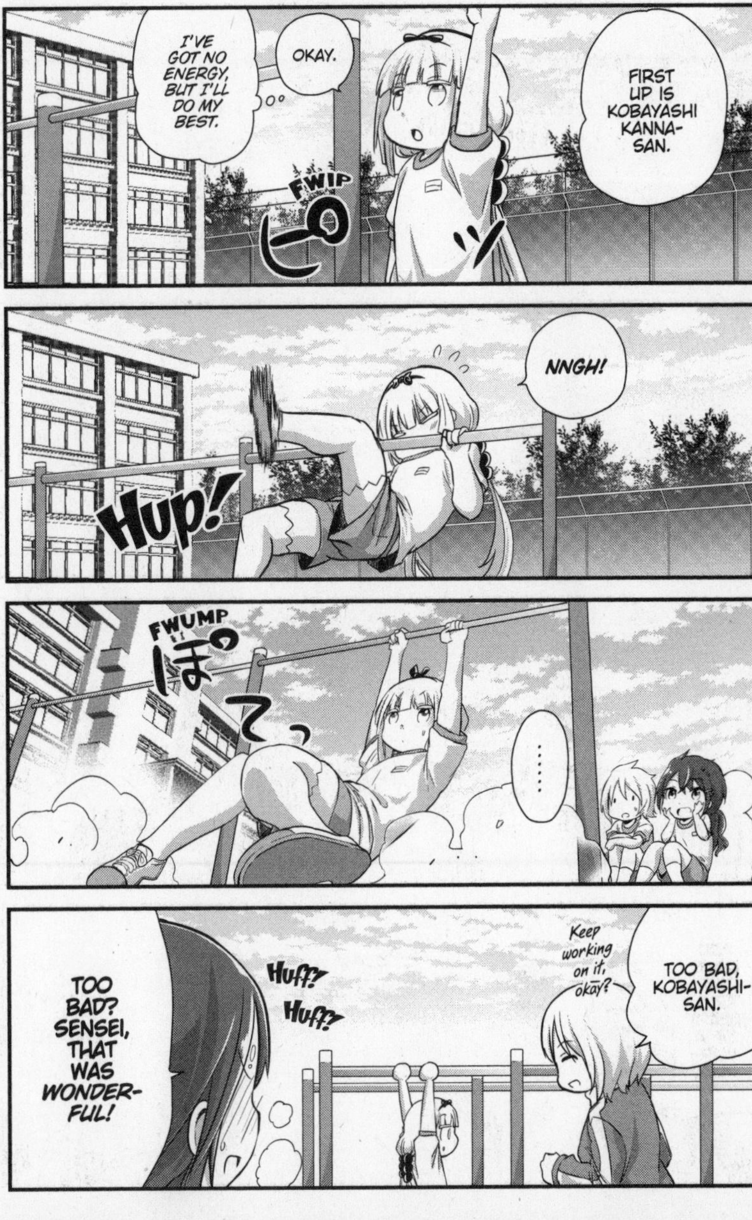
FIRST UP IS KOBAYASHI KANNA-SAN.
OKAY.
I'VE GOT NO ENERGY, BUT I'LL DO MY BEST.
FWIP
NNGH!
HUP!
FWUMP
......
TOO BAD, KOBAYASHI-SAN.
Keep working on it, okay?
Huff?
Huff?
TOO BAD? SENSEI, THAT WAS WONDERFUL!

SAIKAWA-SAN'S GOT SKILLS

YOU CAN DO IT, SAIKAWA.

WATCH AND LEARN, EVERYBODY!

HERE!

NEXT UP, SAIKAWA RIKO-SAN.

YEAH, TOTALLY!

HEH. WOULDN'T IT SUCK IF SHE FAILS AFTER SAYING THAT?

TWITCH

Hup!

I'M SORRY, WHAT WAS THAT?!

WELL DONE AS ALWAYS, SAIKAWA-SAN!

N... NOTHING AT ALL, MA'AM!

Scary!

Eek!

SUPERIOR SPECIES

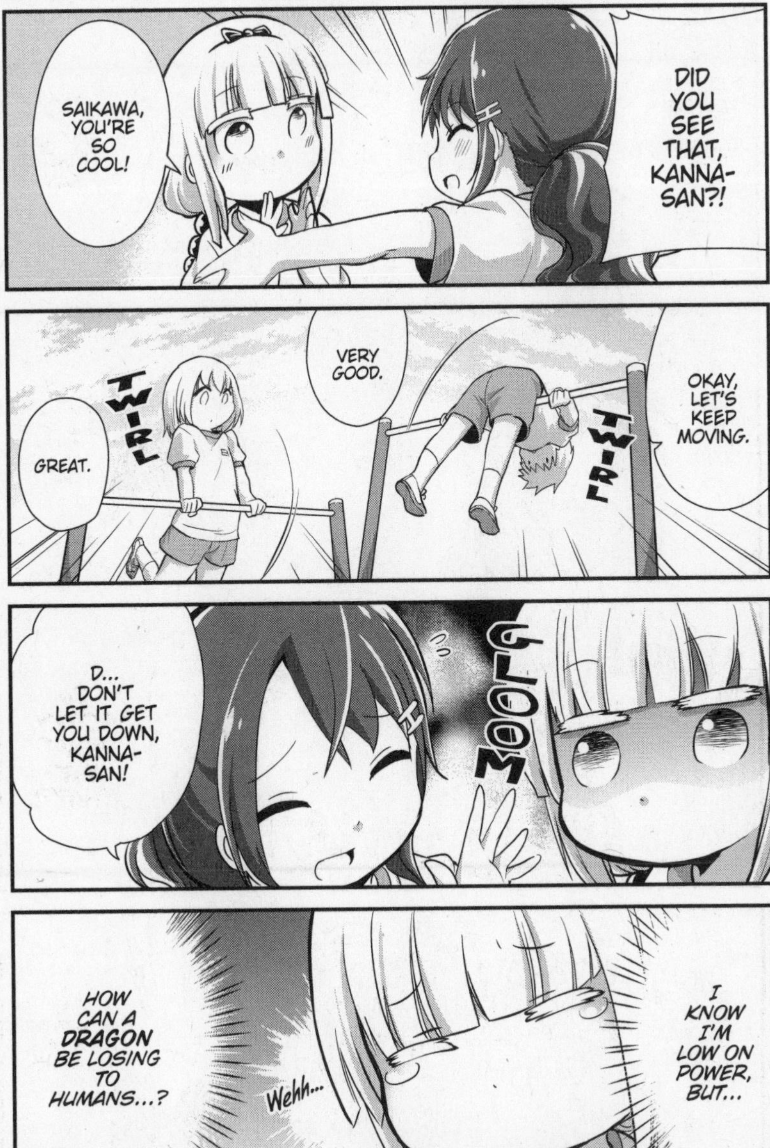

DID YOU SEE THAT, KANNA-SAN?!
SAIKAWA, YOU'RE SO COOL!
OKAY, LET'S KEEP MOVING.
TWIRL
VERY GOOD.
TWIRL
GREAT.
GLOOM
D... DON'T LET IT GET YOU DOWN, KANNA-SAN!
I KNOW I'M LOW ON POWER, BUT...
Wehh...
HOW CAN A DRAGON BE LOSING TO HUMANS...?

GO FOR THE GOLD!

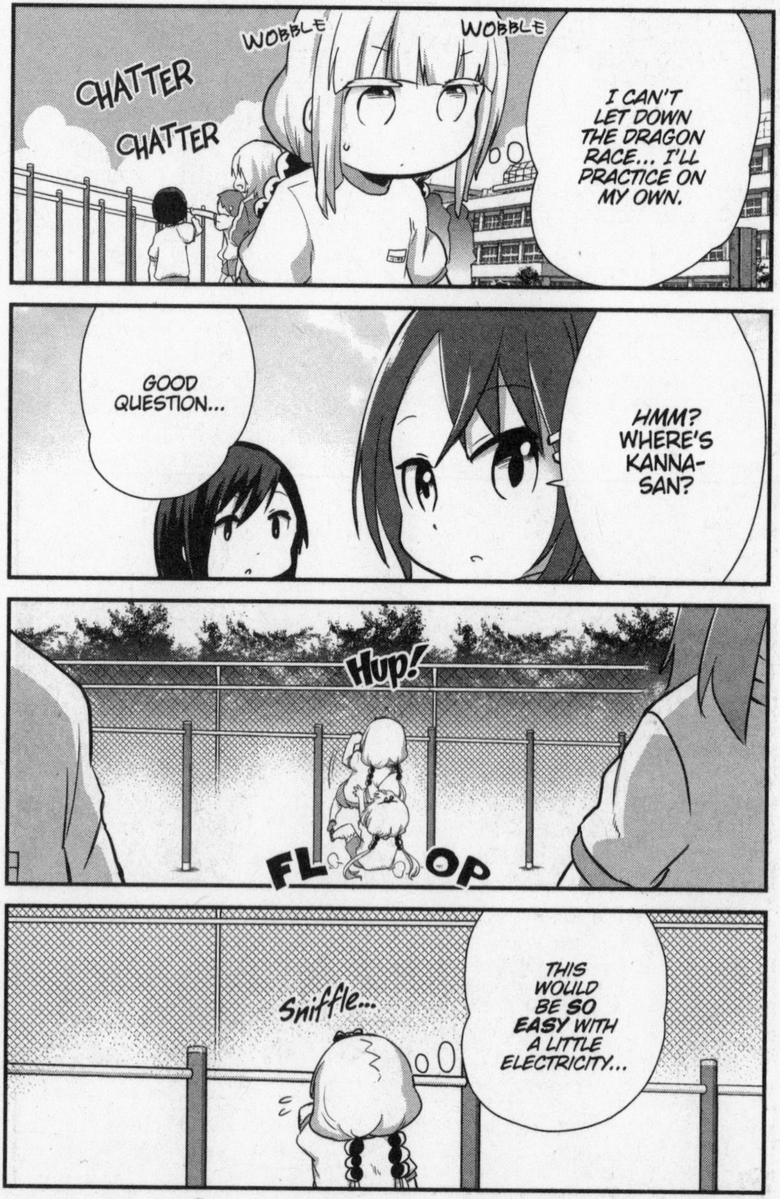
I CAN'T LET DOWN THE DRAGON RACE... I'LL PRACTICE ON MY OWN.
WOBBLE
WOBBLE
CHATTER
CHATTER
HMM? WHERE'S KANNA-SAN?
GOOD QUESTION...
Hup!
FLOP
THIS WOULD BE SO EASY WITH A LITTLE ELECTRICITY...
Sniffle...

A SHOCKING DEVELOPMENT

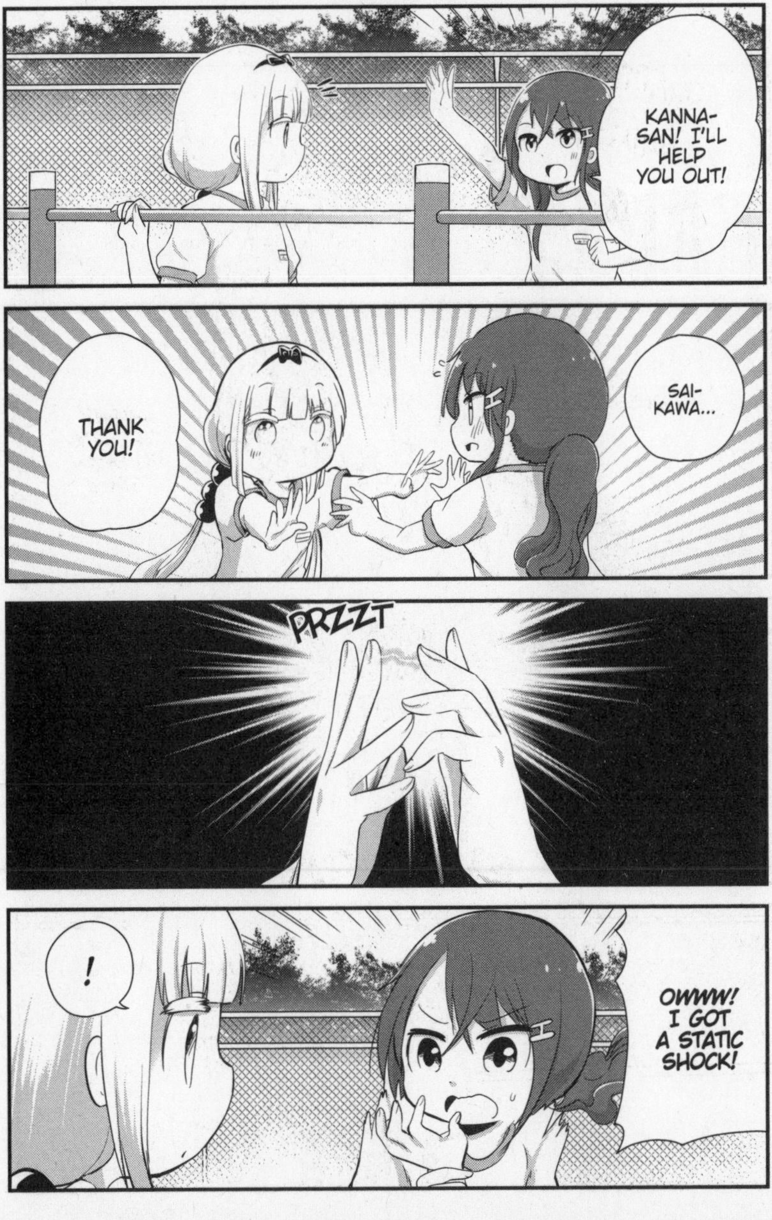
KANNA-SAN! I'LL HELP YOU OUT!
SAI-KAWA...
THANK YOU!
PRZZT
OWWW! I GOT A STATIC SHOCK!
!

SCIENCE LESSON

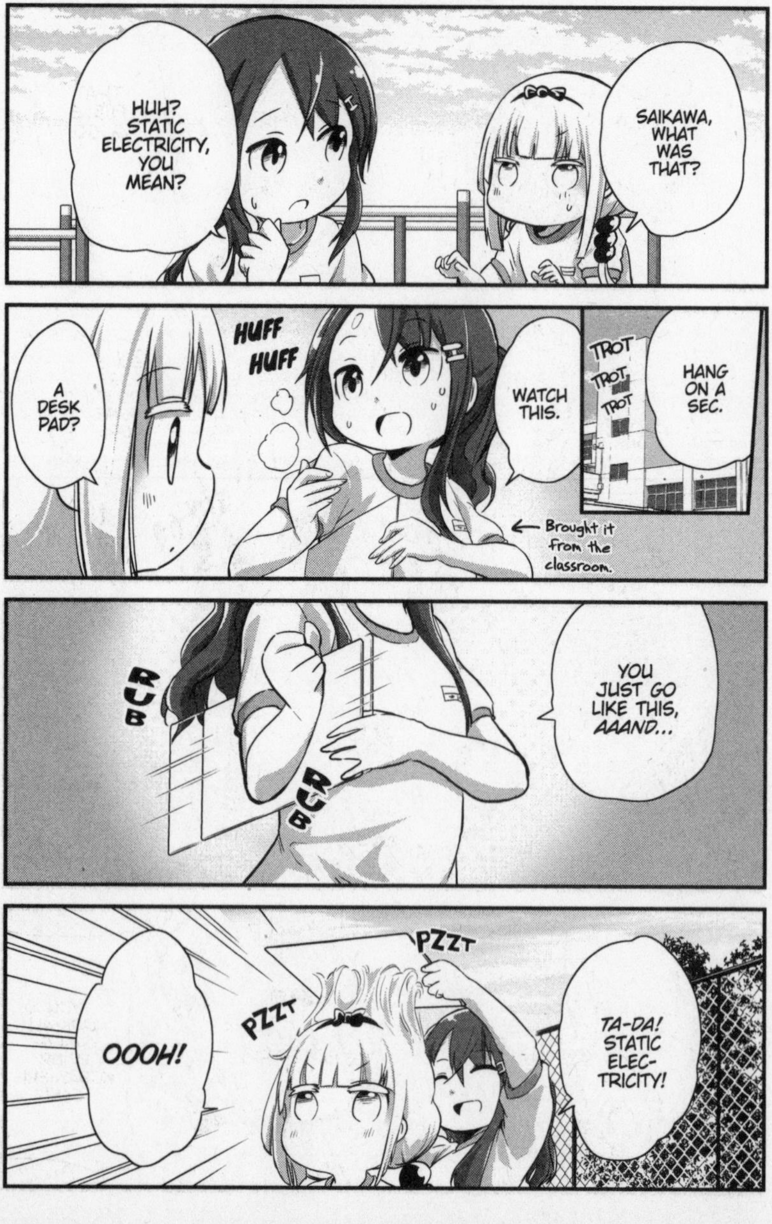
SAIKAWA, WHAT WAS THAT?
HUH? STATIC ELECTRICITY, YOU MEAN?
HANG ON A SEC.
TROT TROT TROT
WATCH THIS.
HUFF HUFF
A DESK PAD?
← Brought it from the classroom.
YOU JUST GO LIKE THIS, AAAND...
RUB RUB
TA-DA! STATIC ELEC-TRICITY!
PZZT
PZZT
OOOH!

SUPER-CHARGED KANNA-CHAN

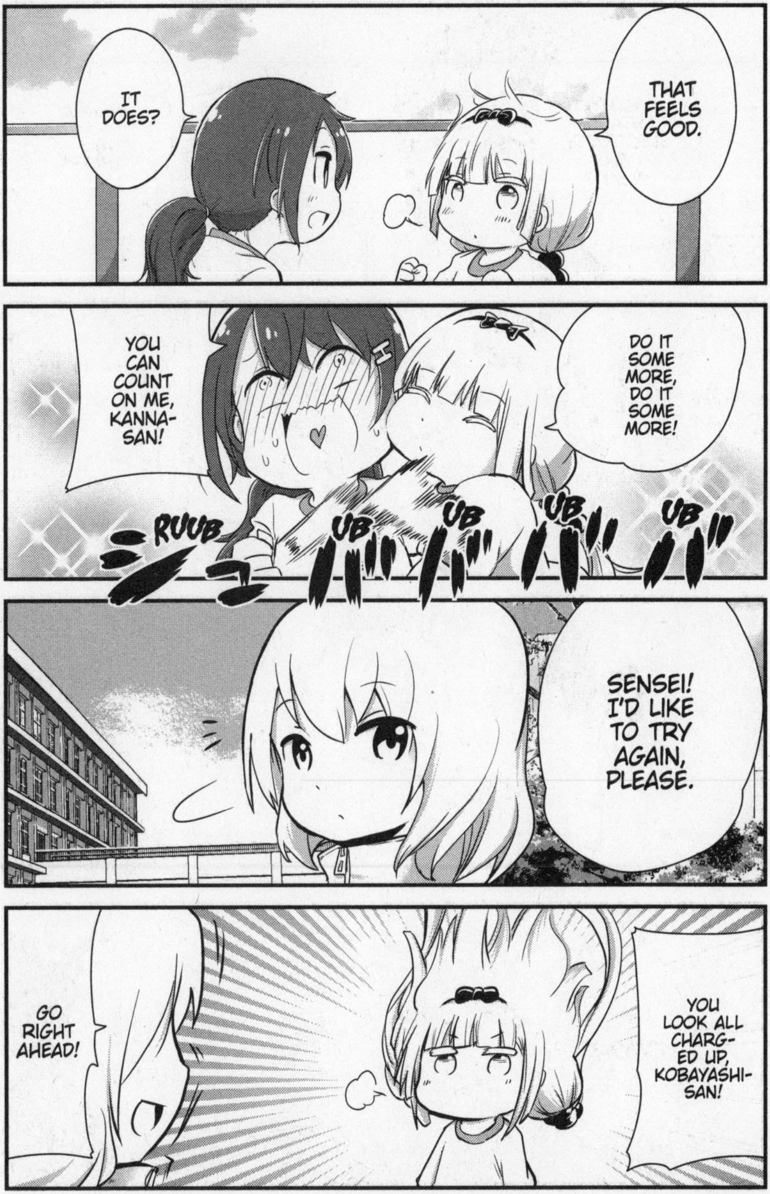
THAT FEELS GOOD.
IT DOES?
DO IT SOME MORE, DO IT SOME MORE!
YOU CAN COUNT ON ME, KANNA-SAN!
RUUB UB UB UB UB
SENSEI! I'D LIKE TO TRY AGAIN, PLEASE.
YOU LOOK ALL CHARG-ED UP, KOBAYASHI-SAN!
GO RIGHT AHEAD!

A DRAGON'S PRIDE

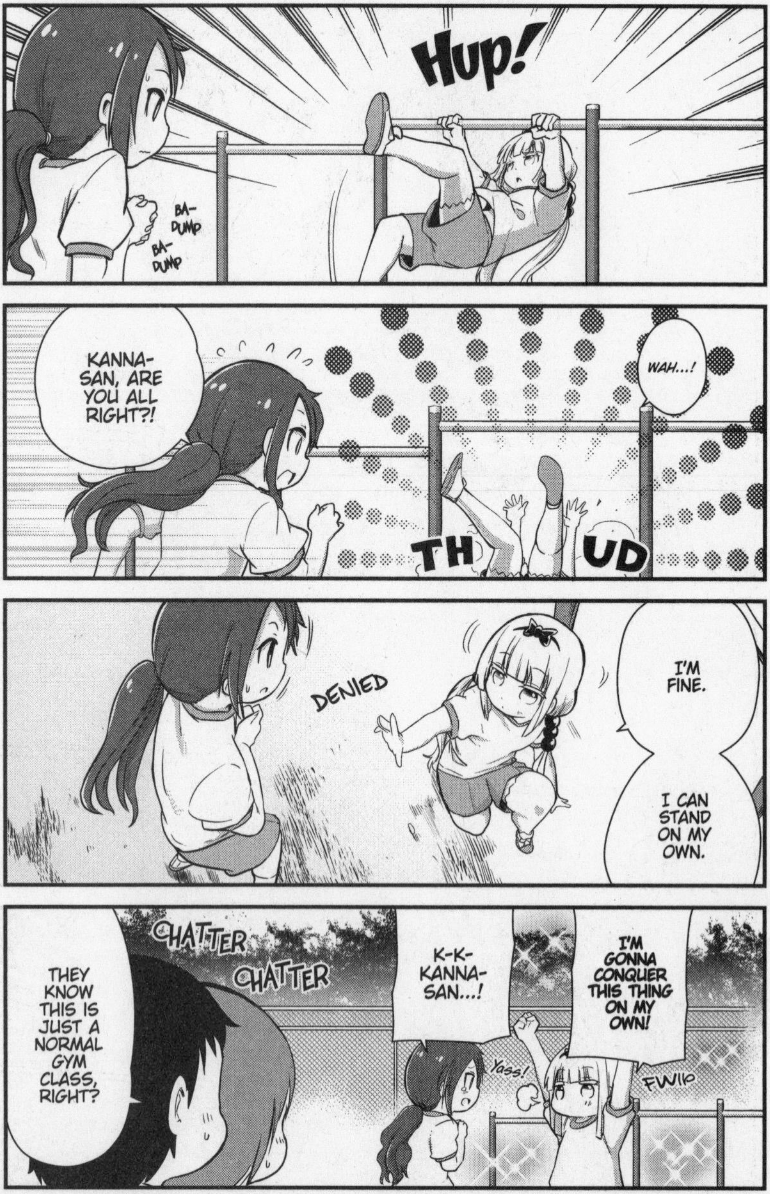
Hup!
BA-DUMP
BA-DUMP
WAH...!
KANNA-SAN, ARE YOU ALL RIGHT?!
THUD
I'M FINE.
I CAN STAND ON MY OWN.
DENIED
I'M GONNA CONQUER THIS THING ON MY OWN!
K-K-KANNA-SAN...!
CHATTER
CHATTER
Yass!
THEY KNOW THIS IS JUST A NORMAL GYM CLASS, RIGHT?

VICTORY!

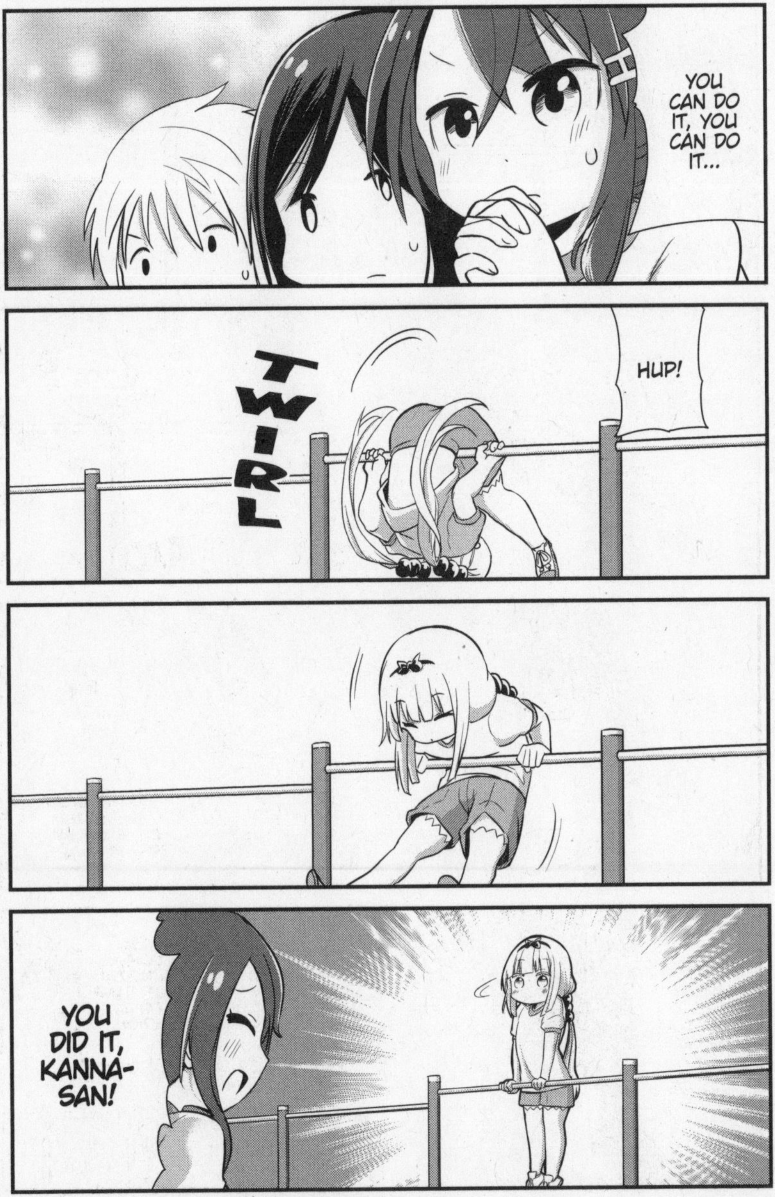
YOU CAN DO IT, YOU CAN DO IT...
HUP!
TWIRL
YOU DID IT, KANNA-SAN!

ABOVE AND BEYOND!

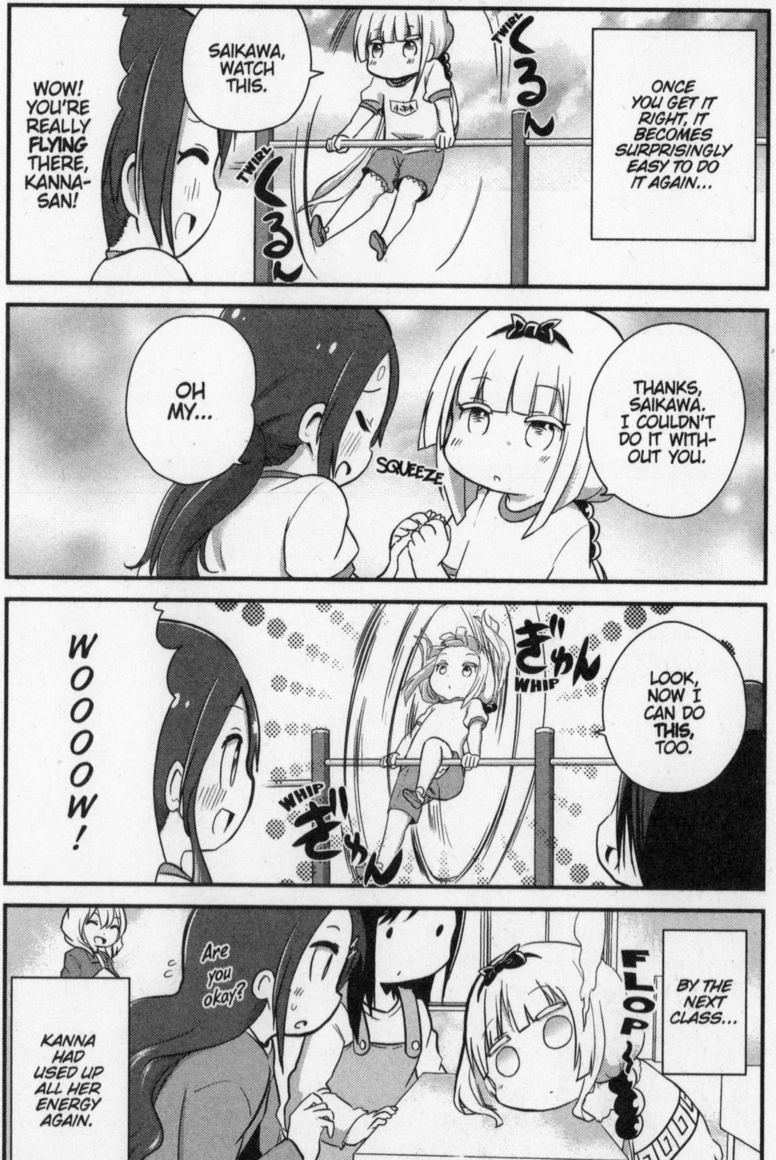
ONCE YOU GET IT RIGHT, IT BECOMES SURPRISINGLY EASY TO DO IT AGAIN...
くるん
TWIRL
SAIKAWA, WATCH THIS.
WOW! YOU'RE REALLY FLYING THERE, KANNA-SAN!
TWIRL
くるん
THANKS, SAIKAWA. I COULDN'T DO IT WITH-OUT YOU.
SQUEEZE
OH MY...
LOOK, NOW I CAN DO THIS, TOO.
ぎゅん
WHIP
WHIP
ぎゅん
WOOOOOOW!
BY THE NEXT CLASS...
FLOP~
Are you okay?
KANNA HAD USED UP ALL HER ENERGY AGAIN.

TIME FOR GYM/END

Oooh...

Miss Kobayashi's Dragon Maid
Kanna's Daily Life

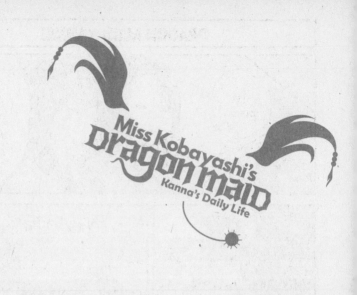

DRAGON MAID KANNA!

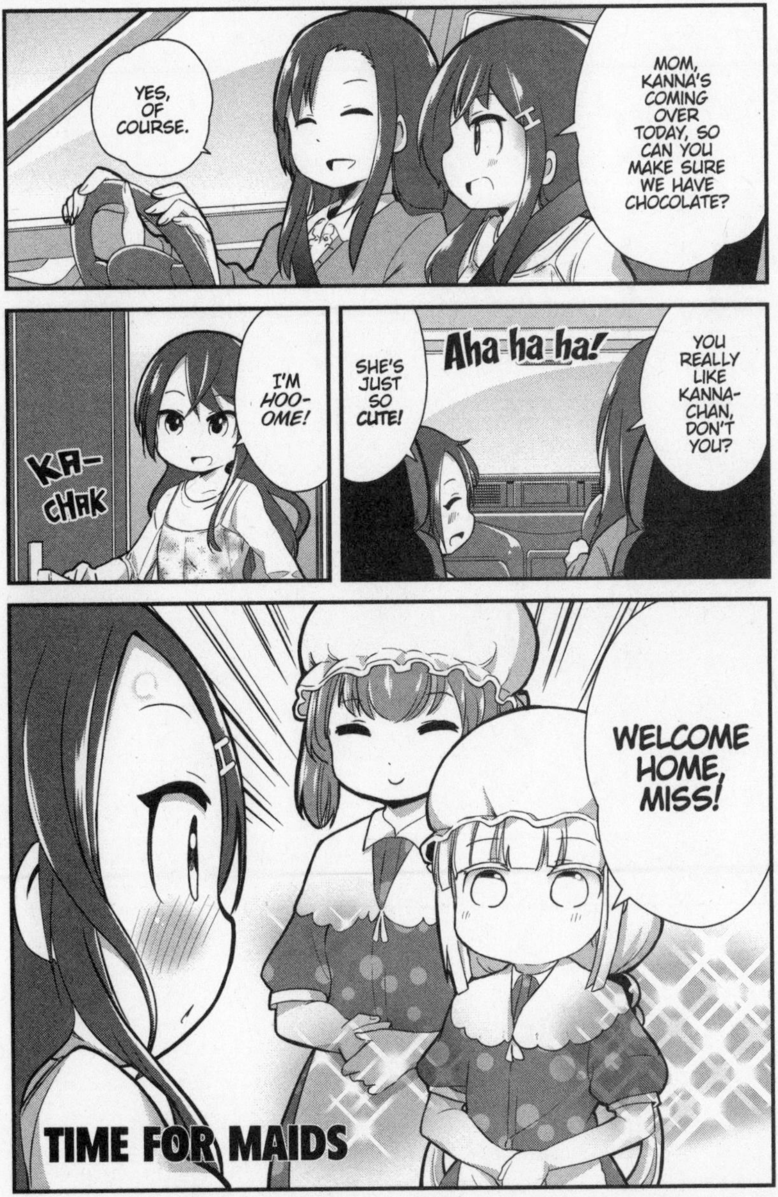
MOM, KANNA'S COMING OVER TODAY, SO CAN YOU MAKE SURE WE HAVE CHOCOLATE?
YES, OF COURSE.
YOU REALLY LIKE KANNA-CHAN, DON'T YOU?
Aha ha ha!
SHE'S JUST SO CUTE!
I'M HOO-OME!
KA-CHAK
WELCOME HOME, MISS!
TIME FOR MAIDS

IS THIS...A DREAM...?!

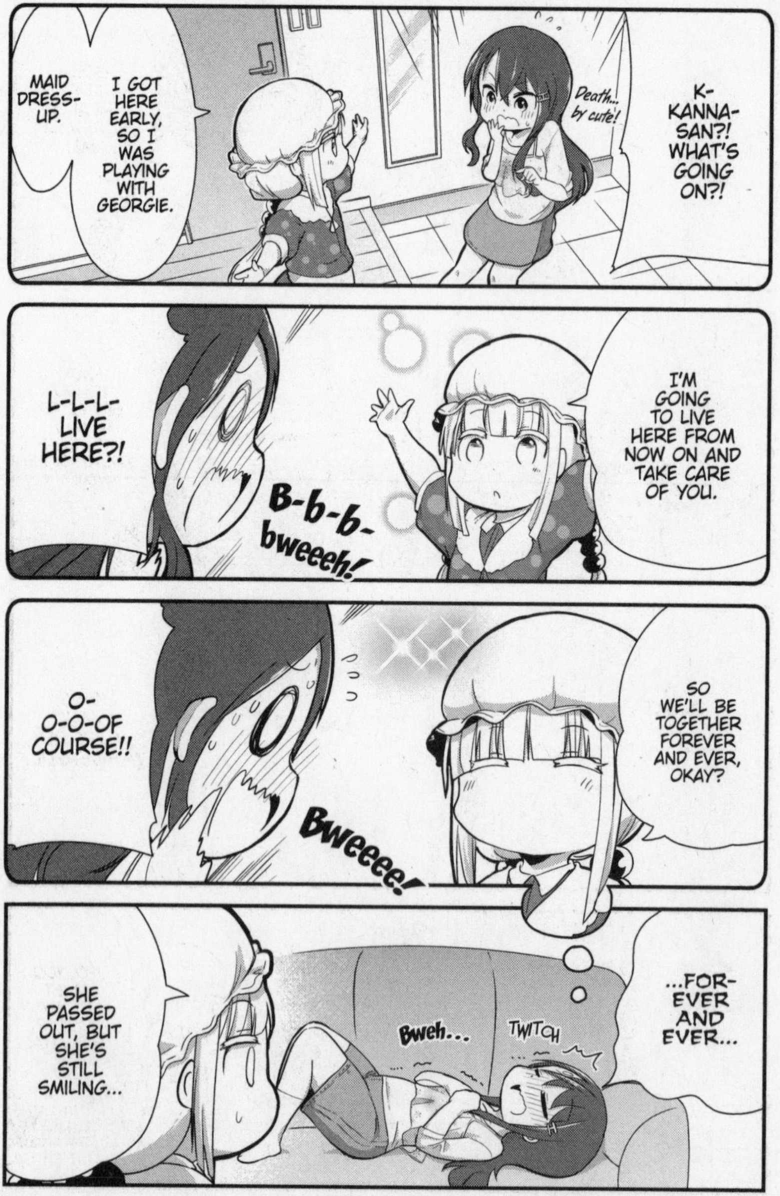
K-KANNA-SAN?! WHAT'S GOING ON?!
Death... by cute!
I GOT HERE EARLY, SO I WAS PLAYING WITH GEORGIE.
MAID DRESS-UP.
I'M GOING TO LIVE HERE FROM NOW ON AND TAKE CARE OF YOU.
B-b-b-bweeeh!
L-L-L-LIVE HERE?!
SO WE'LL BE TOGETHER FOREVER AND EVER, OKAY?
Bweeeee!
O-O-O-OF COURSE!!
...FOR-EVER AND EVER...
TWITCH
Bweh...
SHE PASSED OUT, BUT SHE'S STILL SMILING...

WONDERFUL MAID LIFESTYLE

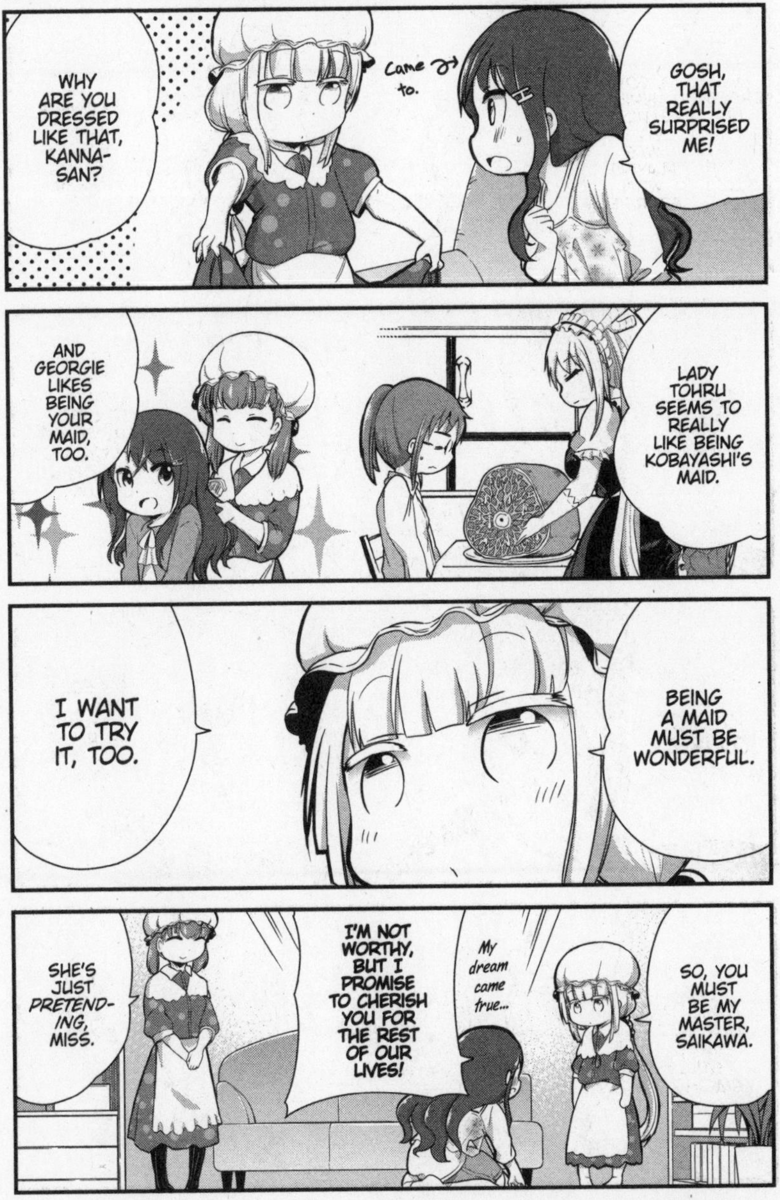
GOSH, THAT REALLY SURPRISED ME!
Came to.
WHY ARE YOU DRESSED LIKE THAT, KANNA-SAN?
LADY TOHRU SEEMS TO REALLY LIKE BEING KOBAYASHI'S MAID.
AND GEORGIE LIKES BEING YOUR MAID, TOO.
BEING A MAID MUST BE WONDERFUL.
I WANT TO TRY IT, TOO.
SO, YOU MUST BE MY MASTER, SAIKAWA.
My dream came true...
I'M NOT WORTHY, BUT I PROMISE TO CHERISH YOU FOR THE REST OF OUR LIVES!
SHE'S JUST PRETENDING, MISS.

REALITY CHECK

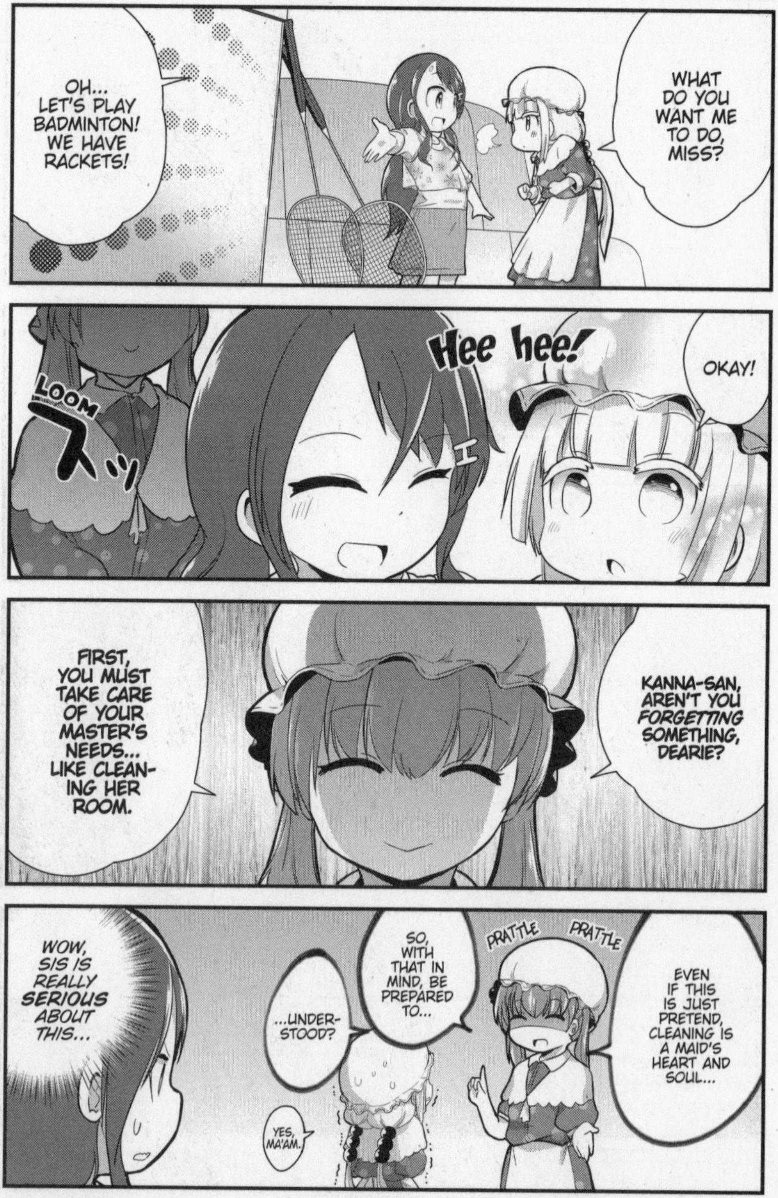
WHAT DO YOU WANT ME TO DO, MISS?
OH... LET'S PLAY BADMINTON! WE HAVE RACKETS!
OKAY!
Hee hee!
LOOM
ズッ
KANNA-SAN, AREN'T YOU FORGETTING SOMETHING, DEARIE?
FIRST, YOU MUST TAKE CARE OF YOUR MASTER'S NEEDS... LIKE CLEAN-ING HER ROOM.
EVEN IF THIS IS JUST PRETEND, CLEANING IS A MAID'S HEART AND SOUL...
PRATTLE
PRATTLE
SO, WITH THAT IN MIND, BE PREPARED TO...
...UNDER-STOOD?
YES, MA'AM.
WOW, SIS IS REALLY SERIOUS ABOUT THIS...

LET'S DO OUR BEST!

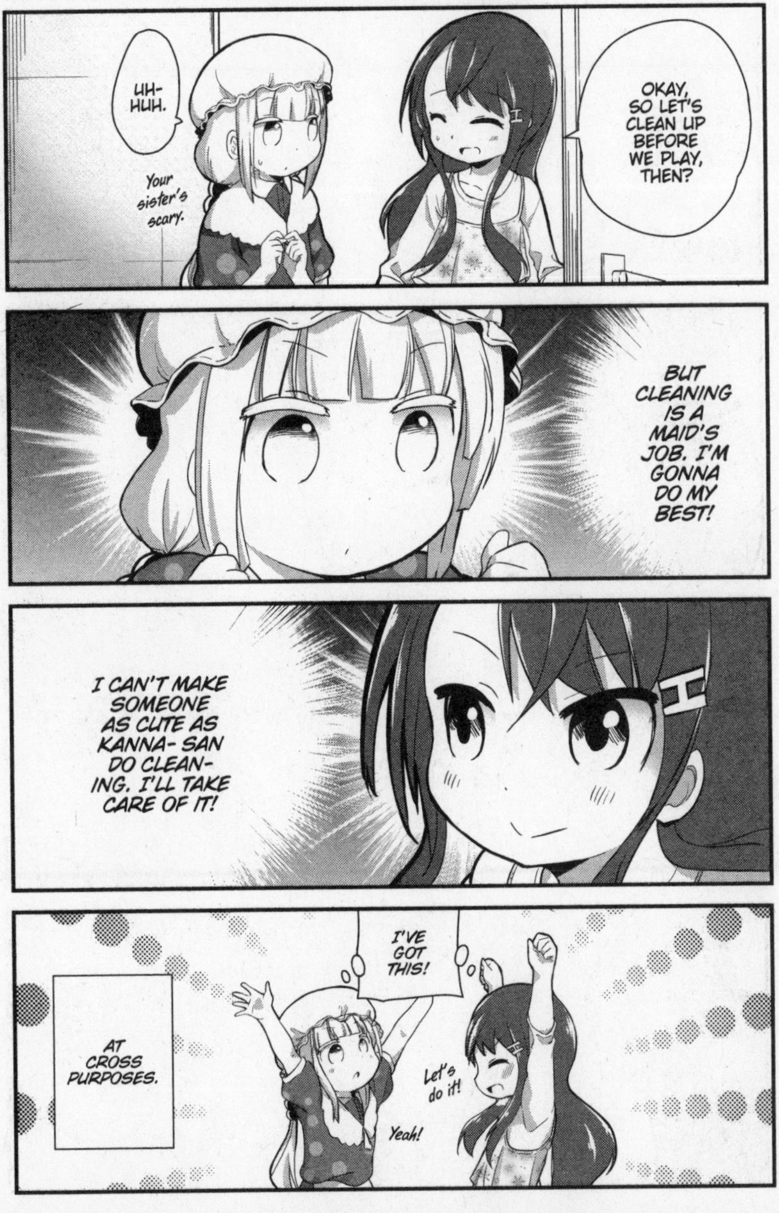

OKAY, SO LET'S CLEAN UP BEFORE WE PLAY, THEN?
UH-HUH.
Your sister's scary.
BUT CLEANING IS A MAID'S JOB. I'M GONNA DO MY BEST!
I CAN'T MAKE SOMEONE AS CUTE AS KANNA-SAN DO CLEAN-ING. I'LL TAKE CARE OF IT!
I'VE GOT THIS!
Let's do it!
Yeah!
AT CROSS PURPOSES.

THAT'S AN ORDER!

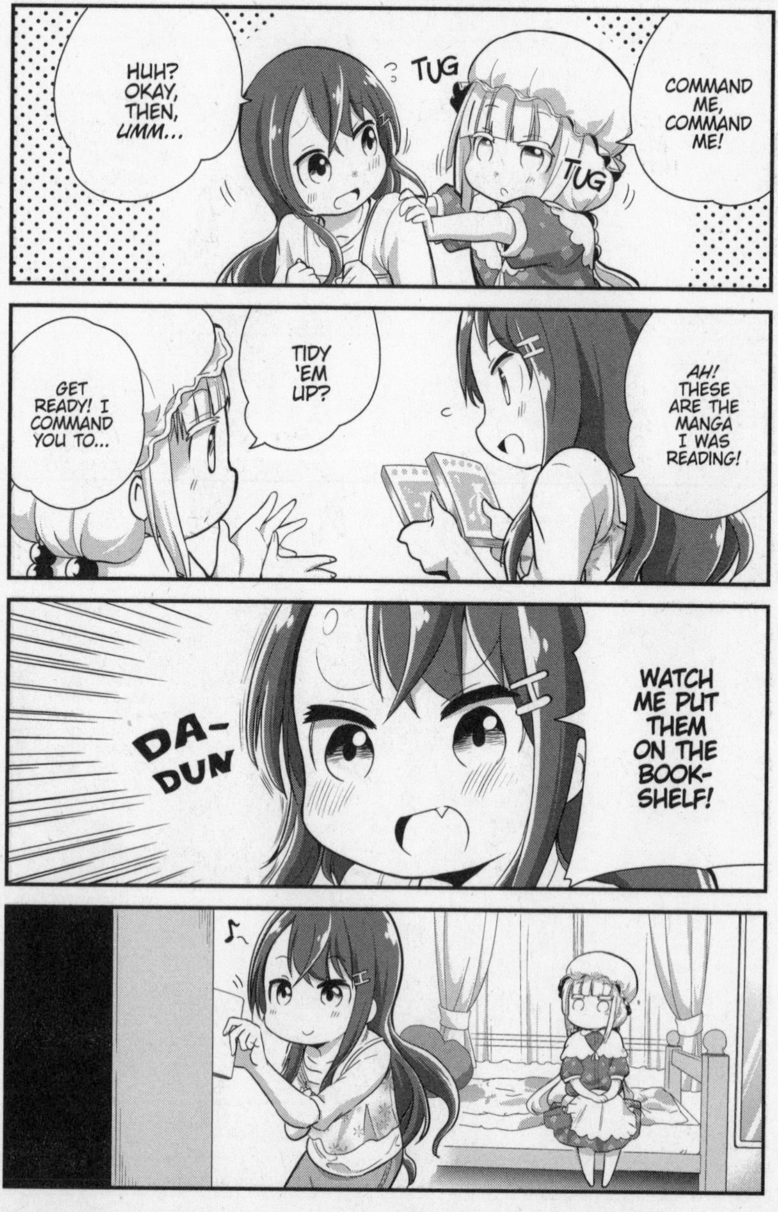
COMMAND ME, COMMAND ME!
TUG
TUG
HUH? OKAY, THEN, UMM...
AH! THESE ARE THE MANGA I WAS READING!
TIDY 'EM UP?
GET READY! I COMMAND YOU TO...
WATCH ME PUT THEM ON THE BOOK-SHELF!
DA-DUN

NATURAL

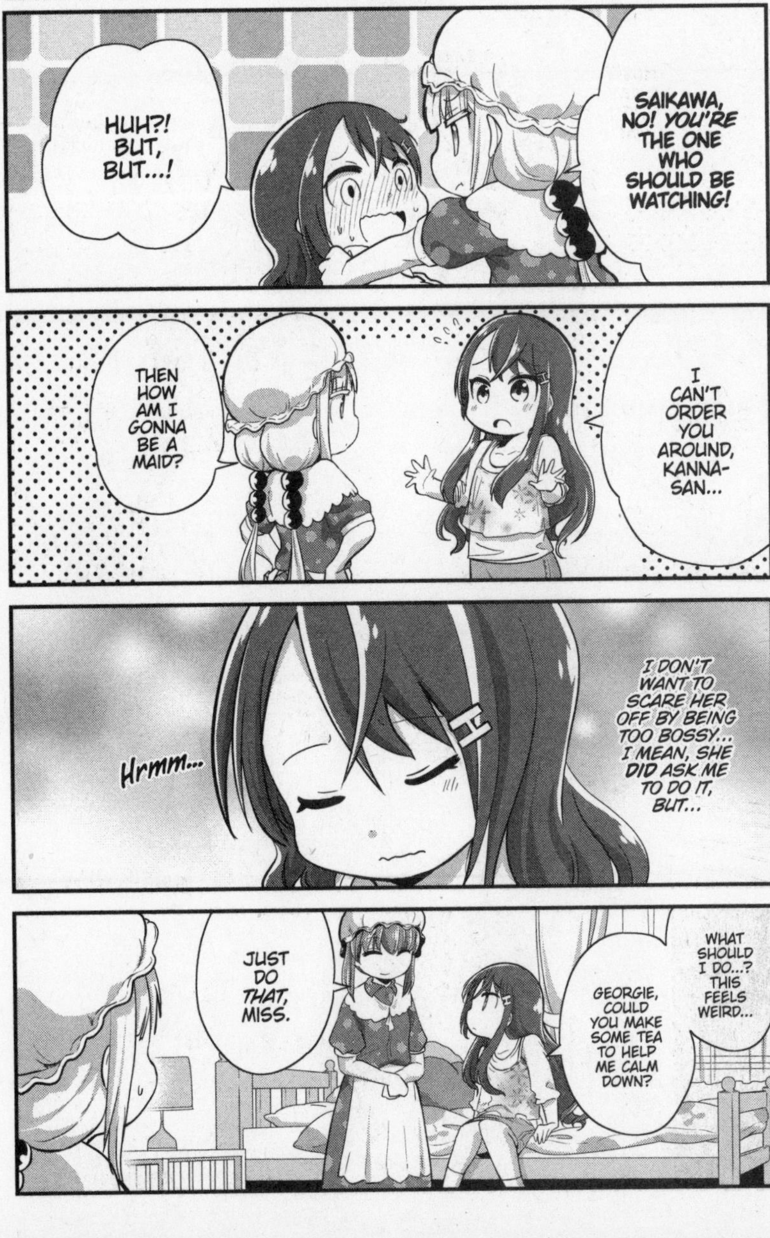
SAIKAWA, NO! YOU'RE THE ONE WHO SHOULD BE WATCHING!
HUH?! BUT, BUT...!
I CAN'T ORDER YOU AROUND, KANNA-SAN...
THEN HOW AM I GONNA BE A MAID?
I DON'T WANT TO SCARE HER OFF BY BEING TOO BOSSY... I MEAN, SHE DID ASK ME TO DO IT, BUT...
Hrmm...
WHAT SHOULD I DO...? THIS FEELS WEIRD...
GEORGIE, COULD YOU MAKE SOME TEA TO HELP ME CALM DOWN?
JUST DO THAT, MISS.

UNCLEAR ON THE CONCEPT

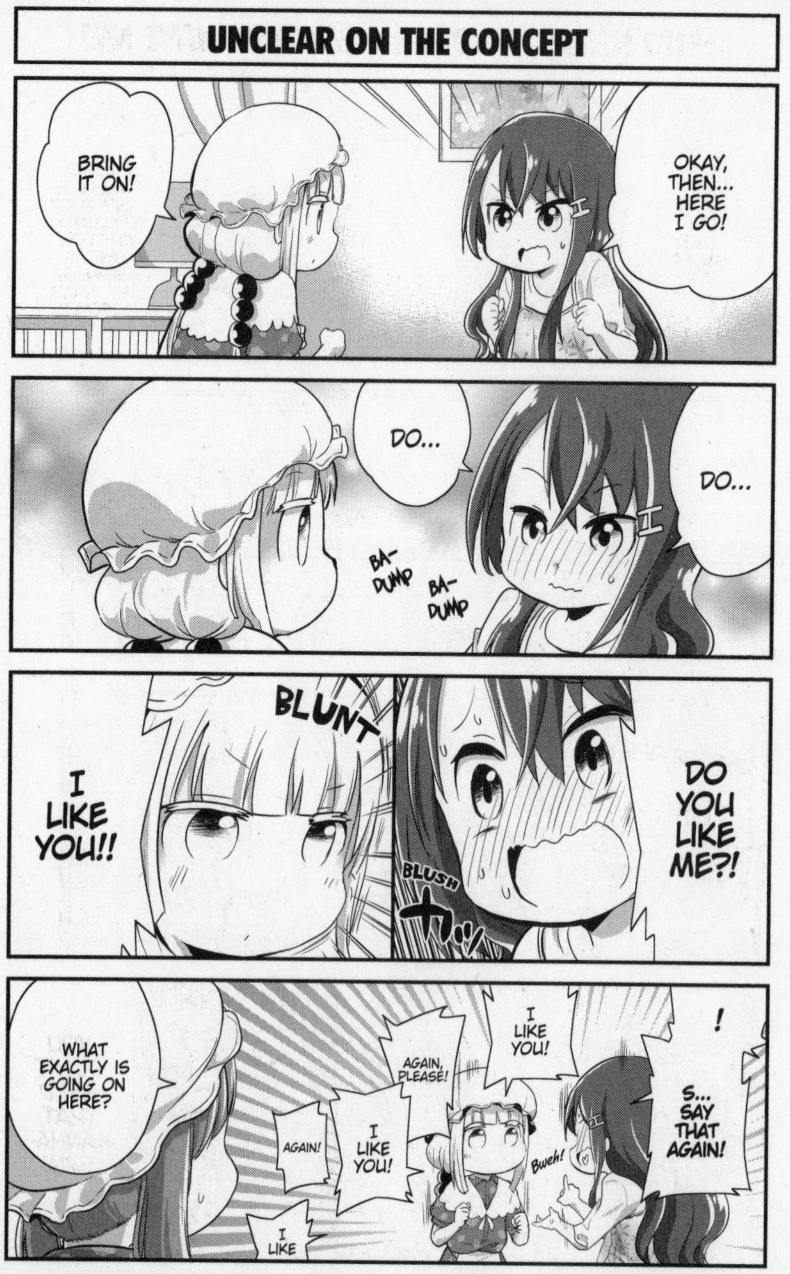
OKAY, THEN... HERE I GO!
BRING IT ON!
DO...
DO...
BA-DUMP
BA-DUMP
DO YOU LIKE ME?!
BLUSH
BLUNT
I LIKE YOU!!
!
S... SAY THAT AGAIN!
Bweh!
I LIKE YOU!
AGAIN, PLEASE!
I LIKE YOU!
AGAIN!
I LIKE
WHAT EXACTLY IS GOING ON HERE?

WHO NEEDS A LADDER WHEN YOU HAVE ME?

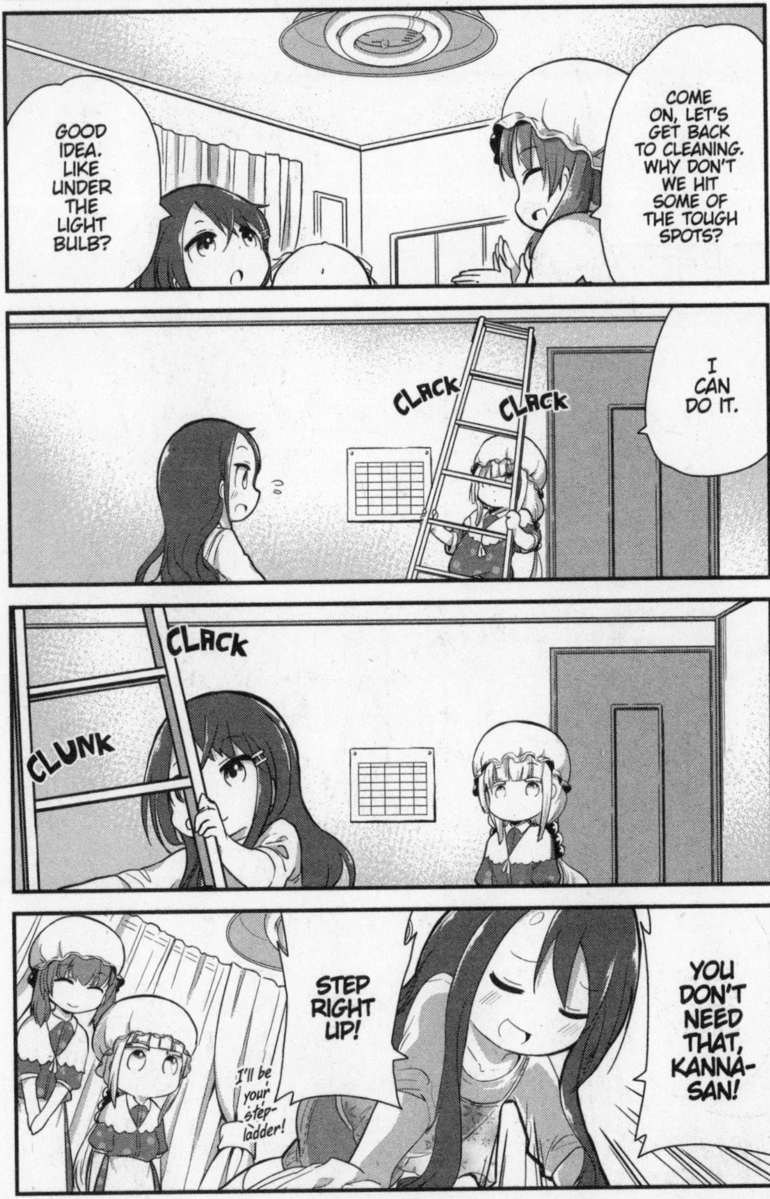
COME ON, LET'S GET BACK TO CLEANING. WHY DON'T WE HIT SOME OF THE TOUGH SPOTS?
GOOD IDEA. LIKE UNDER THE LIGHT BULB?
I CAN DO IT.
CLACK
CLACK
CLACK
CLUNK
YOU DON'T NEED THAT, KANNA-SAN!
STEP RIGHT UP!
I'll be your step-ladder!

GEORGIE GOES ALL OUT

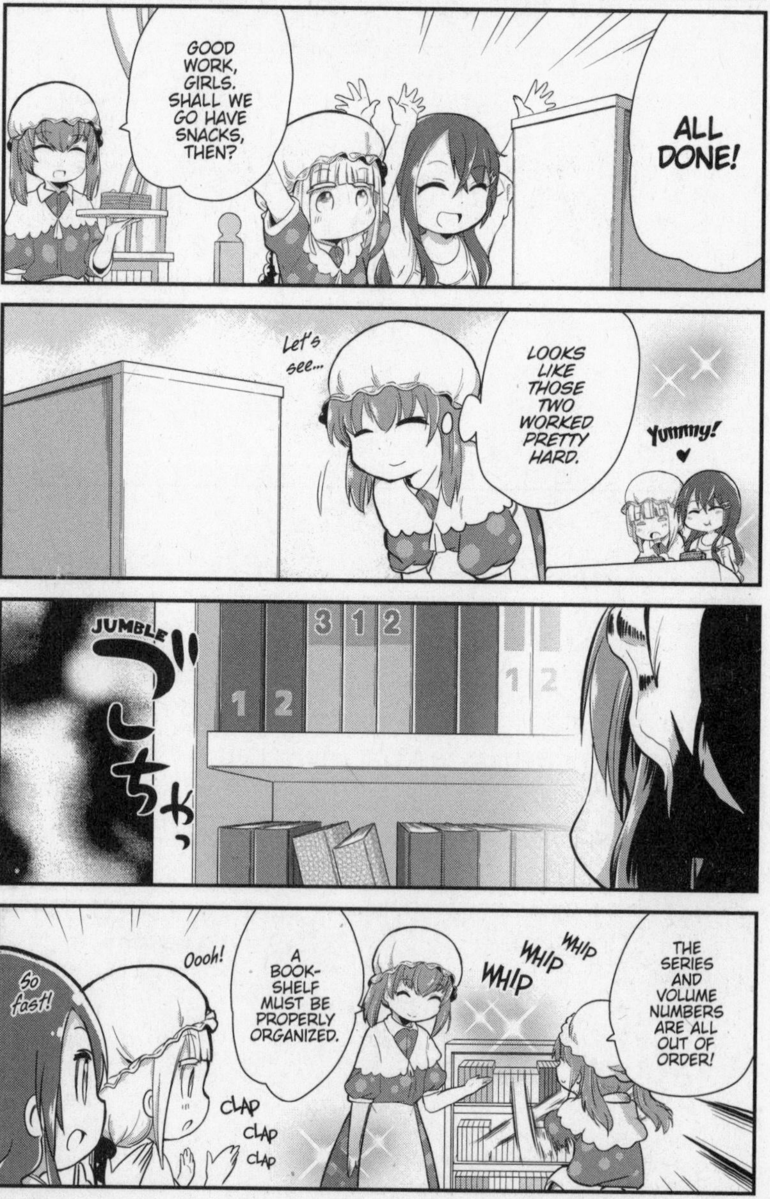

ALL DONE!
GOOD WORK, GIRLS. SHALL WE GO HAVE SNACKS, THEN?
Yummy! ♥
LOOKS LIKE THOSE TWO WORKED PRETTY HARD.
Let's see...
JUMBLE
ごちゃっ
THE SERIES AND VOLUME NUMBERS ARE ALL OUT OF ORDER!
WHIP WHIP WHIP
A BOOK-SHELF MUST BE PROPERLY ORGANIZED.
Oooh!
So fast!
CLAP CLAP CLAP

WHO'S THE MAID AND WHO'S THE MASTER?

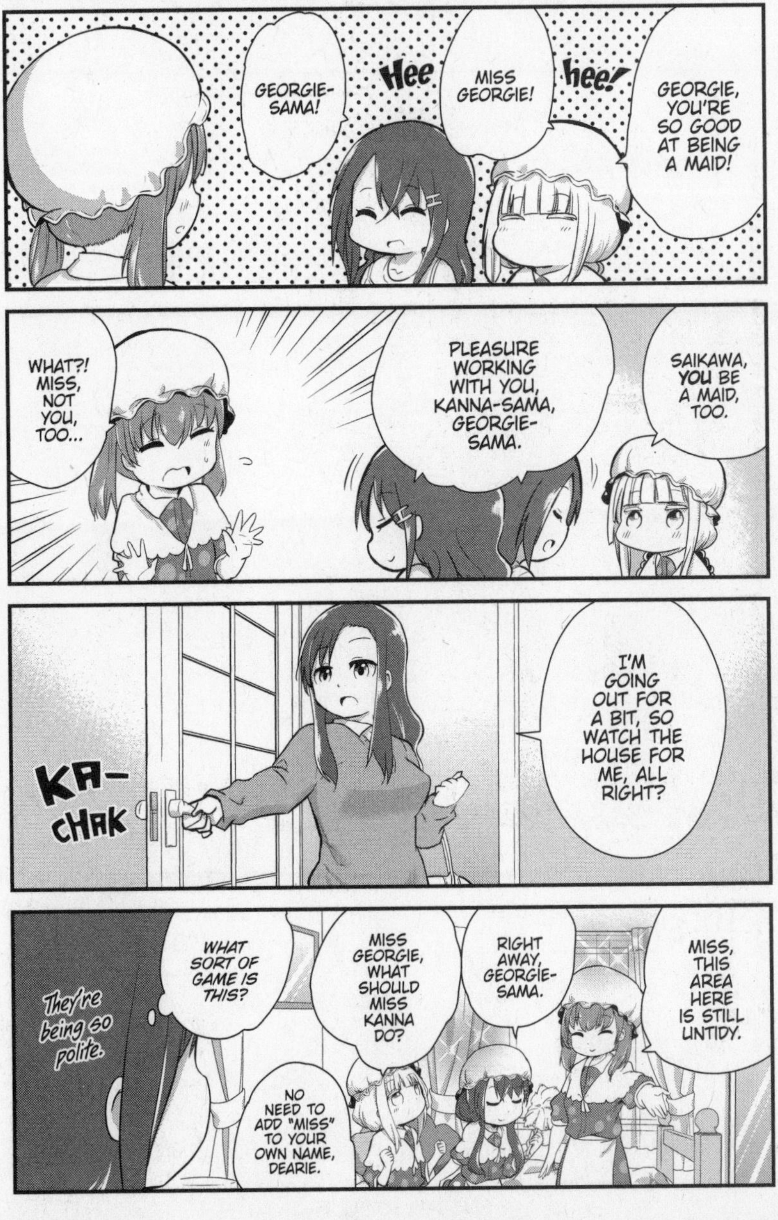
GEORGIE, YOU'RE SO GOOD AT BEING A MAID!
Hee hee!
MISS GEORGIE!
GEORGIE-SAMA!
SAIKAWA, YOU BE A MAID, TOO.
PLEASURE WORKING WITH YOU, KANNA-SAMA, GEORGIE-SAMA.
WHAT?! MISS, NOT YOU, TOO...
I'M GOING OUT FOR A BIT, SO WATCH THE HOUSE FOR ME, ALL RIGHT?
KA-CHAK
MISS, THIS AREA HERE IS STILL UNTIDY.
RIGHT AWAY, GEORGIE-SAMA.
MISS GEORGIE, WHAT SHOULD MISS KANNA DO?
NO NEED TO ADD "MISS" TO YOUR OWN NAME, DEARIE.
WHAT SORT OF GAME IS THIS?
They're being so polite.

MISS KOBAYASHI'S DRAGON MAIDS

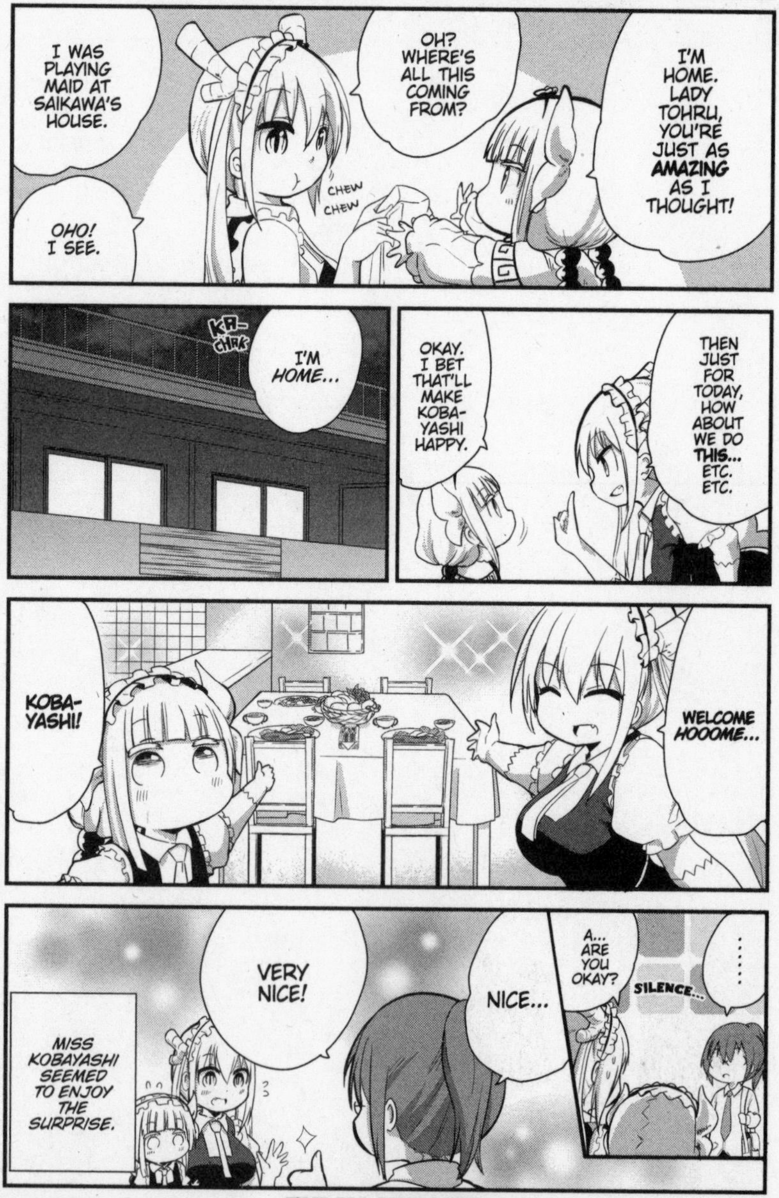
I'M HOME. LADY TOHRU, YOU'RE JUST AS AMAZING AS I THOUGHT!
OH? WHERE'S ALL THIS COMING FROM?
CHEW CHEW
I WAS PLAYING MAID AT SAIKAWA'S HOUSE.
OHO! I SEE.
THEN JUST FOR TODAY, HOW ABOUT WE DO THIS... ETC. ETC.
OKAY. I BET THAT'LL MAKE KOBA-YASHI HAPPY.
KA-CHAK
I'M HOME...
WELCOME HOOOME...
KOBA-YASHI!
......
SILENCE...
A... ARE YOU OKAY?
NICE...
VERY NICE!
MISS KOBAYASHI SEEMED TO ENJOY THE SURPRISE.

TIME FOR MAIDS/END

We are
dragon
maids!

Miss Kobayashi's Dragon Maid

Kanna's Daily Life

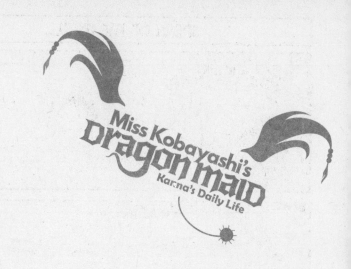

SPEAK OF THE DEVIL...

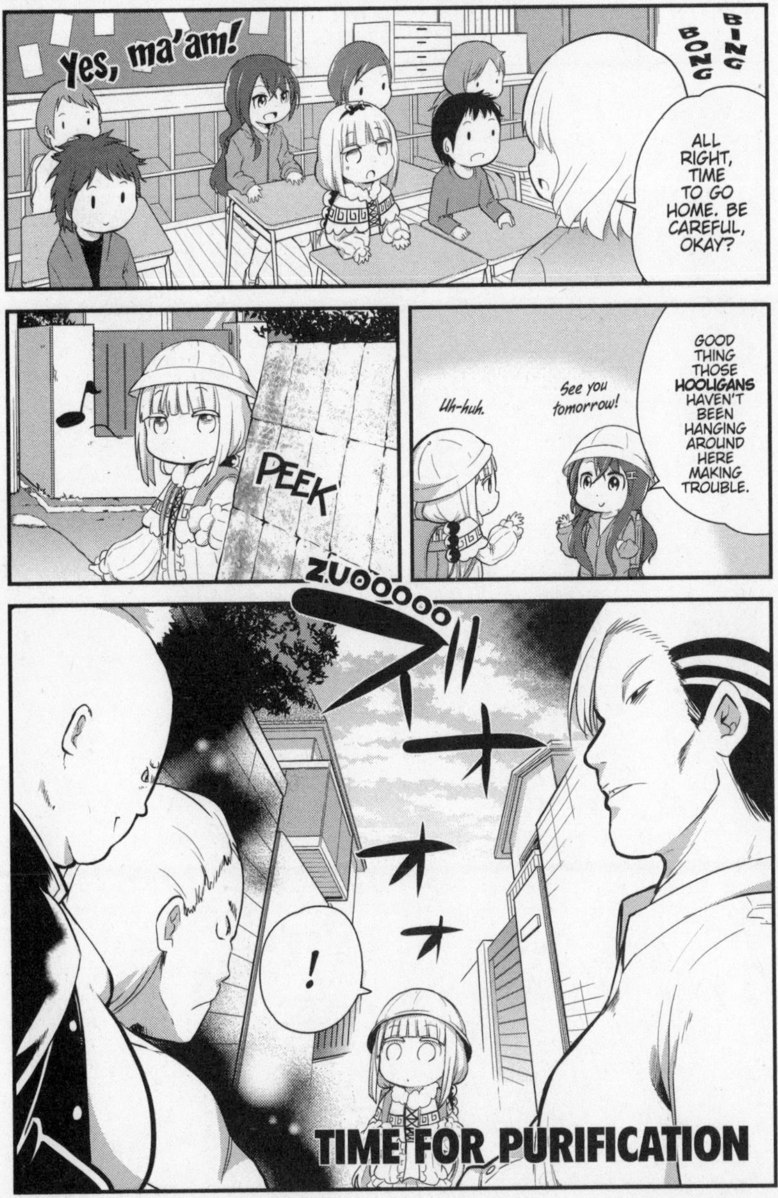
BING BONG
ALL RIGHT, TIME TO GO HOME. BE CAREFUL, OKAY?
Yes, ma'am!
GOOD THING THOSE **HOOLIGANS** HAVEN'T BEEN HANGING AROUND HERE MAKING TROUBLE.
See you tomorrow!
Uh-huh.
PEEK
ZUOOOOO
!
TIME FOR PURIFICATION

THE FEARSOME DRAGON BUSTERS

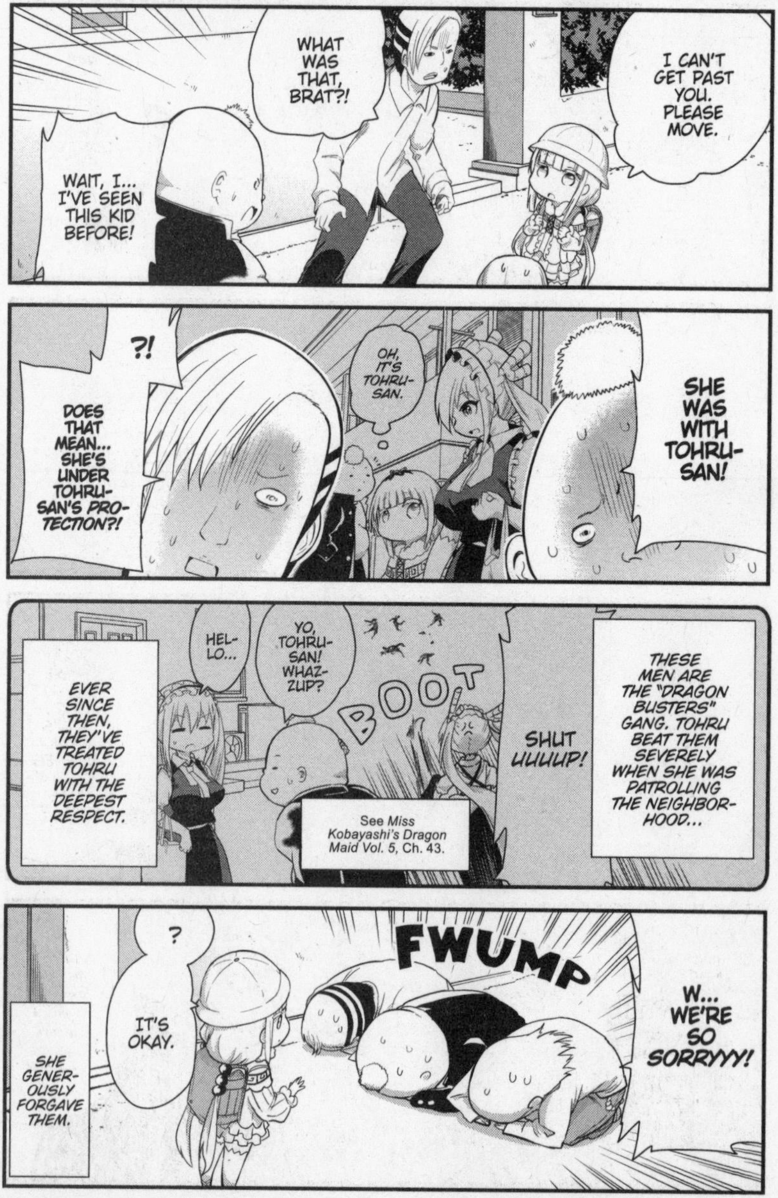
I CAN'T GET PAST YOU. PLEASE MOVE.
WHAT WAS THAT, BRAT?!
WAIT, I... I'VE SEEN THIS KID BEFORE!
SHE WAS WITH TOHRU-SAN!
OH, IT'S TOHRU-SAN.
?!
DOES THAT MEAN... SHE'S UNDER TOHRU-SAN'S *PROTECTION*?!
THESE MEN ARE THE "DRAGON BUSTERS" GANG. TOHRU BEAT THEM SEVERELY WHEN SHE WAS PATROLLING THE NEIGHBORHOOD...
SHUT UUUUP!
BOOT
YO, TOHRU-SAN! WHAZZUP?
HEL-LO...
EVER SINCE THEN, THEY'VE TREATED TOHRU WITH THE DEEPEST RESPECT.
See Miss *Kobayashi's Dragon Maid* Vol. 5, Ch. 43.
W... WE'RE SO *SORRYYY!*
FWUMP
?
IT'S OKAY.
SHE GENEROUSLY FORGAVE THEM.

ON SECOND THOUGHT...

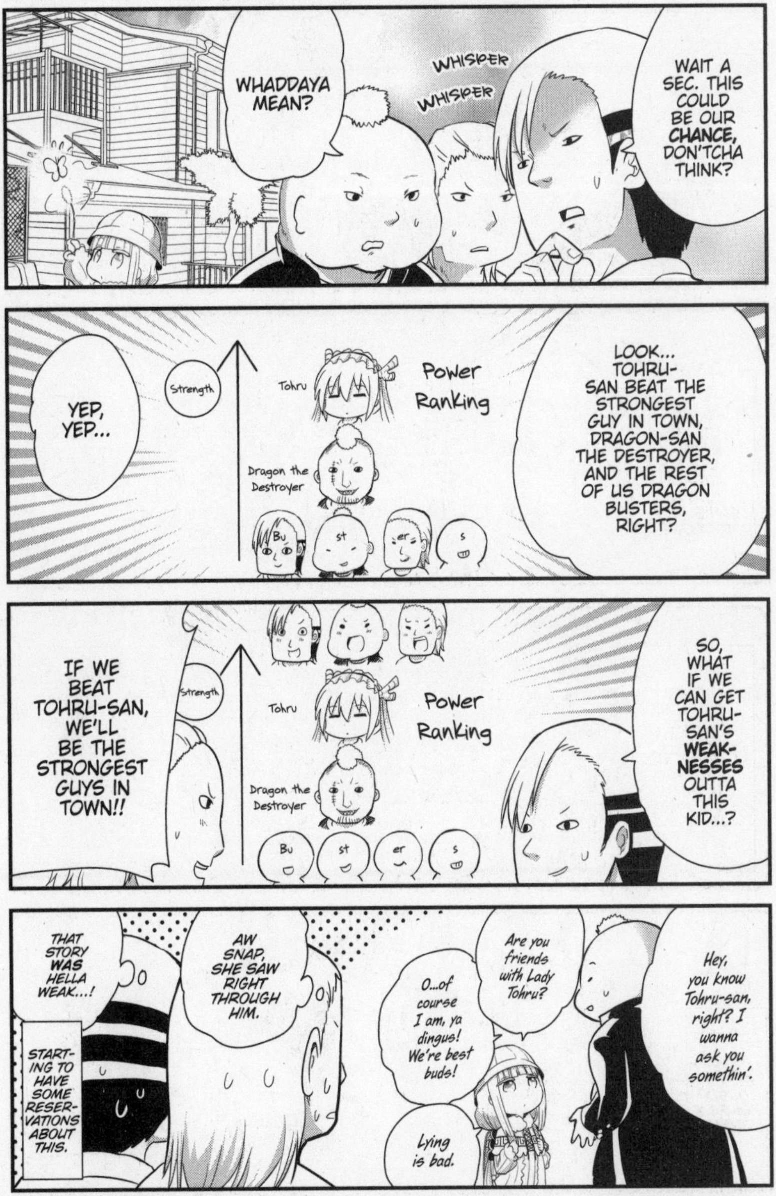
WAIT A SEC. THIS COULD BE OUR CHANCE, DON'TCHA THINK?
WHISPER
WHISPER
WHADDAYA MEAN?
LOOK... TOHRU-SAN BEAT THE STRONGEST GUY IN TOWN, DRAGON-SAN THE DESTROYER, AND THE REST OF US DRAGON BUSTERS, RIGHT?
Power Ranking
Strength
Tohru
Dragon the Destroyer
Bu st er s
YEP, YEP...
SO, WHAT IF WE CAN GET TOHRU-SAN'S WEAKNESSES OUTTA THIS KID...?
Power Ranking
Strength
Tohru
Dragon the Destroyer
Bu st er s
IF WE BEAT TOHRU-SAN, WE'LL BE THE STRONGEST GUYS IN TOWN!!
Hey, you know Tohru-san, right? I wanna ask you somethin'.
Are you friends with Lady Tohru?
O...of course I am, ya dingus! We're best buds!
Lying is bad.
AW SNAP, SHE SAW RIGHT THROUGH HIM.
THAT STORY WAS HELLA WEAK...!
STARTING TO HAVE SOME RESERVATIONS ABOUT THIS.

GOT THAT COVERED

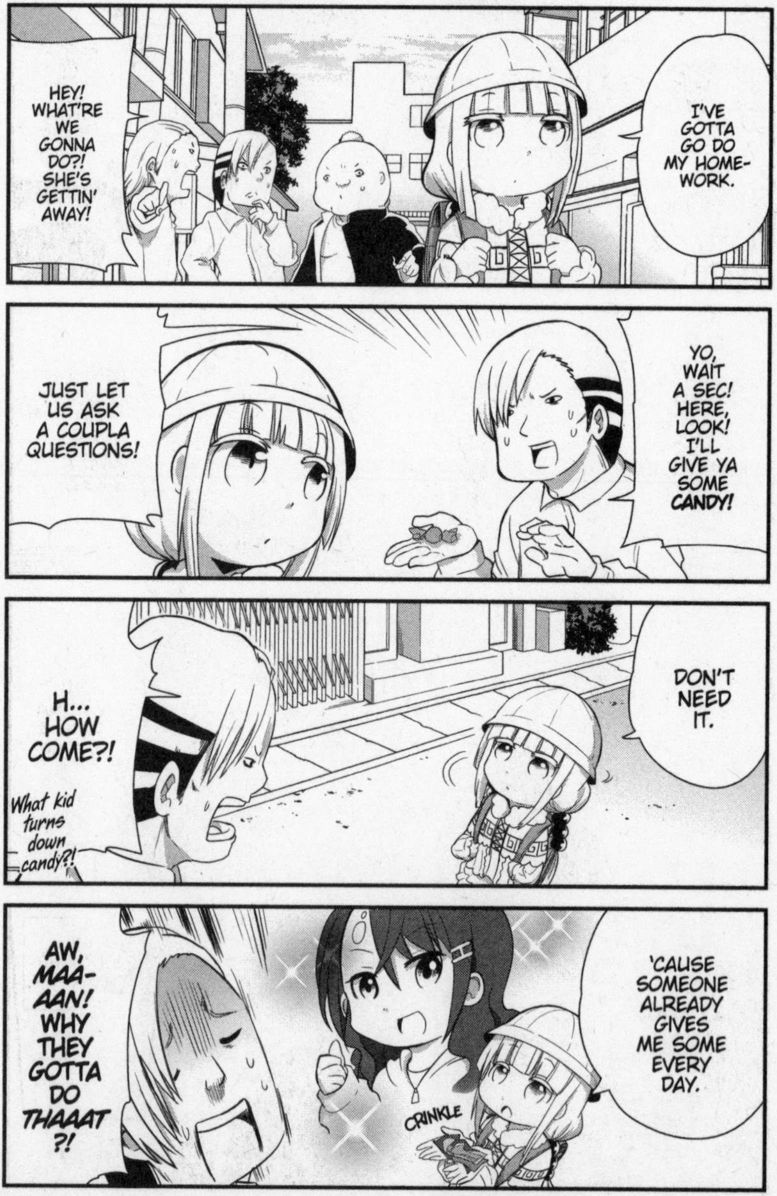
I'VE GOTTA GO DO MY HOME-WORK.
HEY! WHAT'RE WE GONNA DO?! SHE'S GETTIN' AWAY!
YO, WAIT A SEC! HERE, LOOK! I'LL GIVE YA SOME CANDY!
JUST LET US ASK A COUPLA QUESTIONS!
DON'T NEED IT.
H... HOW COME?!
What kid turns down candy?!
'CAUSE SOMEONE ALREADY GIVES ME SOME EVERY DAY.
CRINKLE
AW, MAA-AAN! WHY THEY GOTTA DO THAAAT?!

A HARD BARGAIN

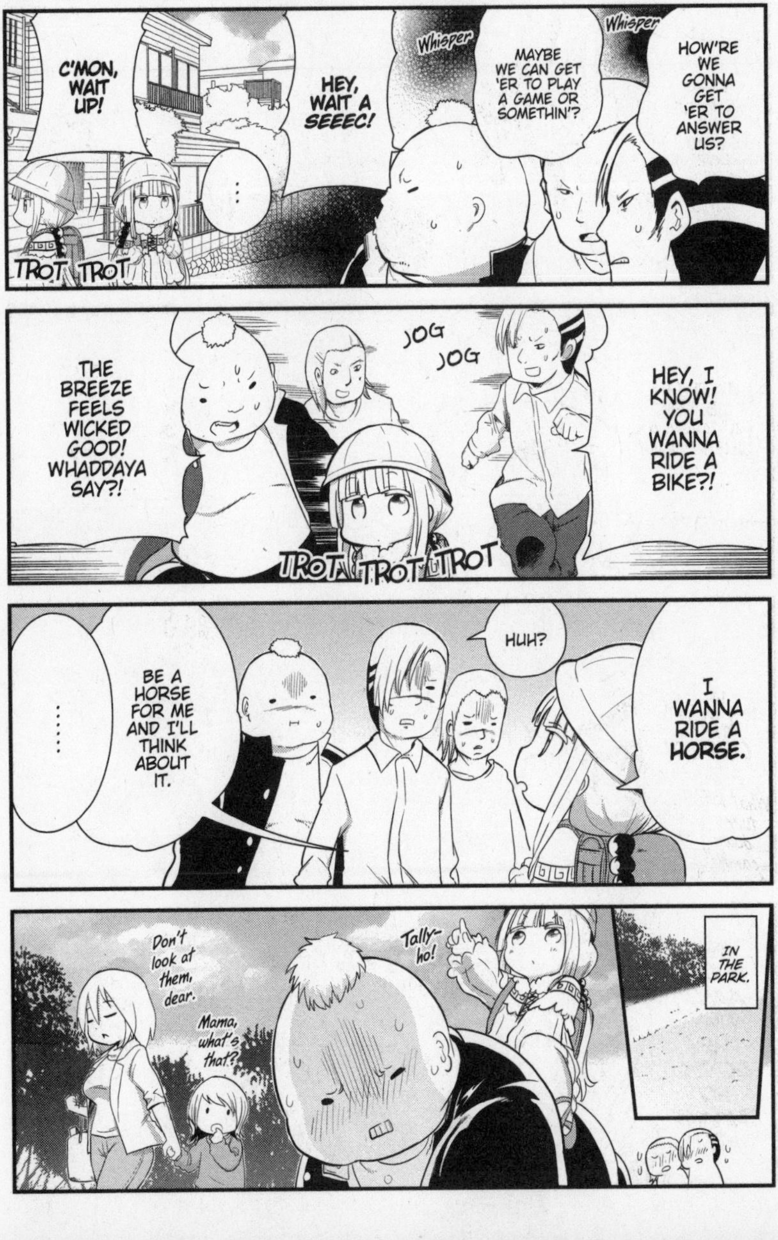
HOW'RE WE GONNA GET 'ER TO ANSWER US?
Whisper
MAYBE WE CAN GET 'ER TO PLAY A GAME OR SOMETHIN'?
Whisper
HEY, WAIT A SEEEC!
...
C'MON, WAIT UP!
TROT TROT
HEY, I KNOW! YOU WANNA RIDE A BIKE?!
JOG JOG
THE BREEZE FEELS WICKED GOOD! WHADDAYA SAY?!
TROT TROT TROT
I WANNA RIDE A HORSE.
HUH?
BE A HORSE FOR ME AND I'LL THINK ABOUT IT.
......
IN THE PARK.
Tally-ho!
Mama, what's that?
Don't look at them, dear.

CAN'T SAY NO TO HER

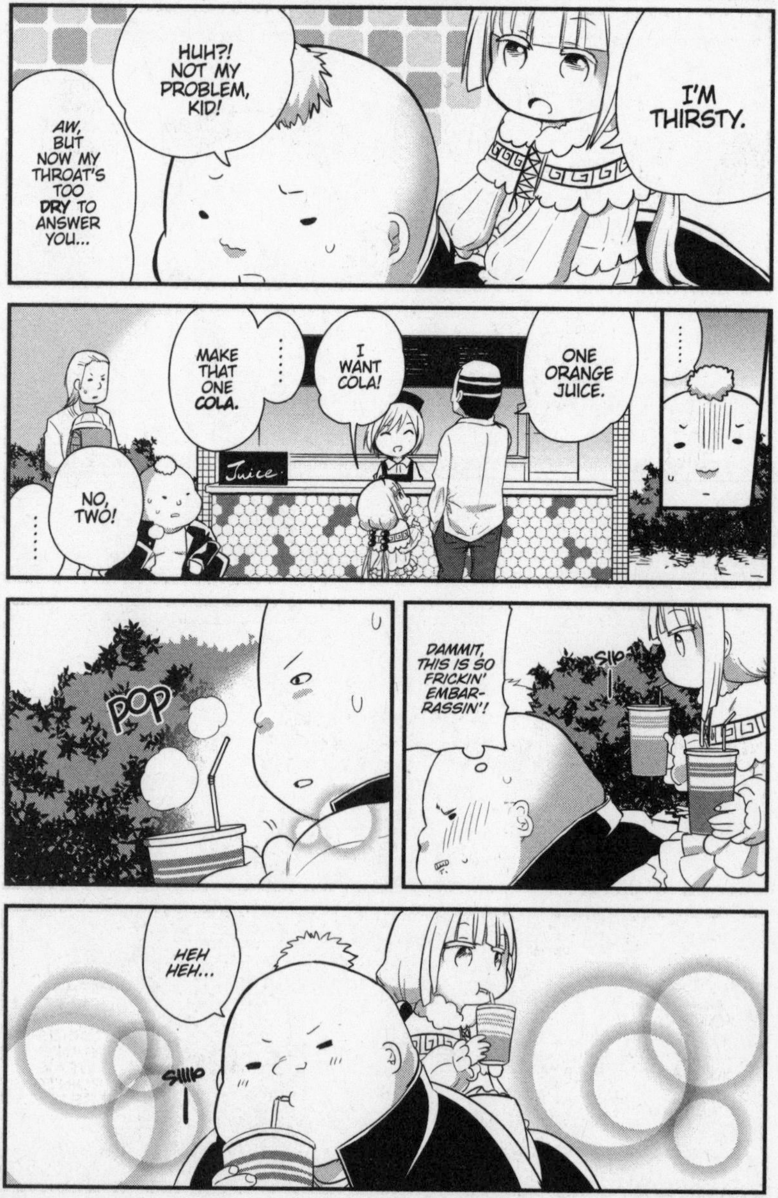
I'M THIRSTY.
HUH?! NOT MY PROBLEM, KID!
AW, BUT NOW MY THROAT'S TOO DRY TO ANSWER YOU...
......
ONE ORANGE JUICE.
I WANT COLA!
......
MAKE THAT ONE COLA.
Juice
NO, TWO!
......
SIP
DAMMIT, THIS IS SO FRICKIN' EMBAR-RASSIN'!
POP
HEH HEH...
SIIIP

CAN'T KEEP UP WITH A (DRAGON) CHILD

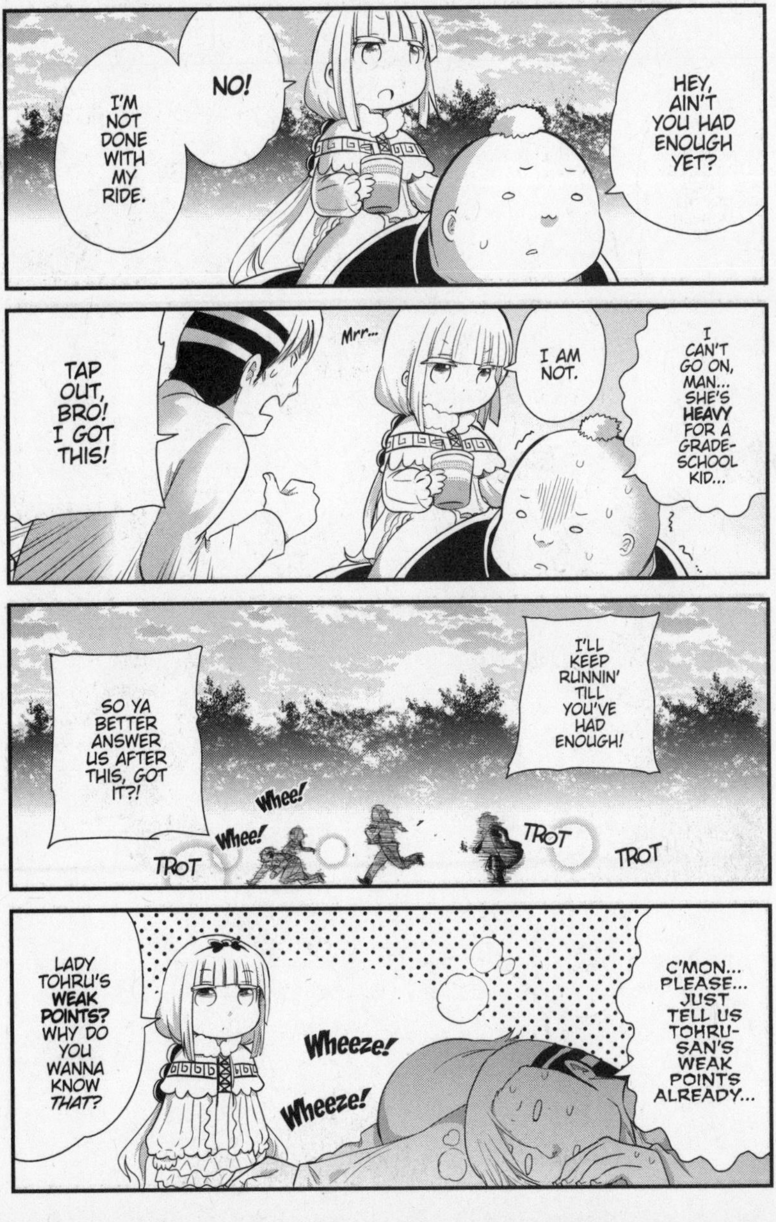
HEY, AIN'T YOU HAD ENOUGH YET?
NO!
I'M NOT DONE WITH MY RIDE.
I CAN'T GO ON, MAN... SHE'S **HEAVY** FOR A GRADE-SCHOOL KID...
I AM NOT.
Mrr...
TAP OUT, BRO! I GOT THIS!
I'LL KEEP RUNNIN' TILL YOU'VE HAD ENOUGH!
TROT
TROT
Whee!
Whee!
TROT
SO YA BETTER ANSWER US AFTER THIS, GOT IT?!
C'MON... PLEASE... JUST TELL US TOHRU-SAN'S WEAK POINTS ALREADY...
Wheeze!
Wheeze!
LADY TOHRU'S **WEAK POINTS?** WHY DO YOU WANNA KNOW *THAT?*

KANNA-CHAN THE GENEROUS

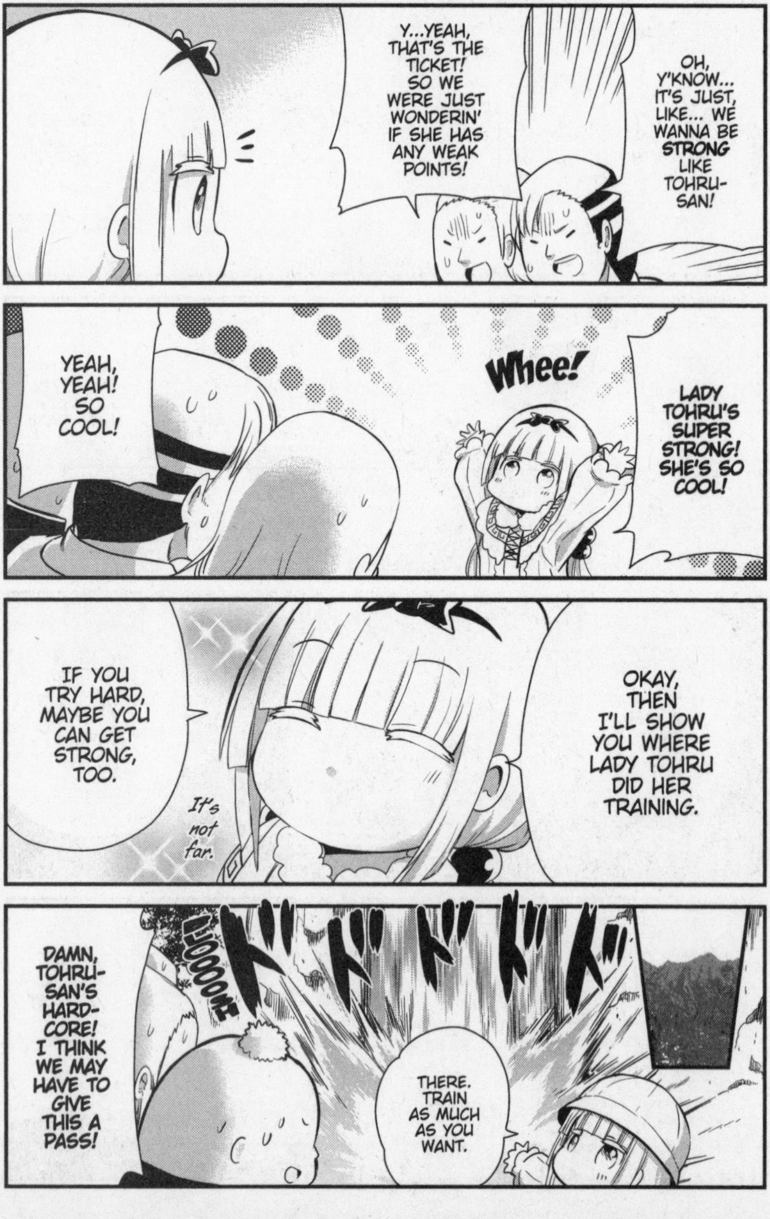
OH, Y'KNOW... IT'S JUST, LIKE... WE WANNA BE **STRONG** LIKE TOHRU-SAN!
Y...YEAH, THAT'S THE TICKET! SO WE WERE JUST WONDERIN' IF SHE HAS ANY WEAK POINTS!
LADY TOHRU'S SUPER STRONG! SHE'S SO COOL!
Whee!
YEAH, YEAH! SO COOL!
OKAY, THEN I'LL SHOW YOU WHERE LADY TOHRU DID HER TRAINING.
IF YOU TRY HARD, MAYBE YOU CAN GET STRONG, TOO.
It's not far.
THERE. TRAIN AS MUCH AS YOU WANT.
DAMN, TOHRU-SAN'S HARD-CORE! I THINK WE MAY HAVE TO GIVE THIS A PASS!

PURIFY YOUR HEARTS, OKAY?

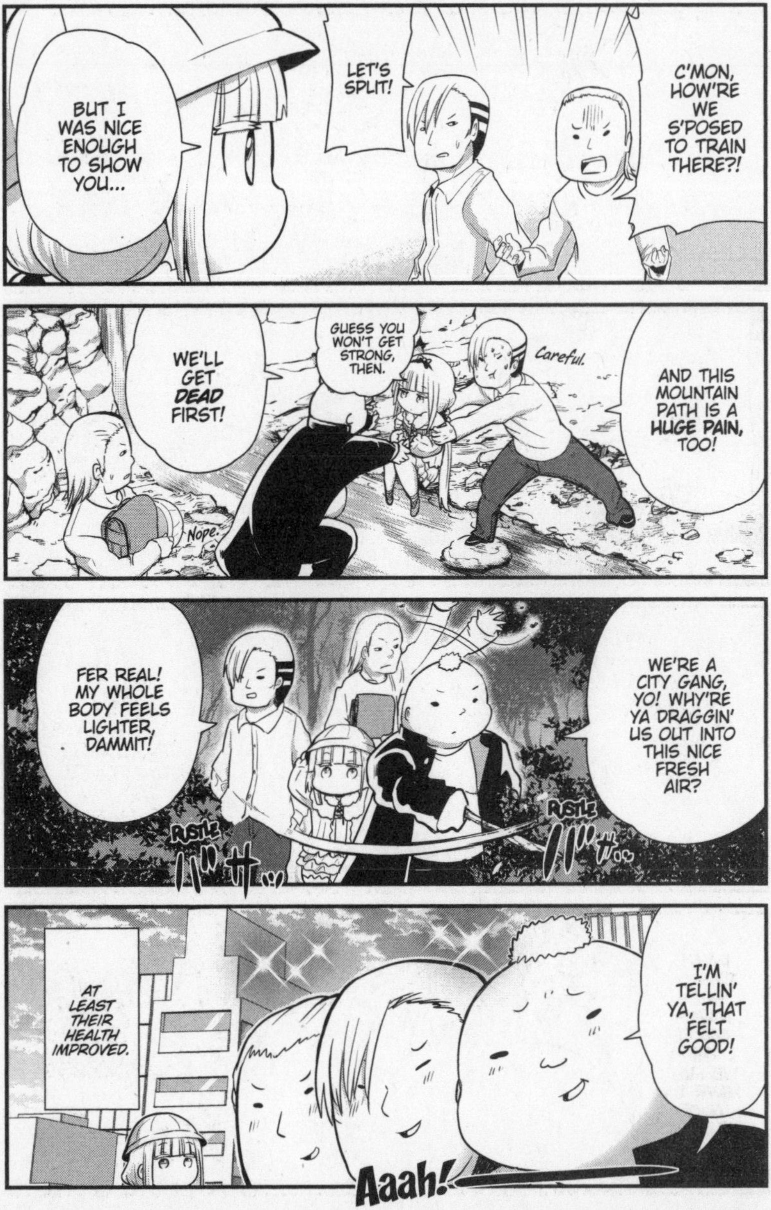
C'MON, HOW'RE WE S'POSED TO TRAIN THERE?!
LET'S SPLIT!
BUT I WAS NICE ENOUGH TO SHOW YOU...
AND THIS MOUNTAIN PATH IS A **HUGE PAIN,** TOO!
Careful.
GUESS YOU WON'T GET STRONG, THEN.
WE'LL GET ***DEAD*** FIRST!
Nope.
WE'RE A CITY GANG, YO! WHY'RE YA DRAGGIN' US OUT INTO THIS NICE FRESH AIR?
RUSTLE
FER REAL! MY WHOLE BODY FEELS LIGHTER, DAMMIT!
RUSTLE
I'M TELLIN' YA, THAT FELT GOOD!
AT LEAST THEIR HEALTH IMPROVED.
Aaah!

TOHRU, THE DRAGON BUSTERS BUSTER!

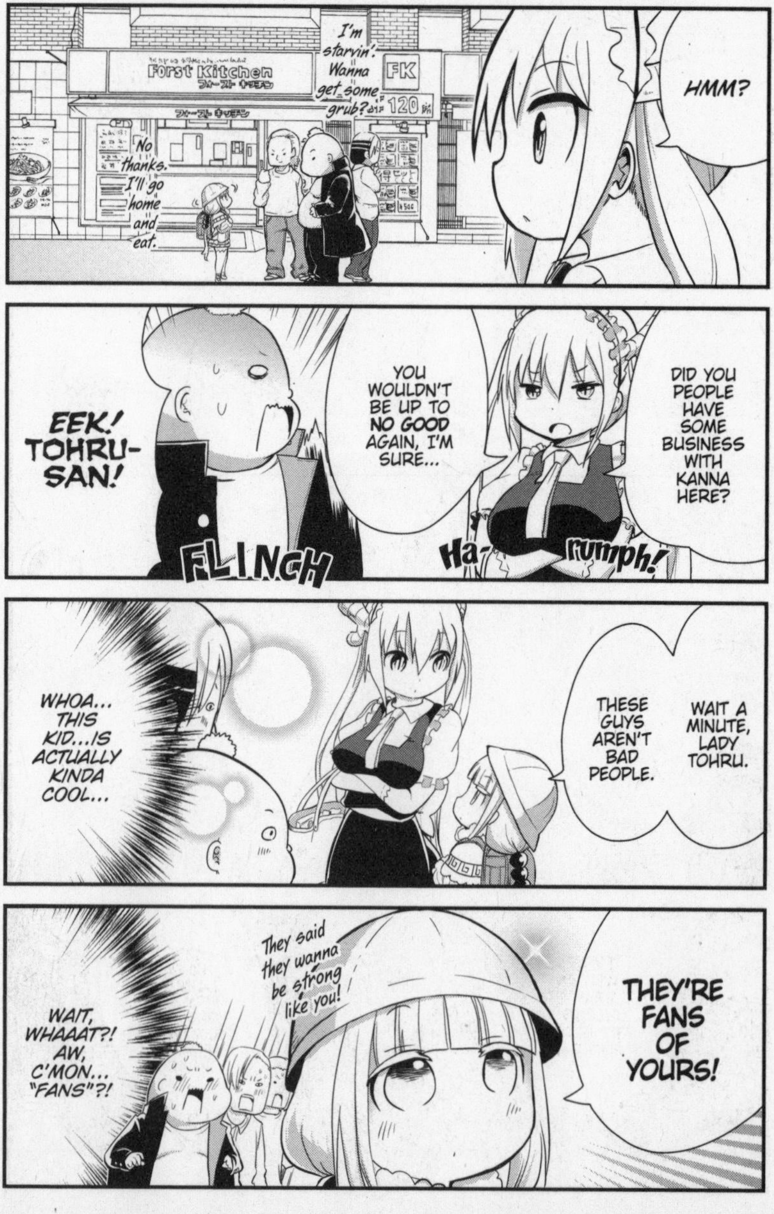
HMM?
Forst Kitchen
FK
120
I'm starvin'. Wanna get some grub?
No thanks. I'll go home and eat.
DID YOU PEOPLE HAVE SOME BUSINESS WITH KANNA HERE?
Ha-rumph!
YOU WOULDN'T BE UP TO NO GOOD AGAIN, I'M SURE...
EEK! TOHRU-SAN!
FLINCH
WAIT A MINUTE, LADY TOHRU.
THESE GUYS AREN'T BAD PEOPLE.
WHOA... THIS KID...IS ACTUALLY KINDA COOL...
THEY'RE FANS OF YOURS!
They said they wanna be strong like you!
WAIT, WHAAAT?! AW, C'MON... "FANS"?!

ARE YOU AN ANGEL?

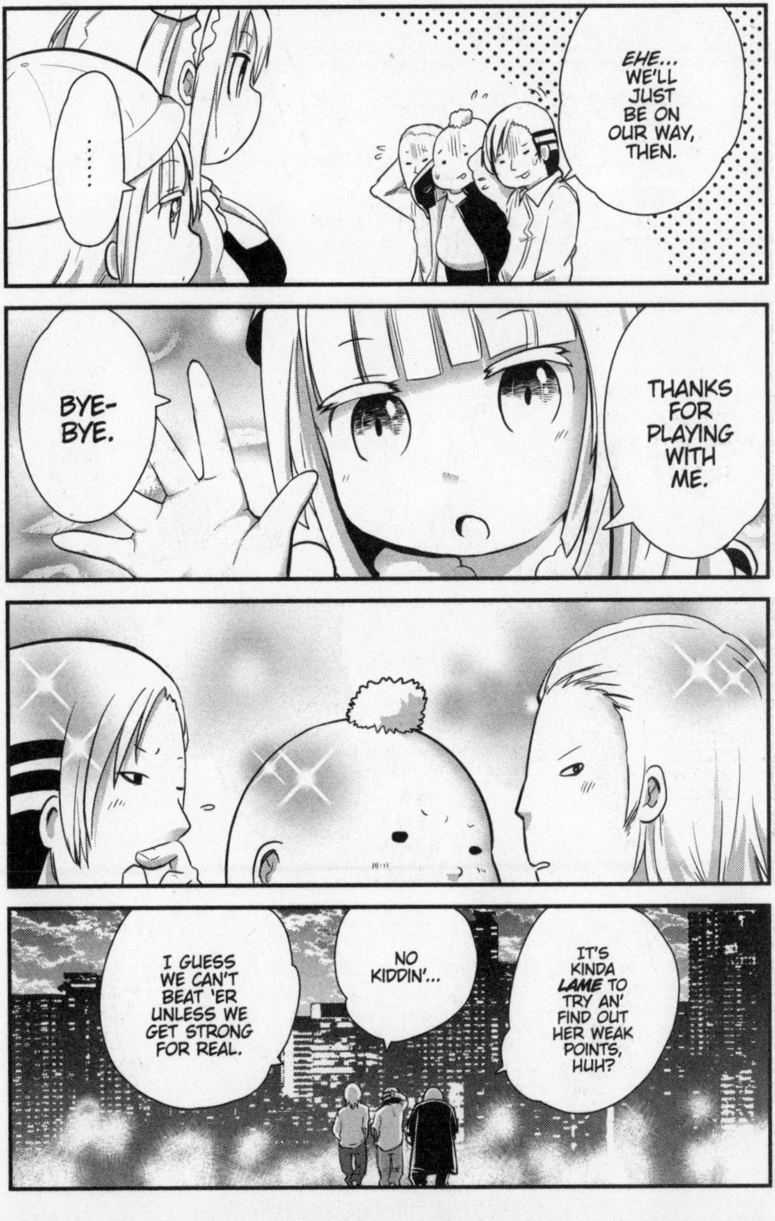
EHE... WE'LL JUST BE ON OUR WAY, THEN.
......
THANKS FOR PLAYING WITH ME.
BYE-BYE.
IT'S KINDA LAME TO TRY AN' FIND OUT HER WEAK POINTS, HUH?
NO KIDDIN'...
I GUESS WE CAN'T BEAT 'ER UNLESS WE GET STRONG FOR REAL.

THE DRAGON BUSTERS, REBORN!

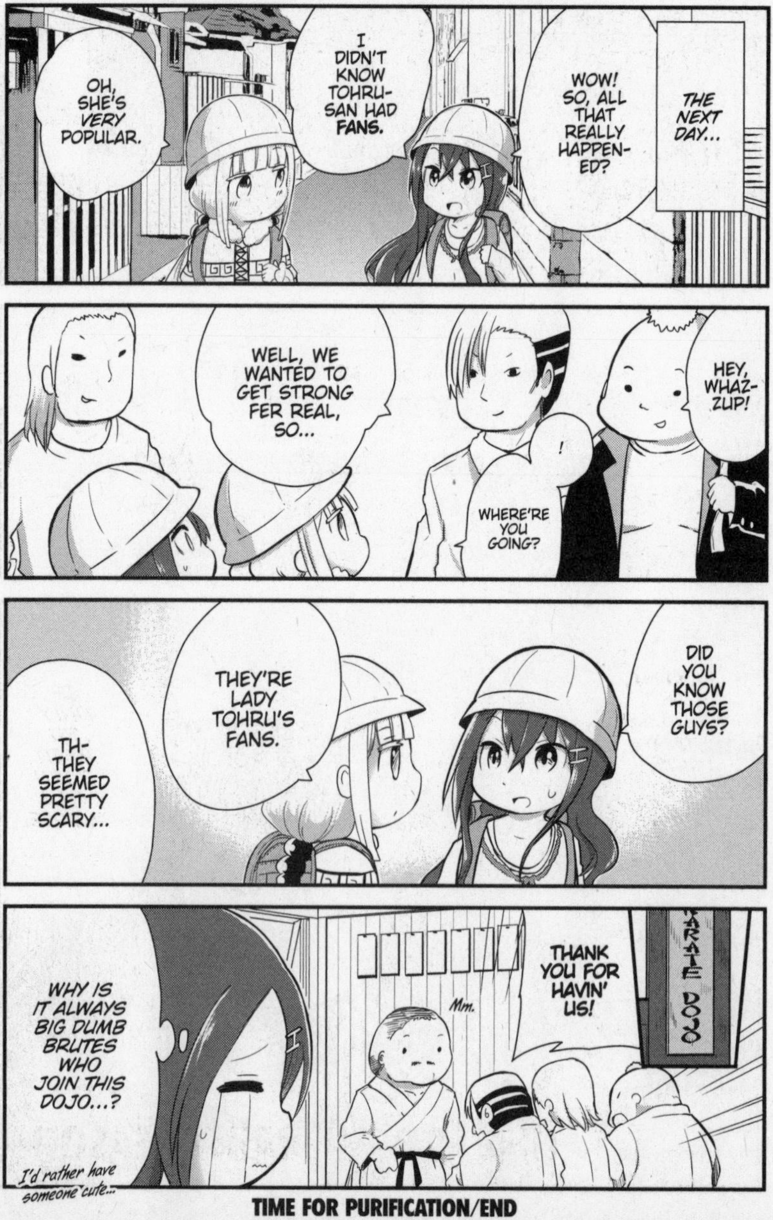
THE NEXT DAY...
WOW! SO, ALL THAT REALLY HAPPENED?
I DIDN'T KNOW TOHRU-SAN HAD FANS.
OH, SHE'S VERY POPULAR.
HEY, WHAZZUP!
!
WHERE'RE YOU GOING?
WELL, WE WANTED TO GET STRONG FER REAL, SO...
DID YOU KNOW THOSE GUYS?
THEY'RE LADY TOHRU'S FANS.
TH-THEY SEEMED PRETTY SCARY...
DOJO
THANK YOU FOR HAVIN' US!
Mm.
WHY IS IT ALWAYS BIG DUMB BRUTES WHO JOIN THIS DOJO...?
I'd rather have someone cute...

TIME FOR PURIFICATION/END

RAINY DAYS GET SAIKAWA-SAN DOWN

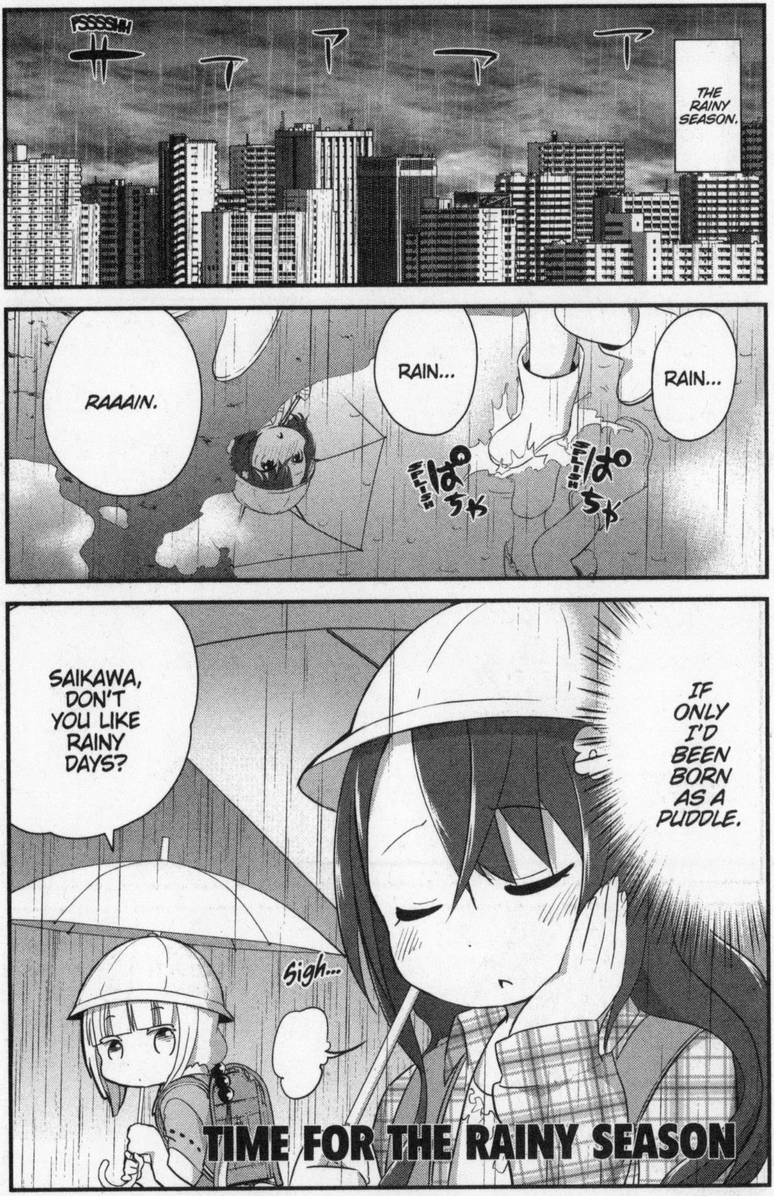
PSSSSHH
ザァ ア ア ア
THE RAINY SEASON.
RAIN...
SPLISH
ぱちゃ
RAIN...
SPLISH
ぱちゃ
RAAAIN.
IF ONLY I'D BEEN BORN AS A PUDDLE.
SAIKAWA, DON'T YOU LIKE RAINY DAYS?
Sigh...
TIME FOR THE RAINY SEASON

STUPID RAIN!

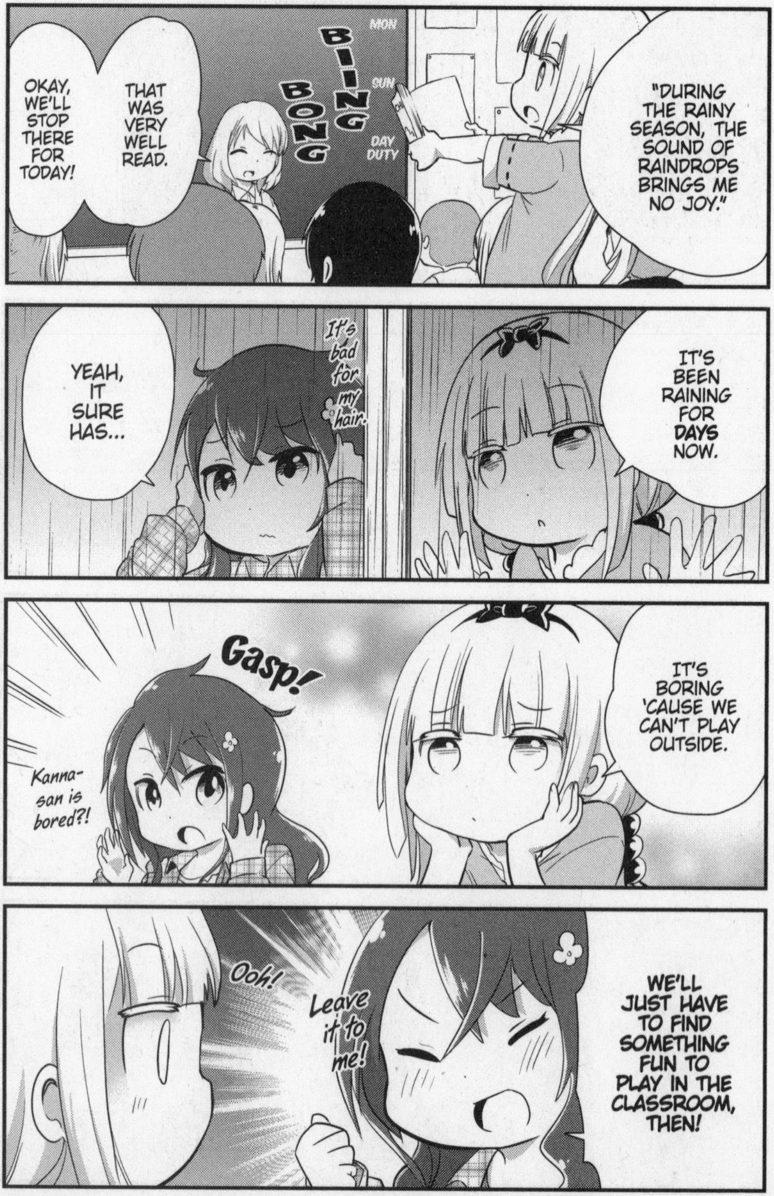
"DURING THE RAINY SEASON, THE SOUND OF RAINDROPS BRINGS ME NO JOY."
MON
SUN
DAY DUTY
BING BONG
THAT WAS VERY WELL READ.
OKAY, WE'LL STOP THERE FOR TODAY!
IT'S BEEN RAINING FOR DAYS NOW.
It's bad for my hair.
YEAH, IT SURE HAS...
IT'S BORING 'CAUSE WE CAN'T PLAY OUTSIDE.
Gasp!
Kanna-san is bored?!
WE'LL JUST HAVE TO FIND SOMETHING FUN TO PLAY IN THE CLASSROOM, THEN!
Leave it to me!
Ooh!

KANNA-CHAN IS TEMPTED

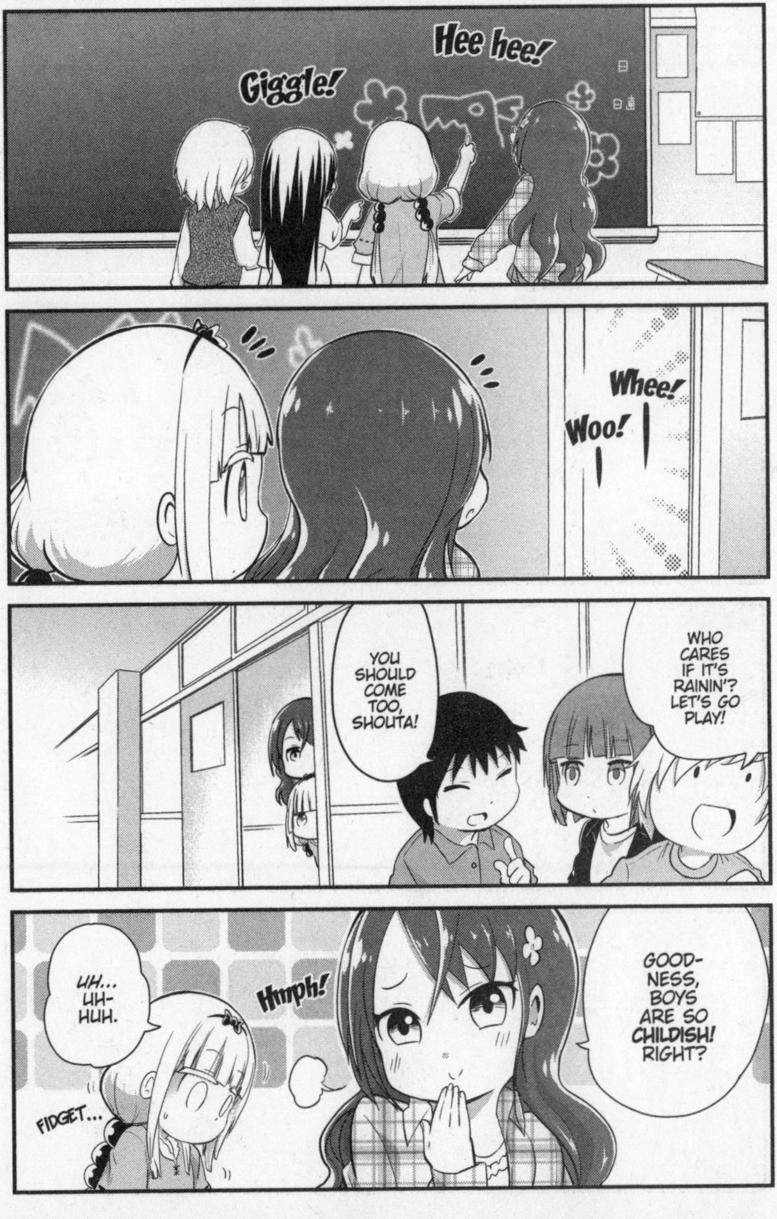
Hee hee!
Giggle!
Whee!
Woo!
WHO CARES IF IT'S RAININ'? LET'S GO PLAY!
YOU SHOULD COME TOO, SHOUTA!
GOOD-NESS, BOYS ARE SO CHILDISH! RIGHT?
Hmph!
UH... UH-HUH.
FIDGET...

DRAT THAT RASCALLY DRAGON

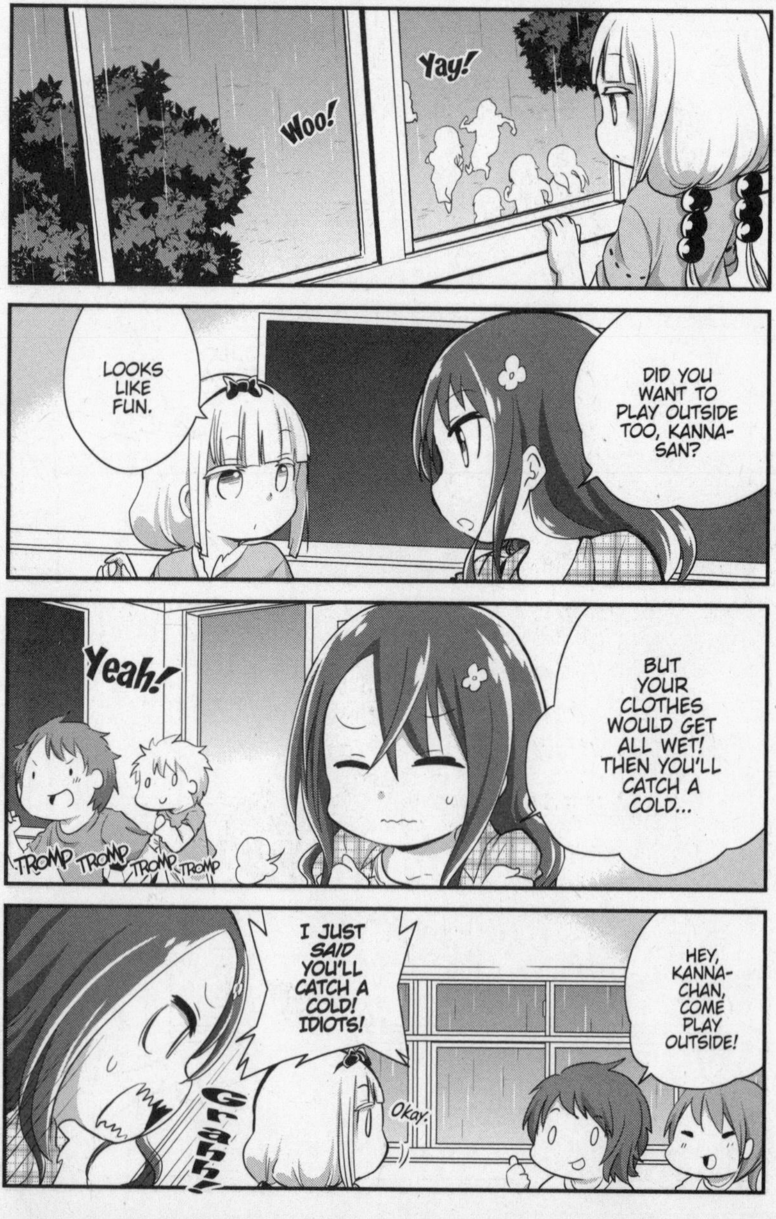
Yay!
Woo!
DID YOU WANT TO PLAY OUTSIDE TOO, KANNA-SAN?
LOOKS LIKE FUN.
BUT YOUR CLOTHES WOULD GET ALL WET! THEN YOU'LL CATCH A COLD...
Yeah!
TROMP TROMP TROMP TROMP
HEY, KANNA-CHAN, COME PLAY OUTSIDE!
I JUST SAID YOU'LL CATCH A COLD! IDIOTS!
Okay.
Grahh!

ANYTHING TO BE WITH YOU

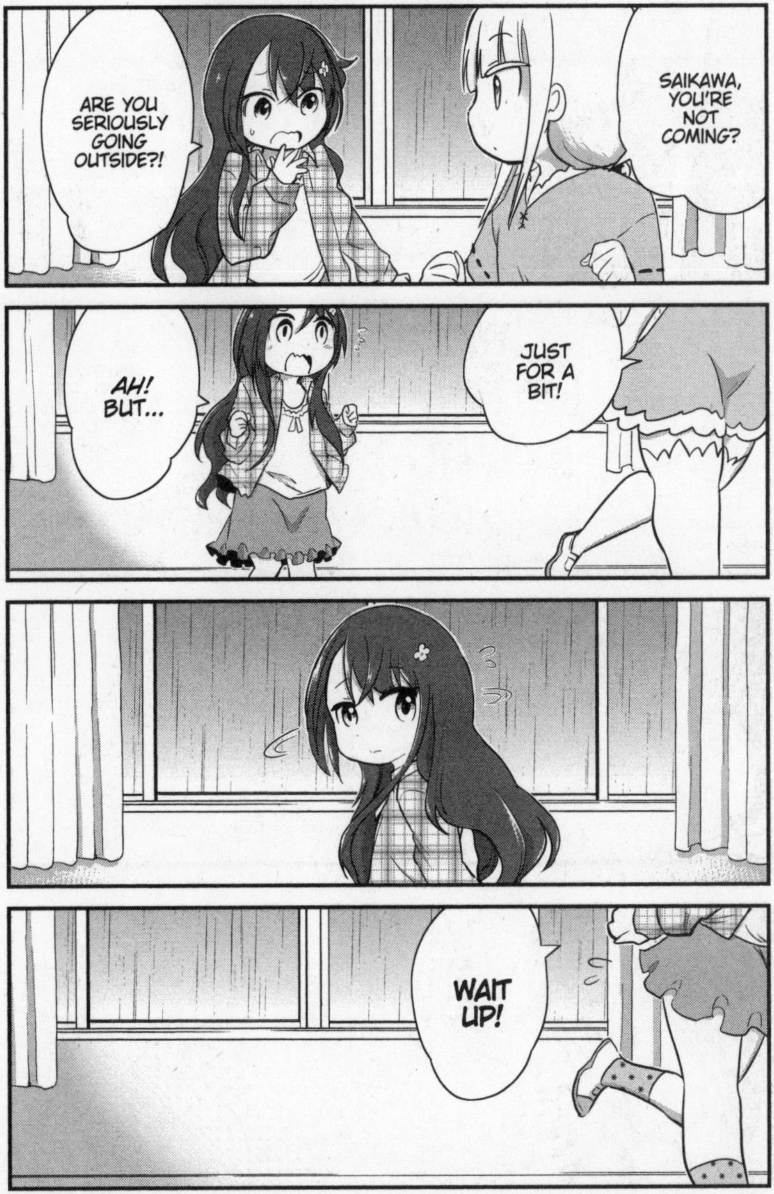
SAIKAWA, YOU'RE NOT COMING?
ARE YOU SERIOUSLY GOING OUTSIDE?!
JUST FOR A BIT!
AH! BUT...
WAIT UP!

WHAT WAS THAT?!

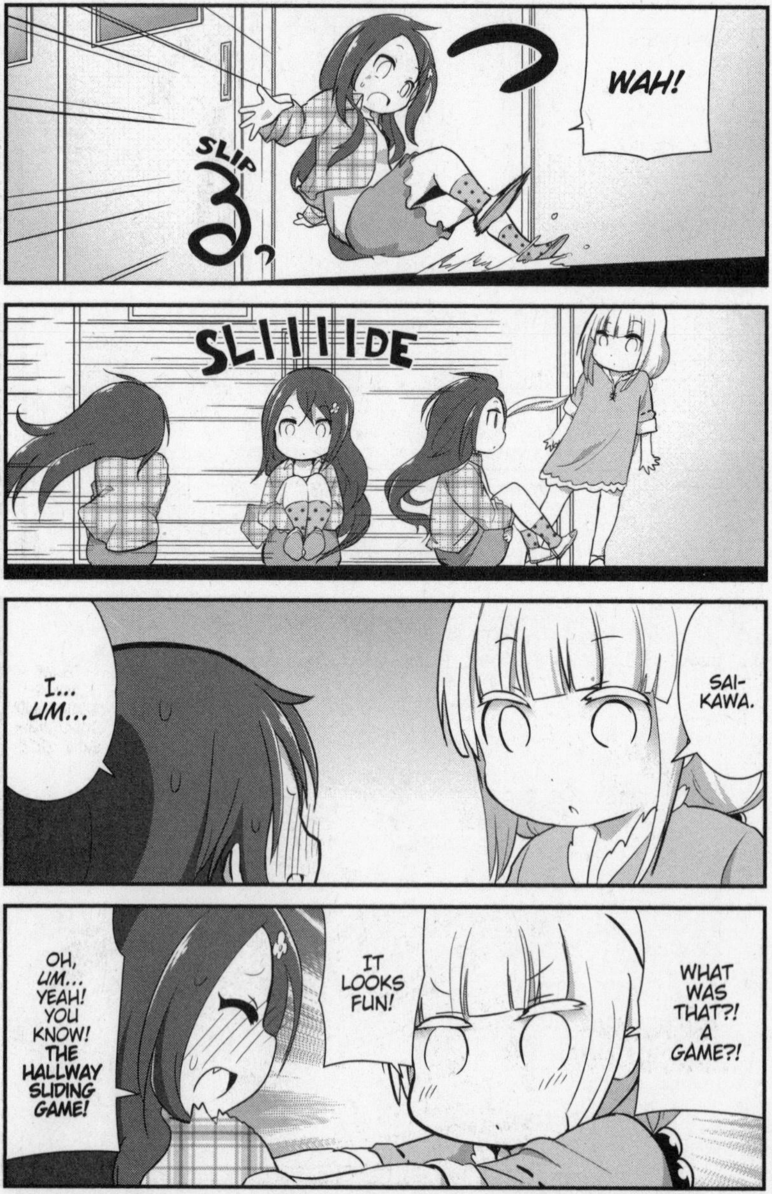
WAH!
SLIP
SLIIIIDE
SAI-KAWA.
I... UM...
WHAT WAS THAT?! A GAME?!
IT LOOKS FUN!
OH, UM... YEAH! YOU KNOW! THE HALLWAY SLIDING GAME!

AWAY SHE GOES!

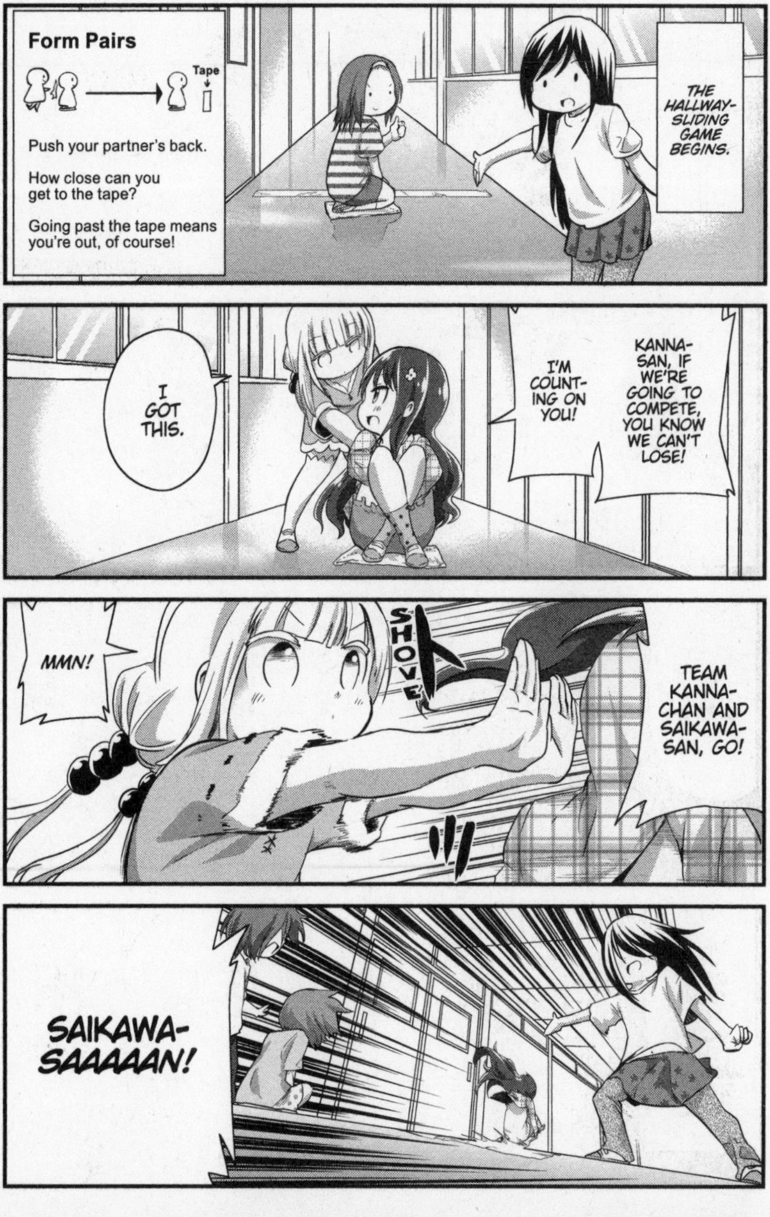
THE HALLWAY-SLIDING GAME BEGINS.
Form Pairs
Tape
Push your partner's back.
How close can you get to the tape?
Going past the tape means you're out, of course!
KANNA-SAN, IF WE'RE GOING TO COMPETE, YOU KNOW WE CAN'T LOSE!
I'M COUNTING ON YOU!
I GOT THIS.
TEAM KANNA-CHAN AND SAIKAWA-SAN, GO!
SHOVE
MMN!
SAIKAWA-SAAAAAN!

KID POWER

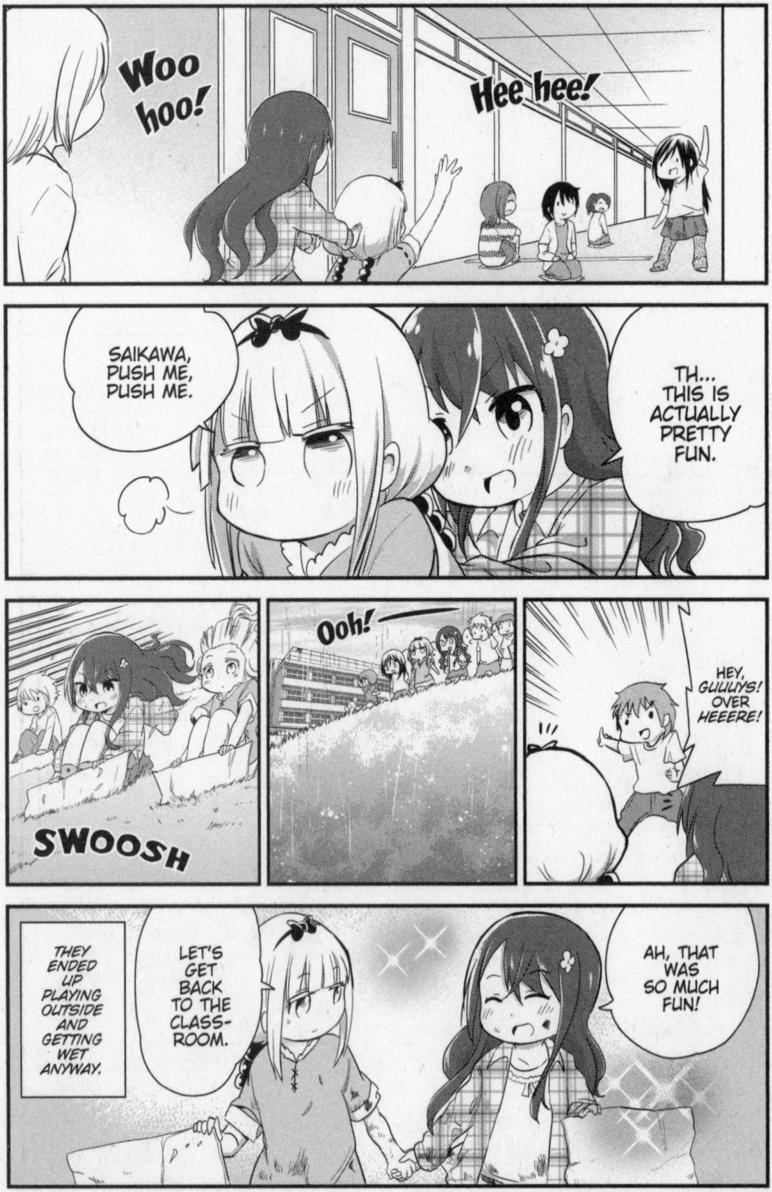
Hee hee!
Woo hoo!
TH... THIS IS ACTUALLY PRETTY FUN.
SAIKAWA, PUSH ME, PUSH ME.
HEY, GUUUYS! OVER HEEERE!
Ooh!
SWOOSH
AH, THAT WAS SO MUCH FUN!
LET'S GET BACK TO THE CLASS-ROOM.
THEY ENDED UP PLAYING OUTSIDE AND GETTING WET ANYWAY.

A SIGHT FOR SAIKAWA EYES

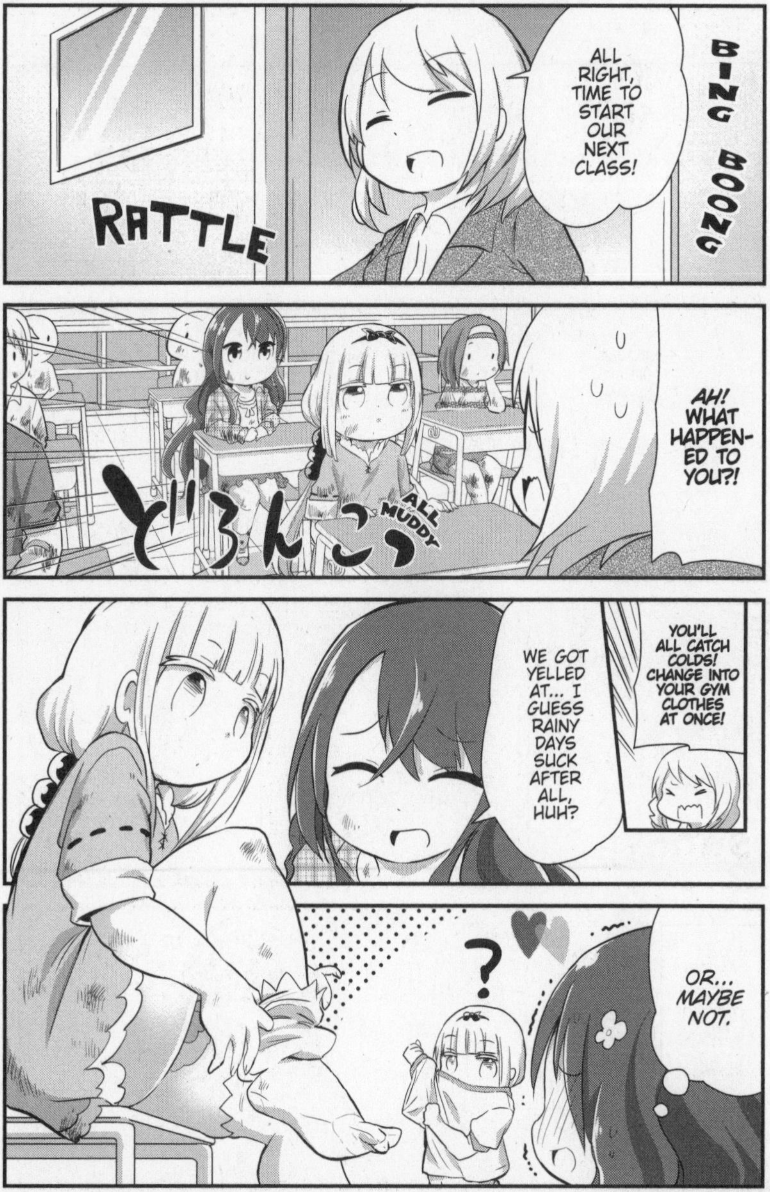
BING BOONG
ALL RIGHT, TIME TO START OUR NEXT CLASS!
RATTLE
AH! WHAT HAPPENED-ED TO YOU?!
ALL MUDDY
どろんこ
YOU'LL ALL CATCH COLDS! CHANGE INTO YOUR GYM CLOTHES AT ONCE!
WE GOT YELLED AT... I GUESS RAINY DAYS SUCK AFTER ALL, HUH?
OR... MAYBE NOT.
?

TERU TERU SAIKAWA-SAN

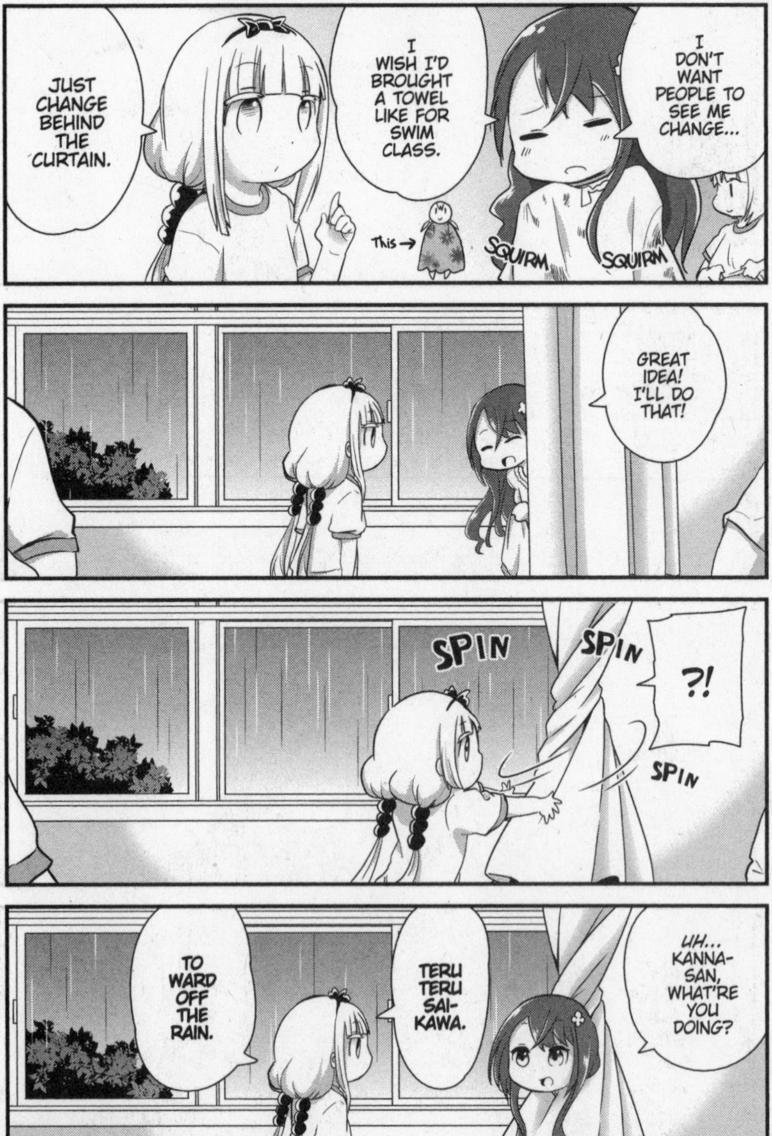
I DON'T WANT PEOPLE TO SEE ME CHANGE...
I WISH I'D BROUGHT A TOWEL LIKE FOR SWIM CLASS.
SQUIRM
SQUIRM
This →
JUST CHANGE BEHIND THE CURTAIN.
GREAT IDEA! I'LL DO THAT!
?!
SPIN
SPIN
SPIN
UH... KANNA-SAN, WHAT'RE YOU DOING?
TERU TERU SAI-KAWA.
TO WARD OFF THE RAIN.

※A reference to teru teru bōzu, which are white cloth dolls believed to get rid of rain.

CAUGHT IN A LOOP?

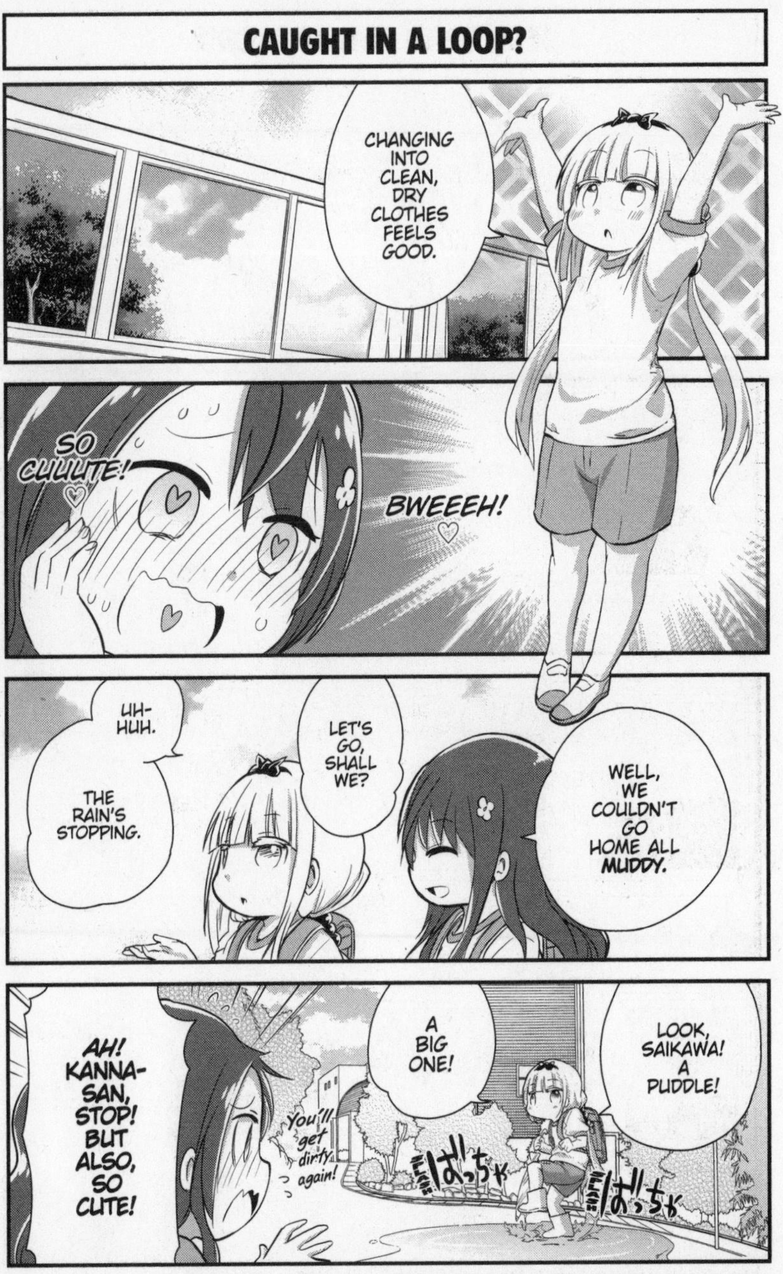
CHANGING INTO CLEAN, DRY CLOTHES FEELS GOOD.
BWEEEH! ♡
SO CUUUTE! ♡
WELL, WE COULDN'T GO HOME ALL MUDDY.
LET'S GO, SHALL WE?
UH-HUH.
THE RAIN'S STOPPING.
LOOK, SAIKAWA! A PUDDLE!
A BIG ONE!
SPLASH ぱっちゃ
SPLASH ぱっちゃ
You'll get dirty again!
AH! KANNA-SAN, STOP! BUT ALSO, SO CUTE!

WHEN THE RAIN STOPS

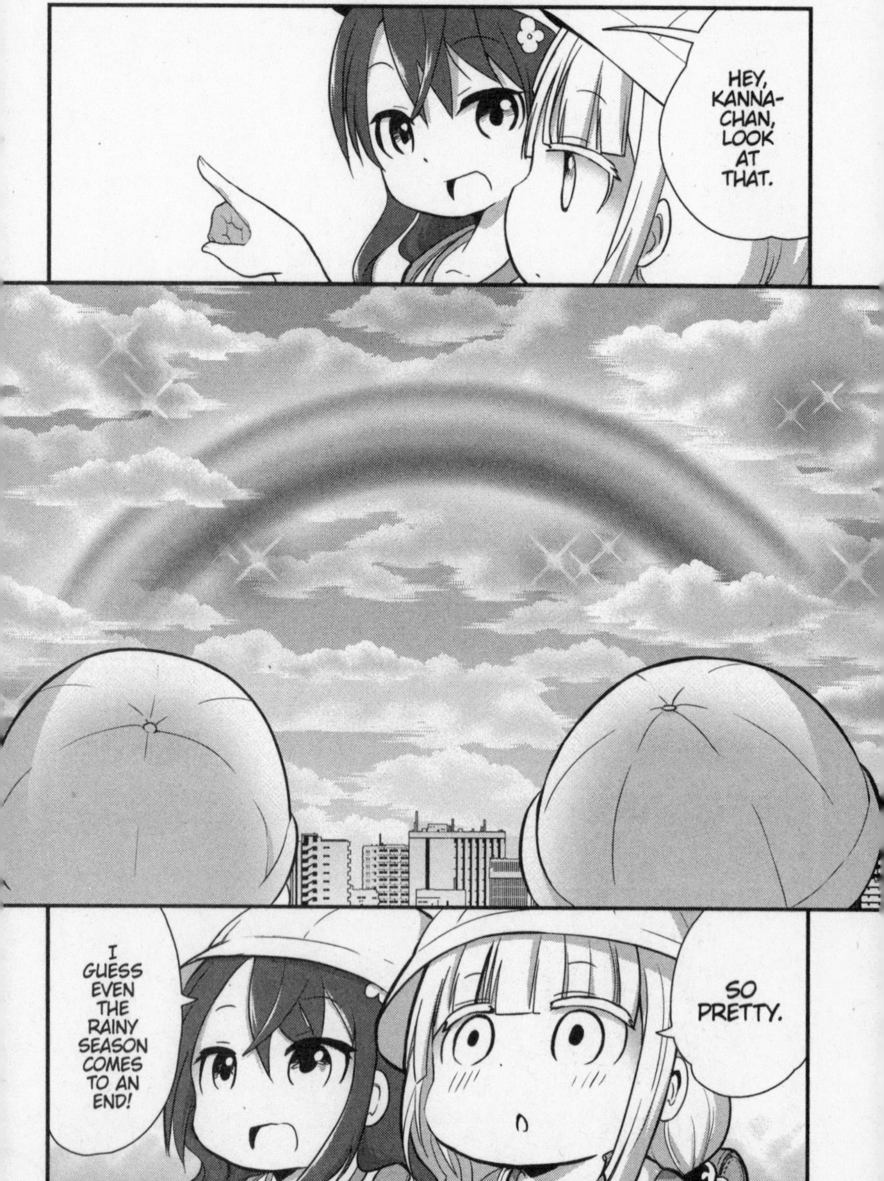
HEY, KANNA-CHAN, LOOK AT THAT.
SO PRETTY.
I GUESS EVEN THE RAINY SEASON COMES TO AN END!

TIME FOR THE RAINY SEASON/END

Miss Kobayashi's Dragon Maid
Kanna's Daily Life

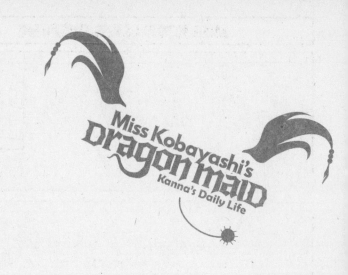

MISS KOBAYASHI'S OVERTIME

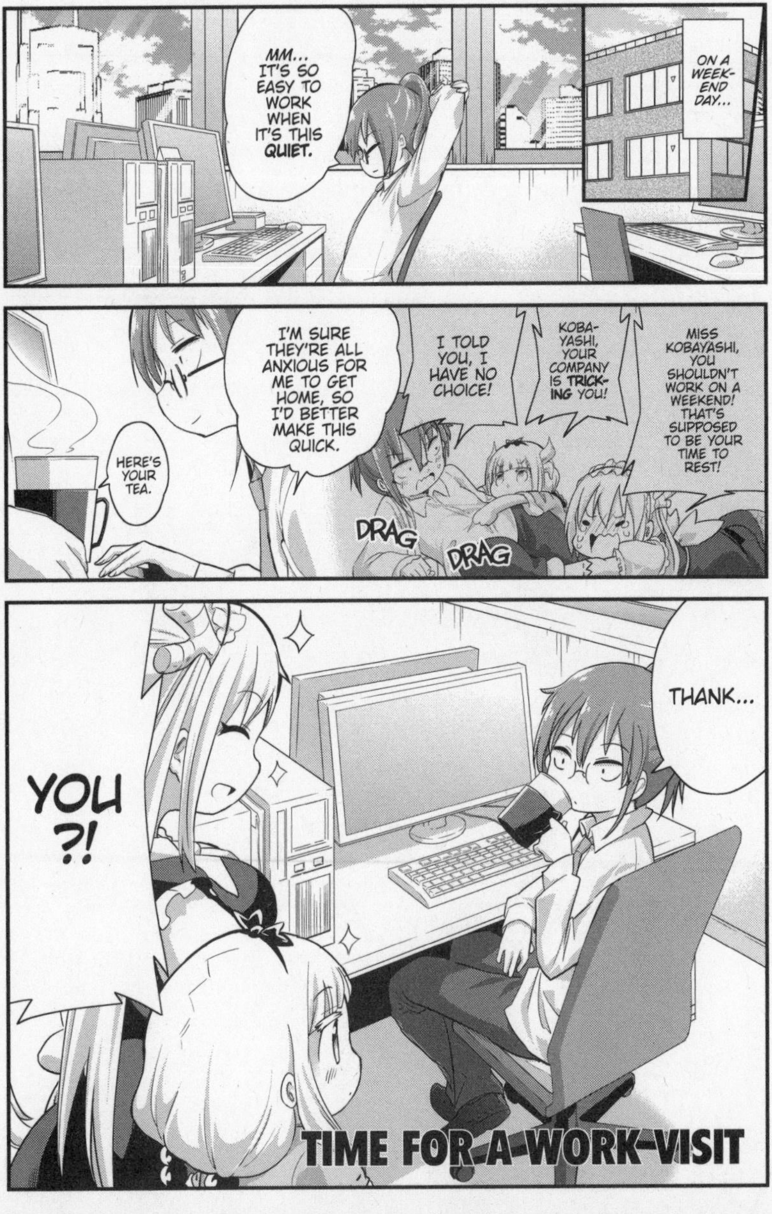
ON A WEEK-END DAY...
MM... IT'S SO EASY TO WORK WHEN IT'S THIS QUIET.
MISS KOBAYASHI, YOU SHOULDN'T WORK ON A WEEKEND! THAT'S SUPPOSED TO BE YOUR TIME TO REST!
KOBA-YASHI, YOUR COMPANY IS TRICK-ING YOU!
I TOLD YOU, I HAVE NO CHOICE!
DRAG
DRAG
I'M SURE THEY'RE ALL ANXIOUS FOR ME TO GET HOME, SO I'D BETTER MAKE THIS QUICK.
HERE'S YOUR TEA.
THANK...
YOU ?!
TIME FOR A WORK-VISIT

DEFEATING THE PURPOSE

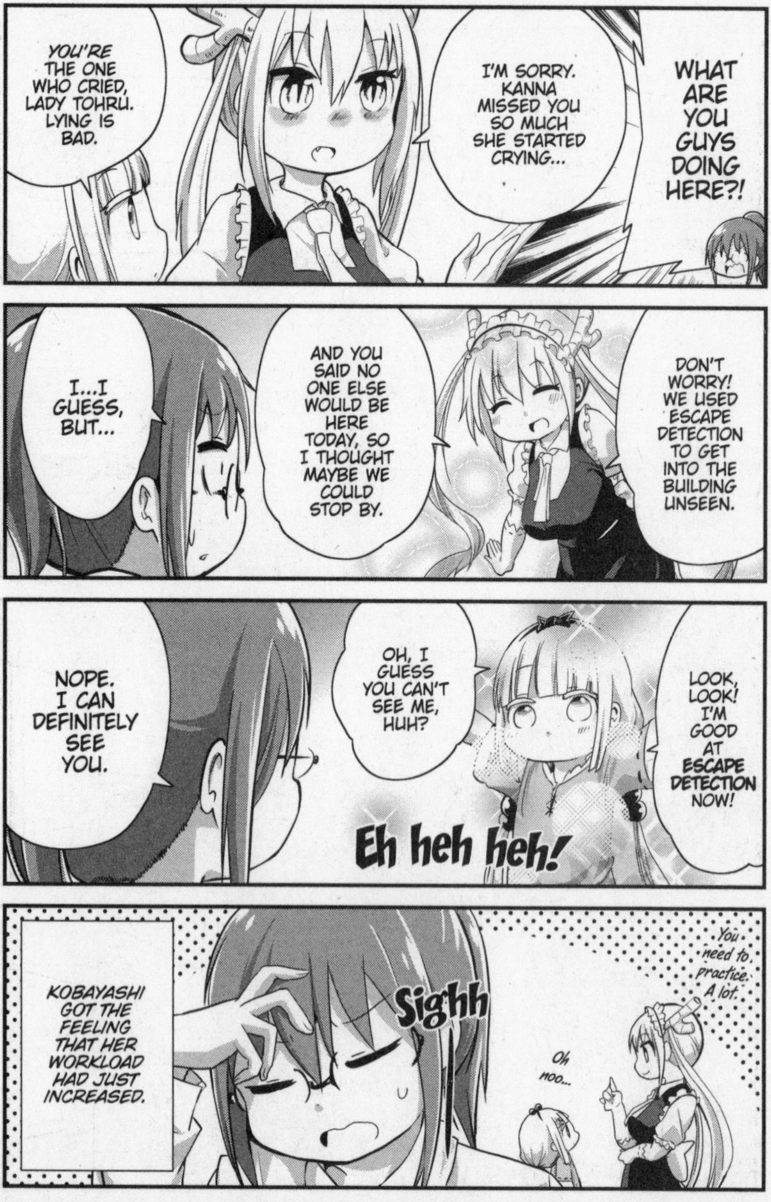
WHAT ARE YOU GUYS DOING HERE?!
I'M SORRY. KANNA MISSED YOU SO MUCH SHE STARTED CRYING...
YOU'RE THE ONE WHO CRIED, LADY TOHRU. LYING IS BAD.
DON'T WORRY! WE USED ESCAPE DETECTION TO GET INTO THE BUILDING UNSEEN.
AND YOU SAID NO ONE ELSE WOULD BE HERE TODAY, SO I THOUGHT MAYBE WE COULD STOP BY.
I...I GUESS, BUT...
LOOK, LOOK! I'M GOOD AT ESCAPE DETECTION NOW!
Eh heh heh!
OH, I GUESS YOU CAN'T SEE ME, HUH?
NOPE. I CAN DEFINITELY SEE YOU.
You need to practice. A lot.
Oh noo...
Sighh
KOBAYASHI GOT THE FEELING THAT HER WORKLOAD HAD JUST INCREASED.

DOESN'T KNOW WHAT SHE'S DOING

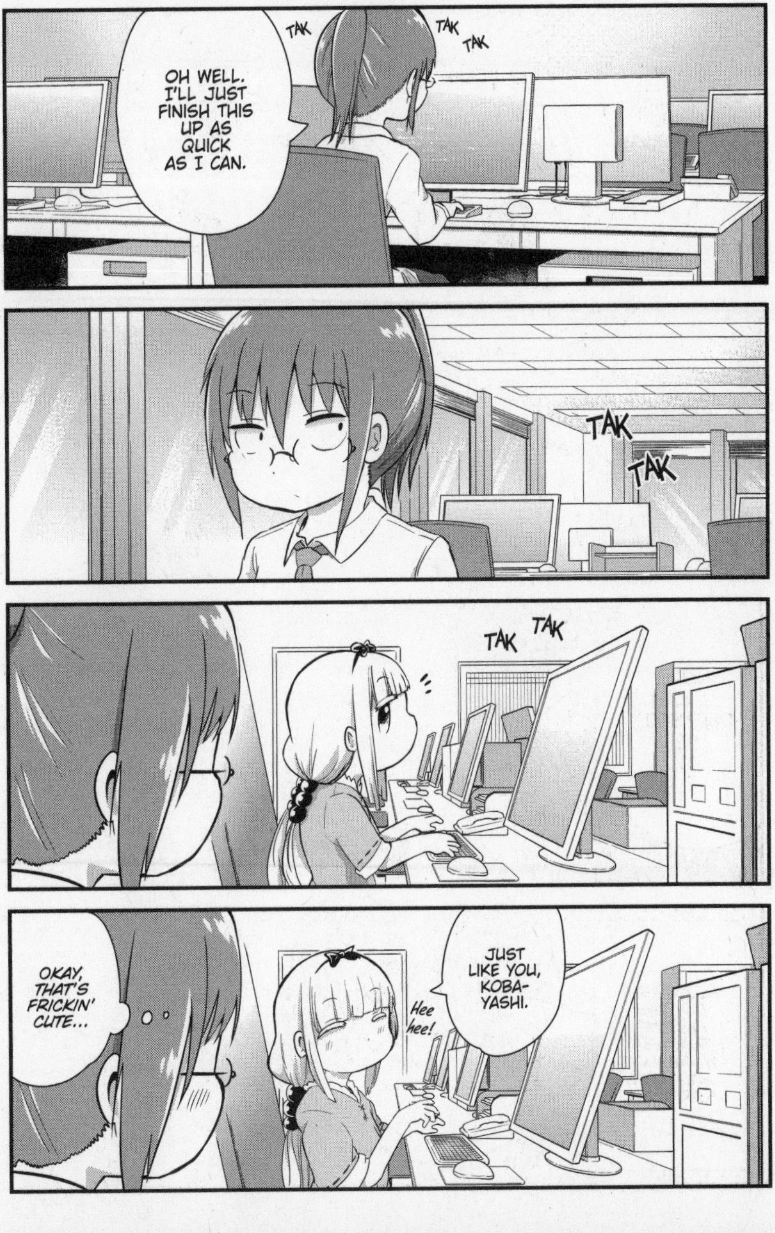
TAK
TAK
OH WELL. I'LL JUST FINISH THIS UP AS QUICK AS I CAN.
TAK
TAK
TAK
TAK
TAK
JUST LIKE YOU, KOBA-YASHI.
Hee hee!
OKAY, THAT'S FRICKIN' CUTE...

ATTENTION DEFICIT

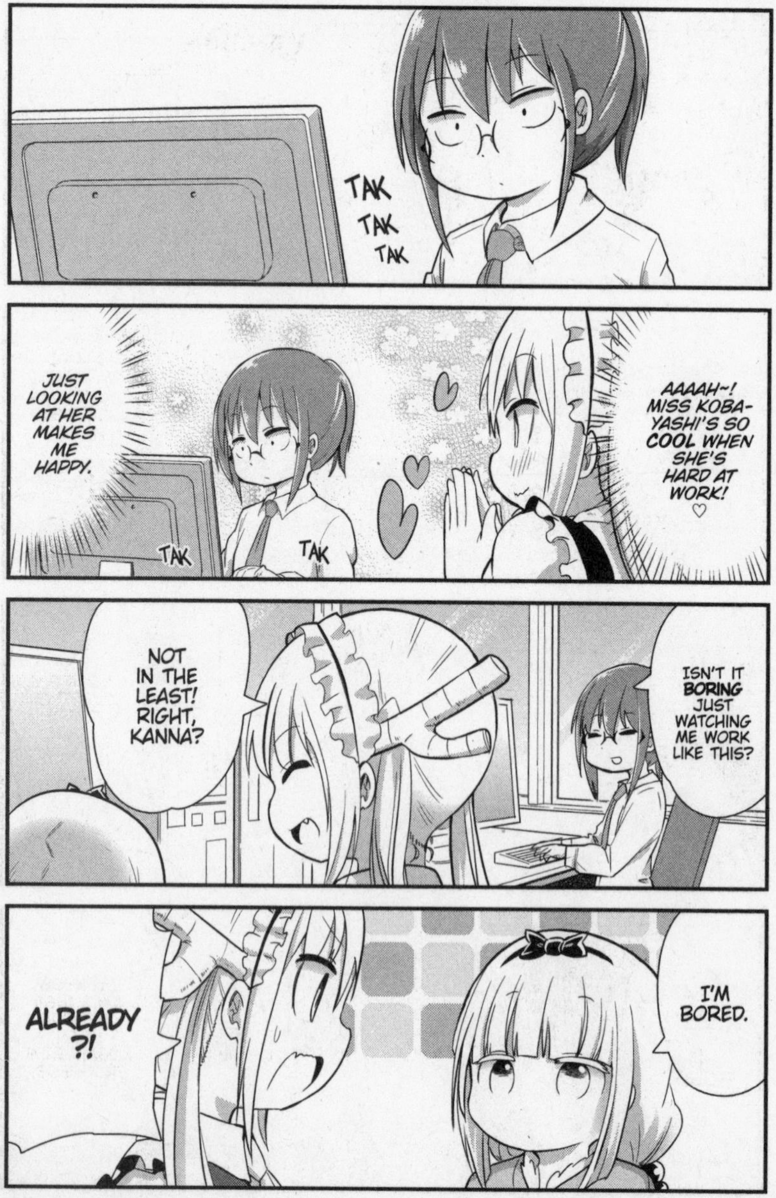
TAK
TAK
TAK
AAAAH~! MISS KOBAYASHI'S SO COOL WHEN SHE'S HARD AT WORK! ♡
JUST LOOKING AT HER MAKES ME HAPPY.
TAK
TAK
ISN'T IT BORING JUST WATCHING ME WORK LIKE THIS?
NOT IN THE LEAST! RIGHT, KANNA?
I'M BORED.
ALREADY ?!

EXECUTIVE PRIVILEGE?

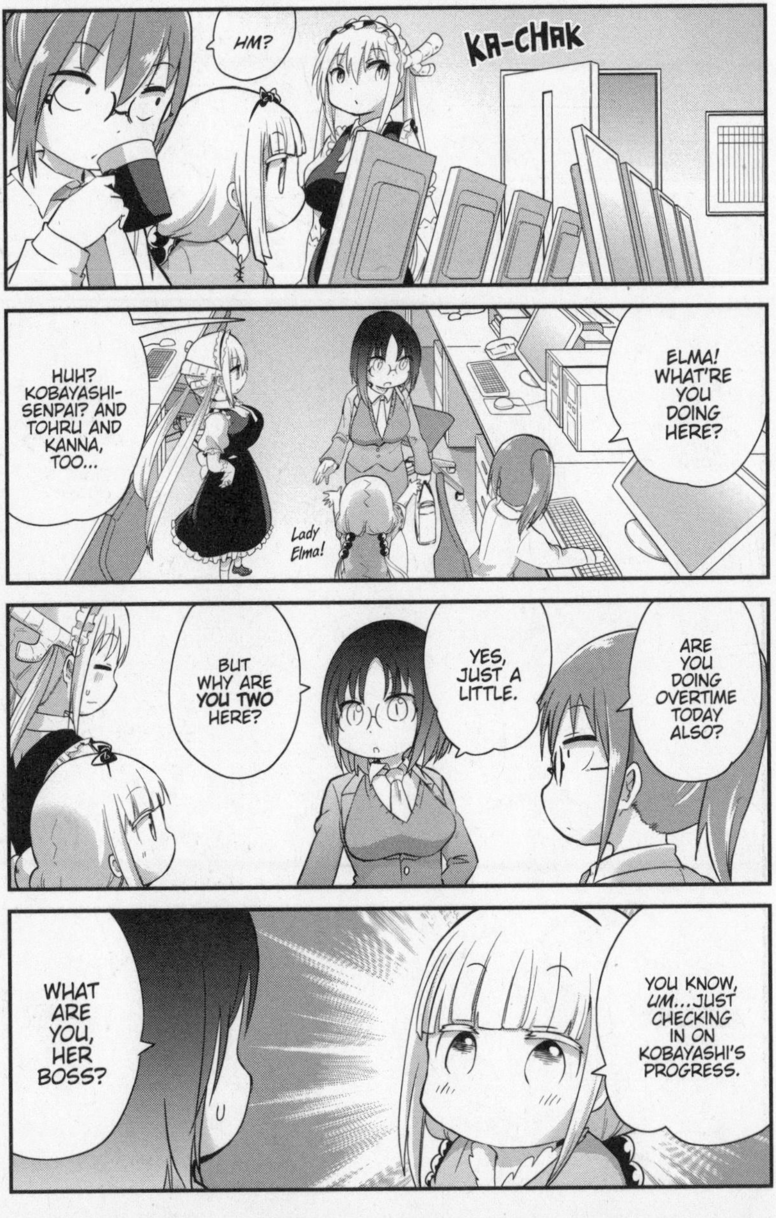
KA-CHAK
HM?
ELMA! WHAT'RE YOU DOING HERE?
HUH? KOBAYASHI-SENPAI? AND TOHRU AND KANNA, TOO...
Lady Elma!
ARE YOU DOING OVERTIME TODAY ALSO?
YES, JUST A LITTLE.
BUT WHY ARE YOU TWO HERE?
YOU KNOW, UM...JUST CHECKING IN ON KOBAYASHI'S PROGRESS.
WHAT ARE YOU, HER BOSS?

ORDERS FROM THE TOP

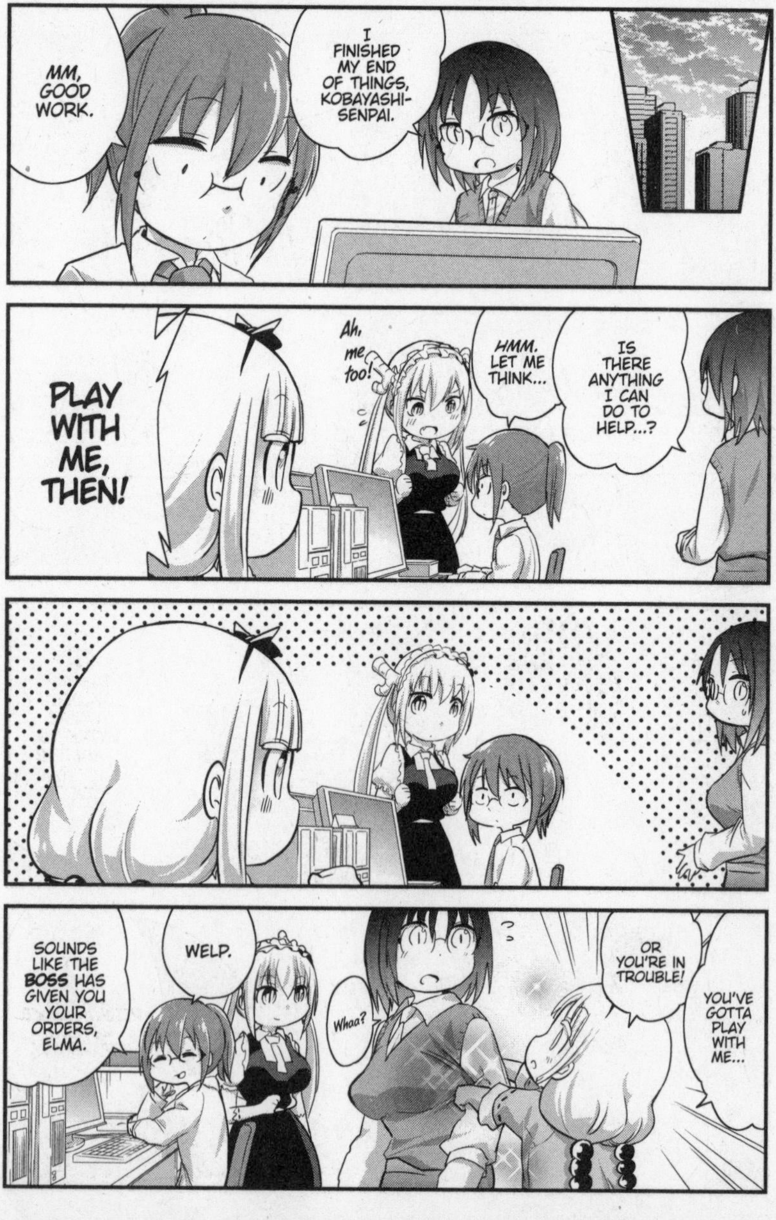
I FINISHED MY END OF THINGS, KOBAYASHI-SENPAI.
MM, GOOD WORK.
IS THERE ANYTHING I CAN DO TO HELP...?
HMM. LET ME THINK...
Ah, me too!
PLAY WITH ME, THEN!
YOU'VE GOTTA PLAY WITH ME...
OR YOU'RE IN TROUBLE!
Whaa?
WELP.
SOUNDS LIKE THE **BOSS** HAS GIVEN YOU YOUR ORDERS, ELMA.

AND TAKIYA-KUN, TOO

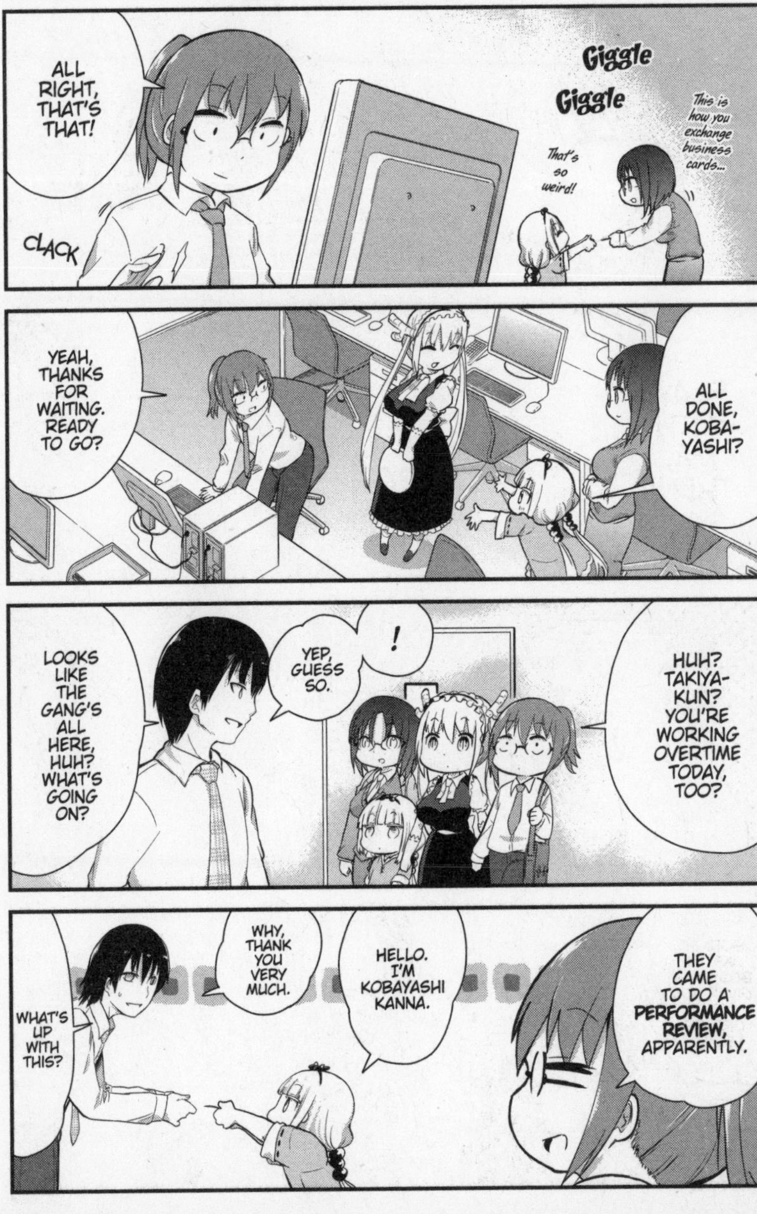

Giggle
Giggle
This is how you exchange business cards...
That's so weird!
ALL RIGHT, THAT'S THAT!
CLACK
ALL DONE, KOBA-YASHI?
YEAH, THANKS FOR WAITING. READY TO GO?
HUH? TAKIYA-KUN? YOU'RE WORKING OVERTIME TODAY, TOO?
!
YEP, GUESS SO.
LOOKS LIKE THE GANG'S ALL HERE, HUH? WHAT'S GOING ON?
THEY CAME TO DO A **PERFORMANCE REVIEW**, APPARENTLY.
HELLO. I'M KOBAYASHI KANNA.
WHY, THANK YOU VERY MUCH.
WHAT'S UP WITH THIS?

I'M ON IT

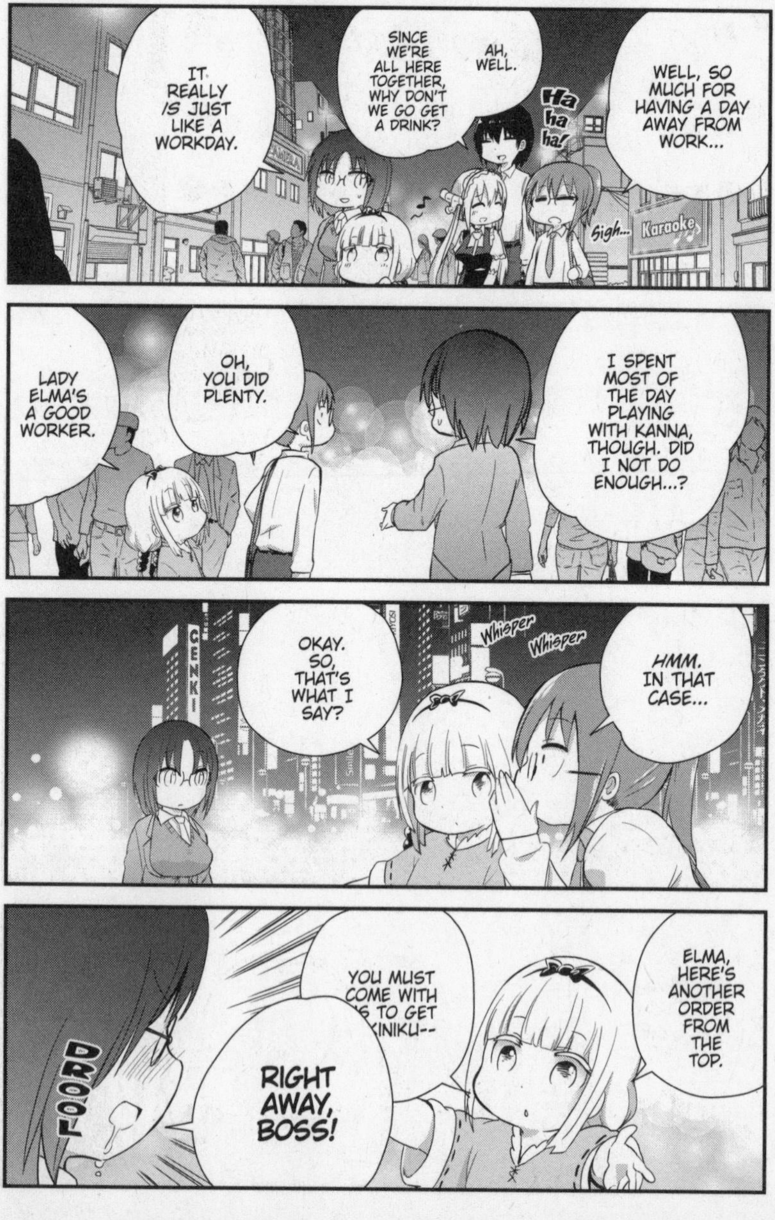

WELL, SO MUCH FOR HAVING A DAY AWAY FROM WORK...
Sigh...
Karaoke
Ha ha ha!
AH, WELL.
SINCE WE'RE ALL HERE TOGETHER, WHY DON'T WE GO GET A DRINK?
IT REALLY IS JUST LIKE A WORKDAY.
CAMERA
I SPENT MOST OF THE DAY PLAYING WITH KANNA, THOUGH. DID I NOT DO ENOUGH...?
OH, YOU DID PLENTY.
LADY ELMA'S A GOOD WORKER.
HMM. IN THAT CASE...
Whisper
Whisper
OKAY. SO, THAT'S WHAT I SAY?
GENKI
ELMA, HERE'S ANOTHER ORDER FROM THE TOP.
YOU MUST COME WITH
S TO GET
KINIKU--
RIGHT AWAY, BOSS!
DROOL

THROUGH A CHILD'S EYES

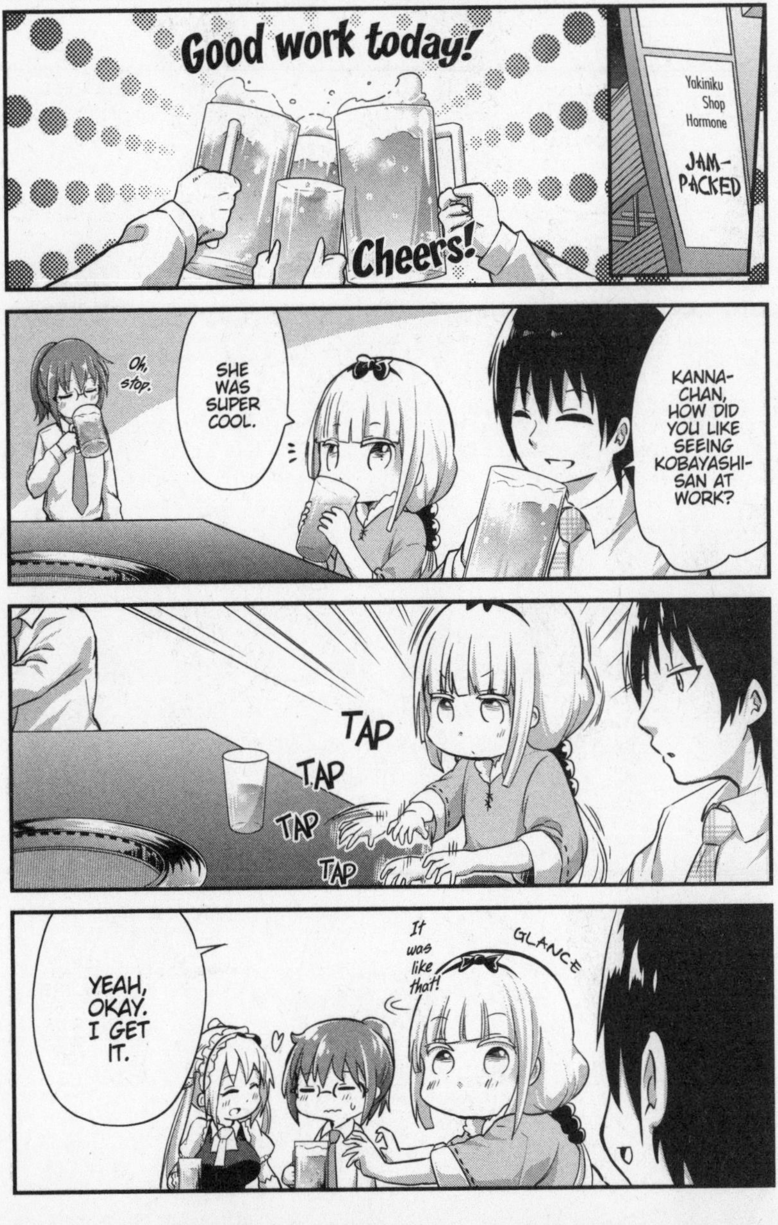
Yakiniku Shop Hormone
JAM-PACKED
Good work today!
Cheers!
KANNA-CHAN, HOW DID YOU LIKE SEEING KOBAYASHI-SAN AT WORK?
SHE WAS SUPER COOL.
Oh, stop.
TAP
TAP
TAP
TAP
GLANCE
It was like that!
YEAH, OKAY. I GET IT.

SUPER-SERIOUS KANNA-CHAN

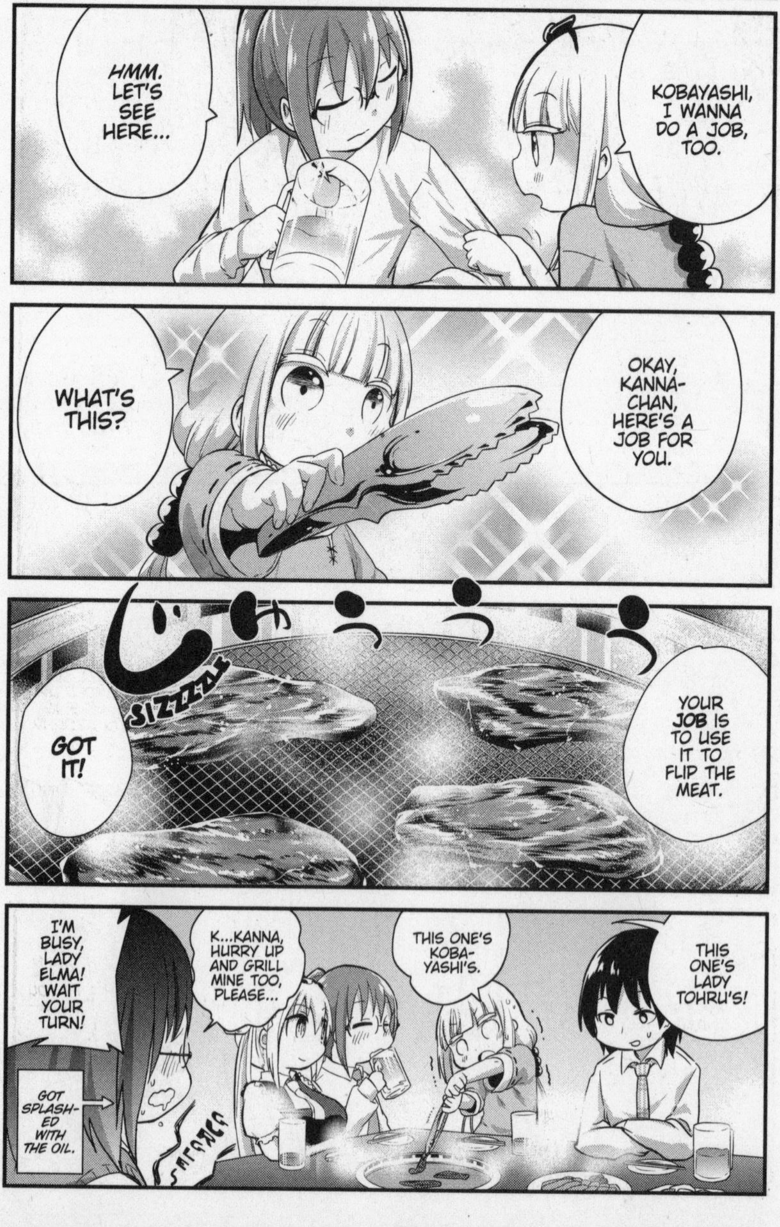

KOBAYASHI, I WANNA DO A JOB, TOO.
HMM. LET'S SEE HERE...
OKAY, KANNA-CHAN, HERE'S A JOB FOR YOU.
WHAT'S THIS?
じゅううう
SIZZZZLE
YOUR JOB IS TO USE IT TO FLIP THE MEAT.
GOT IT!
THIS ONE'S LADY TOHRU'S!
THIS ONE'S KOBA-YASHI'S.
K...KANNA, HURRY UP AND GRILL MINE TOO, PLEASE...
I'M BUSY, LADY ELMA! WAIT YOUR TURN!
GOT SPLASH-ED WITH THE OIL.

I SAID "SOON," NOT "NOW"!

Good night!

THAT MEAT WAS REALLY TASTY!

Not as tasty as my tail, though.

WHEW... I'M PRETTY FULL.

Not at all! ♥

SORRY, YOU TWO. I FEEL LIKE I ENDED UP DRAGGING YOU AROUND ALL DAY.

NEVER UNDERESTIMATE THE POWER OF YOUTHFUL ENERGY!

HUH ?!

THEN LET'S GO PLAY RIGHT NOW!!

I'LL MAKE IT UP TO YOU SOON--

Yaaah!

THE WAY HOME

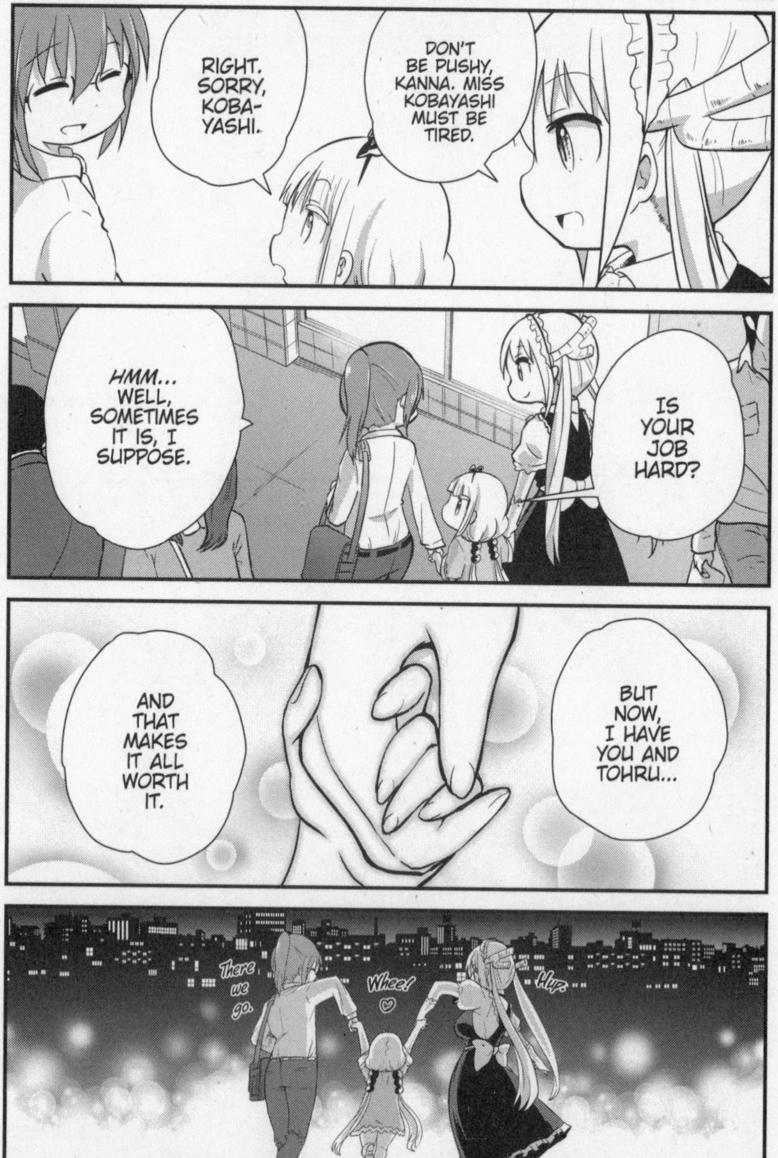
DON'T BE PUSHY, KANNA. MISS KOBAYASHI MUST BE TIRED.
RIGHT. SORRY, KOBA-YASHI.
IS YOUR JOB HARD?
HMM... WELL, SOMETIMES IT IS, I SUPPOSE.
BUT NOW, I HAVE YOU AND TOHRU...
AND THAT MAKES IT ALL WORTH IT.
Hup.
Whee! ♡
There we go.

TIME FOR A WORK VISIT/END

Tight squeeze, huh?

Afterword Manga

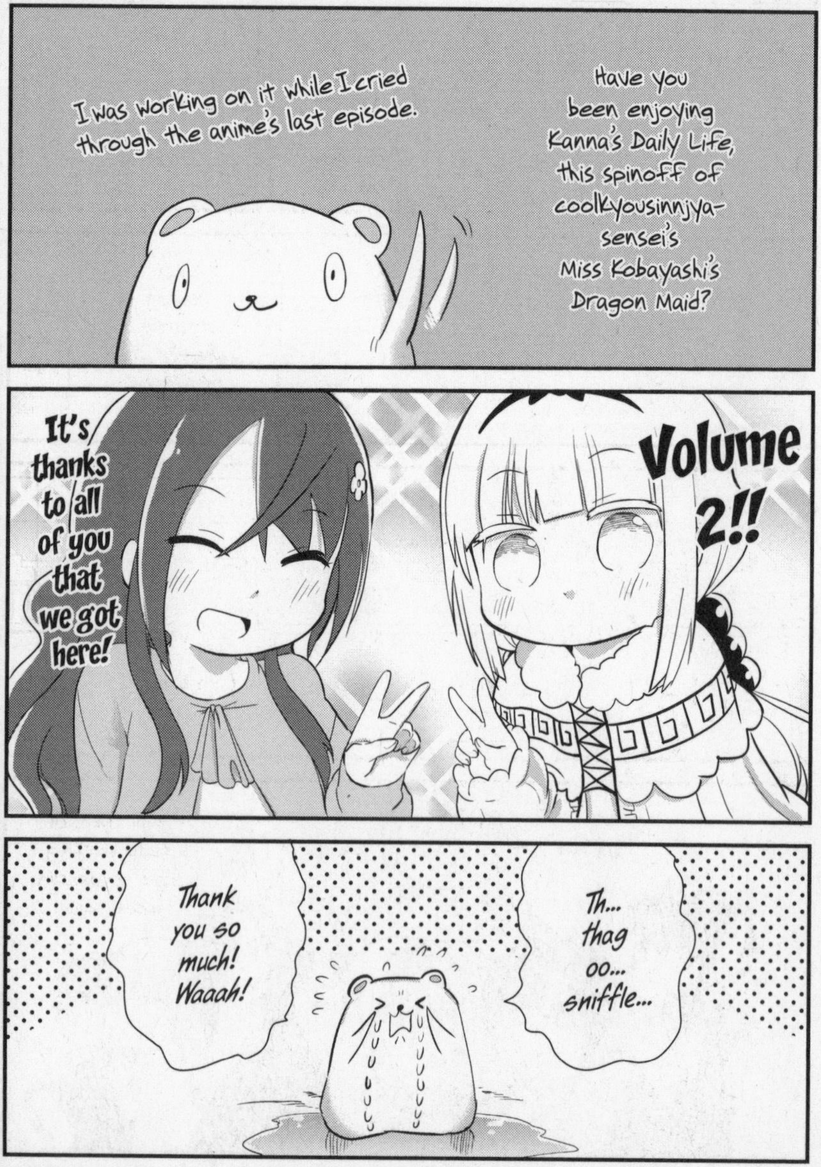

Have you been enjoying Kanna's Daily Life, this spinoff of coolkyousinnjya-sensei's Miss Kobayashi's Dragon Maid?
I was working on it while I cried through the anime's last episode.
Volume 2!!
It's thanks to all of you that we got here!
Th... thag oo... sniffle...
Thank you so much! Waaah!

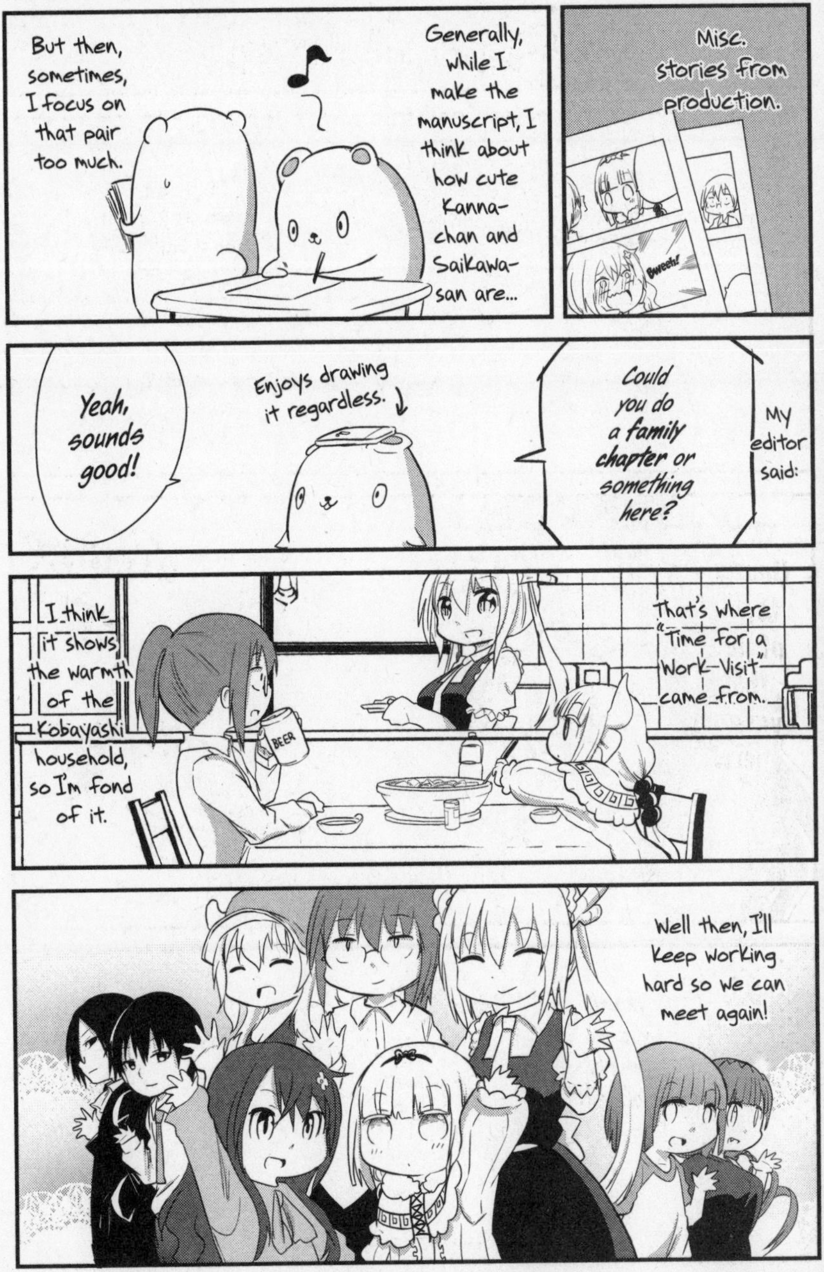
Misc. stories from production.
Bweeh!
Generally, while I make the manuscript, I think about how cute Kanna-chan and Saikawa-san are...
But then, sometimes, I focus on that pair too much.
My editor said:
Could you do a family chapter or something here?
Enjoys drawing it regardless.
Yeah, sounds good!
That's where "Time for a Work Visit" came from.
I think it shows the warmth of the Kobayashi household, so I'm fond of it.
BEER
Well then, I'll keep working hard so we can meet again!

AFTERWORD

COOLKYOUSINNJYA

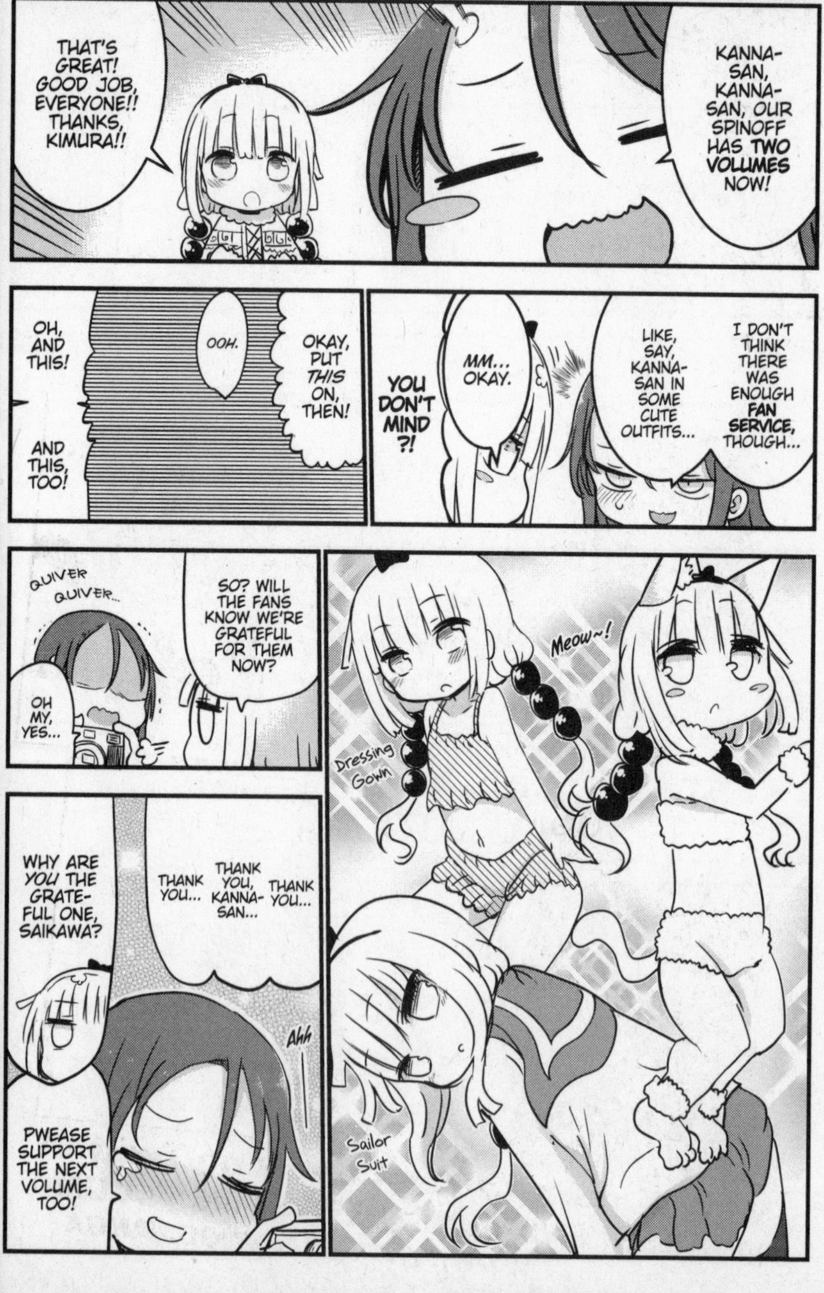
KANNA-SAN, KANNA-SAN, OUR SPINOFF HAS **TWO VOLUMES** NOW!
THAT'S GREAT! GOOD JOB, EVERYONE!! THANKS, KIMURA!!
I DON'T THINK THERE WAS ENOUGH **FAN SERVICE**, THOUGH...
LIKE, SAY, KANNA-SAN IN SOME CUTE OUTFITS...
MM... OKAY.
YOU DON'T MIND ?!
OKAY, PUT *THIS* ON, THEN!
OOH.
OH, AND THIS!
AND THIS, TOO!
Meow~!
Dressing Gown
Sailor Suit
SO? WILL THE FANS KNOW WE'RE GRATEFUL FOR THEM NOW?
QUIVER QUIVER...
OH MY, YES...
THANK YOU...
THANK YOU, KANNA-SAN...
THANK YOU...
WHY ARE *YOU* THE GRATEFUL ONE, SAIKAWA?
Ahh
PWEASE SUPPORT THE NEXT VOLUME, TOO!

SEVEN SEAS ENTERTAINMENT PRESENTS

Miss Kobayashi's
Dragon Maid
Kanna's Daily Life VOL.2

original story by **coolkyousinnjya**   story and art by **Mitsuhiro Kimura**

TRANSLATION
Jenny McKeon

ADAPTATION
Shanti Whitesides

LETTERING
Jennifer Skarupa

LOGO DESIGN
KC Fabellon

COVER DESIGN
Nicky Lim

PROOFREADING
Stephanie Cohen

ASSISTANT EDITOR
Jenn Grunigen

PRODUCTION ASSISTANT
CK Russell

PRODUCTION MANAGER
Lissa Pattillo

EDITOR-IN-CHIEF
Adam Arnold

PUBLISHER
Jason DeAngelis

Seven Seas books may be purchased in bulk for promotional, educational, or
business use. Please contact your local bookseller or the Macmillan Corporate
and Premium Sales Department at 1-800-221-7945, extension 5442, or by
e-mail at MacmillanSpecialMarkets@macmillan.com.

Seven Seas and the Seven Seas logo are trademarks of
Seven Seas Entertainment, LLC. All rights reserved.

ISBN: 978-1-626927-93-3

Printed in Canada

First Printing: June 2018

10 9 8 7 6 5 4 3 2 1

2366 49001

FOLLOW US ONLINE: www.sevenseasentertainment.com

READING DIRECTIONS

This book reads from *right to left*, Japanese style.
If this is your first time reading manga, you start
reading from the top right panel on each page and
take it from there. If you get lost, just follow the
numbered diagram here. It may seem backwards at
first, but you'll get the hang of it! Have fun!!

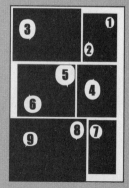